ENDORSEMENTS

"Rev. Earl is a God loving, God fearing, lifelong student of God's word; constantly seeking the truth, not afraid to challenge that which needs to be challenged, who loves and serves Christ with the heart and enthusiasm of a child. *Jesus and the Gospel Timeline* reconciles the four Gospels in a straight forward, side by side manner. The book made me re-examine how I learn—to study the Gospels in their entirety, rather than independently. I found jewels of truth that I had missed in prior studies. A recommended read for all seekers of truth in our Lord and Savior, Jesus Christ!" – Paul Sammons

"I like *Jesus and the Gospel Timeline* because it is much easier to follow and has good and relevant comments. A lay person or someone with more Bible knowledge could follow the Gospels without difficulty. I always enjoy writers who stick to the Word instead of just their opinions. Your book sticks to the Word. The comments are good."
– Cindy Lewis

"I very much appreciate your story telling reference with the topography and cultural traditions of the period in a palatable and quickly understood manner. Today, only a faithful minority have the right to be called the 'the righteous remnant' and in fact many Orthodox synagogues are named 'Shearith Israel' Remnant of Israel. This weeding out is called in the Torah 'The Sifting.'"– David Aarons, Jerusalem

"As a layman I have read and studied the Gospels for years. As a Sunday school teacher I strive to present Scripture accurately and understandably that it may be applied in the student's daily life. Earl David's *Jesus and the Gospel Timeline* along with the companion volume *The 8 Days of Holy Week* enables the reader to gain understanding and to consider various ways to model the example of our Savior. Beyond being a 'parallel' study this also gives the chronology. In doing so a whole new perspective is presented causing one to consider the Gospels in a different and unique approach." – Mike Willis

JESUS AND THE GOSPEL TIMELINE

BOOK I

THE BEGINNING

As reported in

The Gospels of

Mark

Matthew

Luke

John

BY
EARL C. DAVID, JR.

Intermedia Publishing Group

THE BEGINNING

Published by:
Intermedia Publishing Group, Inc.
P.O. Box 2825
Peoria, Arizona 85380
www.intermediapub.com

ISBN 978-1-935906-16-2

Copyright © 2011 by Earl C. David, Jr.
Printed in the United States of America

No part of this publication may be reproduced, stored in a retrieval system, or transmitted in any form or by any means—electronic, mechanical, digital photocopy, recording, or any other without the prior permission of the author.

Scripture quotations are from the Revised Standard Version of the Bible (unless indicated otherwise), copyright © 1946, 1952, and 1971 the National Council of the Churches of Christ in the USA. Used by permission. All rights reserved.

Preface

Jesus and the Gospel Timeline is a new way of studying the Gospels.

The basic premise of ***Jesus and the Gospel Timeline*** is every event occurs on a timeline within a given context and has a beginning, middle, and end. To illustrate this idea think of a train. The train runs on a track, and in this instance the track represents history. The train represents an event that is taking place somewhere on the timeline of history. As long as the train is running smoothly it moves in a line, from its beginning toward its destination. However; should a derailment occur the cars could be scattered in a random fashion. It would take a master list to correctly realign them. So each car is explored individually, to ascertain what its relationship is to the others. So it is with ***Jesus and the Gospel Timeline***. I have explored each of the different cars of this train and reassembled them in what appears to me to be a realistic replacement on the timeline, from the time of the Announcement of Jesus' birth, through his ministry to his ascension into heaven. Every event recorded in the Four Gospels takes place somewhere on the timeline of history and each of these events is part of a specific context.

The goal of ***Jesus and the Gospel Timeline*** is to establish as accurately as possible the timeline of Jesus' birth, life, ministry, and ascension. Since no one gospel provides this information per se, I have connected the points of information found within the four Gospels.

The birth stories are found in the opening chapters of Matthew and Luke. Each of the four Gospels closes with Holy Week. All the material between these two events is what I call the train wreck. These events are scattered throughout the four Gospels and are generally camouflaged by many stories, events, parables, etc.

Jesus and the Gospel Timeline carefully examines these seemingly random, scattered pieces of the Gospel record and places them within the scriptural context. The results is a portrayal of Jesus' biography that may be followed in a more consistent and understandable manner.

Obviously, the Gospel writers were not concerned about stating exactly where and when Jesus spoke or healed. Occasionally they do tell us that it was morning, evening, or at a particular location but this was not of great importance to them. If we could ask such a question of them, I would not be surprised to get a blank stare and perhaps hear them say, "What difference does it make?" The difference for me is clarity.

It is also worth remembering that chapters and verses were added to the text hundreds of years after the entire Bible had become the acknowledged book of faith for the Christian community.

There will be times when you will be shocked as you read and understand exactly what Jesus said to his audiences. We preachers, in our sermonizing, often sugarcoat the words and water them down for fear of hurting people's feelings and possibly even driving them away. I believe that it is imperative that we understand exactly what Jesus said and what he meant by what he said.

I have chosen to use the Revised Standard Version of the New Testament as my textual source. I reached this conclusion on the basis that the two best word-for-word translations that we have access to in the English language are the King James Version and the Revised Standard Version. I prefer the language of the Revised Standard Version; therefore, that is the text I follow.

Acknowledgements

To Elizabeth, my wife and soul mate who listened to all of my frustrations and victories and maintained the courage to tell me the truth without any sugar coating. Without her I may have never finished this "labor of love."

Jim Ross, author of two books, ***The Last Reunion*** and ***The Snake's Hand***, who took time from his writing to read and offer clarity and sincere interest in my work. To Lucy Ross who gave me unending encouragement. To Mike Willis who has read these pages almost as many times as I have and who is teaching it to his Sunday School Class.

I am deeply grateful to Dr. Donald Strobe who shared with me his amazingly clear and concise depiction of Israel's early history and geography and his permission to use it in this work. Special thanks to Deborah Murdock who has patiently guided me through my legal questions.

This work would never have been done without two persons who were absolutely indispensible. To John Uran, whose computer skills have paved a way for me to use this wonderful invention. And to my friend and guide David Aaron, who has shown me my "Spiritual Homeland."

I simply cannot say enough about the adult students who made time in their busy schedules to become a focus group. They listened as I taught the lessons in ***Jesus and the Gospel Timeline*** and engaged me as they raised questions and helped me create more clarity within the book.

Without all of you this book would never have become a book.

Thanks
Rev. Earl

Table of Contents

Chapter 1 *page 1*

We begin with a backward look at the long history of the Jews. Matthew's version of the family tree mentions women of significant importance in the history of Israel. Luke names only the male side of the family tree.

Chapter 2 *page 7*

Herod and his boys are trouble with a big T. Zechariah has an unexpected visitor, the angel. The angel's message is spellbinding. The angel's next visit is to a girl named Mary. The birth of John the Baptist answers many questions.

Chapter 3 *page 21*

All four Evangelists contribute to the entrance of the world's most unique person. The very "Word" of God is about to become flesh and blood. The Angel Gabriel visits Mary and startles her saying, "Hail, O favored one." She is going to have a baby, but more than that. To comfort and assure her he tells her that Elizabeth is already with child. Conditions swerve off course causing Joseph to resolve to divorce her quietly. The plot thickens as the Emperor of Rome becomes a player.

Chapter 4 *page 49*

John the Baptist makes his entry as an evangelist. His mission is to prepare the way of the Lord. He presents the kingdom of heaven. When questioned, he confesses he is not the Christ. He is baptizing in a place known as Bethany beyond the Jordan. He tells them to look for one that is coming, who is mightier than himself. When questioned by authorities from the Temple he refers to them as a brood of vipers.

Chapter 5 *page 69*

Jesus departs from Nazareth for his baptism. John is reluctant to baptize Jesus. John proclaims, "Behold, the Lamb of God." Jesus emerges from the water. The Spirit drives/ leads Jesus into the wilderness. The temptations Jesus faced. Jesus returned to Galilee. Four men leave their livelihood to follow Jesus. Jesus and new disciples visit Capernaum and the home of Simon Peter. The Sabbath contained worship, healing, and sundown. The next morning Jesus talks with a would-be disciple, and attends the wedding at Cana.

Chapter 6 *page 95*

Jesus' family and disciples visit Capernaum. The Passover is at hand, the first Passover mentioned during Jesus' ministry. When Jesus cleansed the Temple he created uproar. The Temple authorities demanded a sign for doing this. In the darkness Jesus met Nicodemus. John's disciples have a dispute with the Jews about purifying. The plan of salvation is revealed. Jesus converses with the Samarian woman. Herod Antipas has John arrested. Returning to Galilee, Jesus heals the son of a town official.

Chapter 7 *page 117*

Jesus heals the Leper and orders him to tell no one. The healed man ignored Jesus' prohibition and joyfully told everyone. As Jesus entered Capernaum a Centurion asked him to heal his servant. In the process the Centurion displayed a faith unlike any Jesus had yet seen. At Nain Jesus raised the son of a widow from the dead. Here we find a major undercurrent in Jesus' ministry. At home (Nazareth) he heals a paralytic. Matthew leaves a lucrative business to follow Jesus.

Chapter 8 *page 143*

Jesus heals the man with the withered hand. The Pharisees and the Herodians conspire against Jesus. Jesus is concerned about "crowd control." Jesus interacts with the demons. The religious leadership declares Jesus heals by the power of Satan. The unforgivable sin is committed. Jesus and his family experience times of conflict.

Chapter 9
page 167

Jesus sleeps through a bad storm. Jesus and Legion meet. The hogs stampede. Jesus is asked to please go away. Legion gets a new calling. A young girl is near death. A mature woman sees Jesus as her last hope. The girl is restored to life. Jesus tells the parable of the Sower. A reference to the Garden of Eden is made.

Chapter 10
page 211

While the Inner-Circle is on mission Jesus goes to Jerusalem. John, in prison, hears about Jesus. Jesus charges the people saying you do not really like me or John. Jesus talks about trees. Jesus goes to Jerusalem without the Inner-Circle. Jesus ends up in a whole lot of trouble.

Chapter 11
page 231

The Inner-Circle reported back to Jesus after their missionary journey. The Pharisees become upset, because Jesus' disciples do not wash their hands before eating. A lawyer, scribe, is upset by what Jesus said to him. Jesus has intermittent conflict with the Pharisees. The world will always experience temptations but woe to the one who brings it.

Chapter 12
page 245

Here we have the entire Sermon on the Mount with the addition of Luke's comments that are pertinent.

Chapter 13
page 285

Jesus learns that John the Baptist has been executed. A Pharisee invites Jesus to his home for a meal. While eating, a woman from the street came in and broke open an alabaster jar of ointment and anointed Jesus' feet. Then she dried them with her hair. Who are the women that follow Jesus? Jesus feeds the 5,000. Jesus invites Peter to walk on water with him. Jesus states that he is the bread of life. Jesus experiences conflict with the people of Capernaum.

Chapter 14 *page 309*

There is conflict between Jesus and his brothers. Jesus goes to Jerusalem for the feast of the Tabernacles. The chief priest orders Jesus arrested. In an effort to trap Jesus in a misstatement the Pharisees bring to him a woman who has been caught in the act of adultery. Jesus accuses the Pharisees of wanting to kill him.

Chapter 15 *page 335*

Jesus has a conversation with the Syrophoenician mother. Jesus feeds the four thousand. A woman who had an issue of blood for eighteen years touches Jesus' garment.

Chapter 16 *page 351*

The final preparation for Jerusalem begins now. Jesus is transfigured before Peter, James, and John's very eyes. Peter makes the mistake of trying to tell Jesus how to conduct his ministry. At the foot of the mountain a father brought his possessed son for healing. Jesus returns to Galilee.

Chapter 17 *page 371*

The disciples engage in a conversation as to who among them will be greatest in Jesus' Kingdom. Jesus warns do not mess with the children. Jesus encounters would-be disciples. Jesus sends out seventy on a mission trip. Jesus delivers the parable of the Good Samaritan.

Chapter 18 *page 387*

Jesus is accused of inviting sinners to eat with him. Jesus speaks of precious things that have become lost. Jesus tells the story of a dishonest servant. You cannot serve God and wealth at the same time. Jesus warns that they will look for him but they will not find him. Jesus tells the story of a judge that did not fear God nor cared for man. Jesus returned to Jerusalem for the Feast of Dedication.

Chapter 19 *page 415*

Jesus speaks of divorce. Jesus is displeased with the disciples because they refused to let little children come to him. Jesus encounters a man who asked the question, "What can I do to inherit eternal life?" Jesus tells the parable of the rich man and Lazarus. Jesus warned it will be hard for rich men to get into heaven. There will be many people in the kingdom of heaven. Jesus heals again on the Sabbath. Jesus tells the parable of the rich man hiring workers for his vineyard.

Chapter 20 *page 437*

Jesus announces they are going up to Jerusalem. James and John ask Jesus for the most important positions in his kingdom. At Jericho Jesus meets blind Bartimaeus. Mary and Martha send for Jesus. Jesus raises Lazarus from the dead. Passover is close at hand.

Study Guide *page 457*

Sample page

This is a sample page to illustrate the most valuable way to read and study, *Jesus and the Gospel Timeline.*

This column will always contain the passage to be studied. Here is an example: **Six days before Passover** (Passage heading) **John 12:1-2** (Text to be examined) A single reference means this information is found only in the Gospel cited. If there is more than one Gospel that contains a similar account the Book and Passage will be cited. The order of citation will be: Mark, Matthew, Luke, or John. This ordering is based on the earliest writing to the last.	This column will always contain the commentary associated to the passage.

Comments beneath the columns appear at the points where valuable information is given to help enlighten the passage from sources other than the Bible. These can also be personal comments by the author.

Chapter 1

Introduction To The Life And Ministry Of Jesus The Christ

Luke 1:1-4	Comment
1 Inasmuch as many have undertaken to compile a narrative of the things which have been accomplished among us, 2 just as they were delivered to us by those who from the beginning were eyewitnesses and ministers of the word, 3 it seemed good to me also, having followed all things closely for some time past, to write an orderly account for you, most excellent Theoph'ilus, 4 that you may know the truth concerning the things of which you have been informed.	**Luke 1:1-4** Only Luke gives us an introduction to his Gospel. It is believed by many that *Theophilus* was a person having influence and at least some degree of authority in Rome where Paul was awaiting trial. Luke's gospel and the book of Acts may have been written as a defense of Paul and his evangelist fervor.

Matthew's version of the family tree

Matthew's version of the family tree is arranged in three sections. These three sections are based on the great stages of Jewish history.

Section one begins with Abraham and leads to King David. David was the shepherd boy who became king. It was David who brought together all of the twelve tribes under the leadership of one powerful man. David's leadership wielded the people into a powerful nation.

The second phase of the history continues the story from David to the exile of Israel by the Babylonians. This period in history exposes the shame, tragedy, and disasters that befell Israel's great leaders.

The third stage of this history moves from the great exile in Babylon to the birth of Jesus Christ. It is Jesus who will liberate mankind from slavery to sin. Just as Moses had delivered the children of Israel out of bondage in Egypt, Jesus will lead mankind into restoration with Almighty God. Here we find the tragedy of the preceding history turned into victory for the future.

Jesus' Family Tree According to Matthew	*Jesus' Family Tree According to Matthew*
Matthew 1:1-17 1 The book of the genealogy of Jesus Christ, the son of David, the son of Abraham. 2 Abraham was the father of Isaac, and Isaac the father of Jacob, and Jacob the father of Judah and his brothers, 3 and Judah the father of Perez and Zerah by Tamar, and Perez the father of Hezron, and Hezron the father of Ram, 4 and Ram the father of Ammin'adab, and Ammin'adab the father of Nahshon, and Nahshon the father of Salmon, 5 and Salmon the father of Bo'az by Rahab, and Bo'az the father of Obed by Ruth, and Obed the father of Jesse, 6 and Jesse the father of David the king.	**Comment** **Matthew 1:1-17** Matthew begins the genealogy of Jesus with Abraham and ends with Joseph. Matthew includes the names of several mothers whose sons are listed in his genealogy. He tells us Judah and Tamar had Perez, Boaz and Ruth had Obed, the grandfather of King David. Matthew said Solomon son of King David "by the wife of Uriah." I find it interesting that the innocent victim of David's adultery is remembered in this genealogy while the more famous Bathsheba's name is deliberately omitted.

And David was the father of Solomon by the wife of Uri'ah, 7 and Solomon the father of Rehobo'am, and Rehobo'am the father of Abi'jah, and Abi'jah the father of Asa, 8 and Asa the father of Jehosh'aphat, and Jehosh'aphat the father of Joram, and Joram the father of Uzzi'ah, 9 and Uzzi'ah the father of Jotham, and Jotham the father of Ahaz, and Ahaz the father of Hezeki'ah, 10 and Hezeki'ah the father of Manas'seh, and Manas'seh the father of Amos, and Amos the father of Josi'ah, 11 and Josi'ah the father of Jechoniah and his brothers, at the time of the deportation to Babylon.

12 And after the deportation to Babylon: Jechoni'ah was the father of She-al'ti-el, and She-al'ti-el the father of Zerub'babel, 13 and Zerub'babel the father of Abi'ud, and Abi'ud the father of Eli'akim, and Eli'akim the father of Azor, 14 and Azor the father of Zadok, and Zadok the father of Achim, and Achim the father of Eli'ud, 15 and Eli'ud the father of Elea'zar, and Elea'zar the father of Matthan, and Matthan the father of Jacob, 16 and Jacob the father of Joseph the husband of Mary, of whom Jesus was born, who is called Christ.

17 So all the generations from Abraham to David were fourteen generations, and from David to the deportation to Babylon fourteen generations, and from the deportation to Babylon to the Christ fourteen generations.

The message from the Family Tree

It is amazing that we find women listed in this family tree. It is a rare thing indeed in Jewish history for women to be included in the family tree. Women were generally considered slightly above the status of chattel mortgage. The father or husband had total control over the life and death of the women of his house. Women had no legal rights. Jewish men often prayed that they were glad God had not made them a Gentile, a slave, or a woman.

Rahab was a harlot of Jericho, see Joshua 2:1-7.

Ruth was not even a Jew she was a Moabite. Her story is told in the short book titled Ruth.

Deuteronomy 23:3 says neither Ammonite nor Moabite shall enter into the congregation of the Lord; even to the tenth generation, shall they not enter into the congregation of the Lord for ever.

Tamar was a deliberate seducer and adulteress. Her story is found in the thirty-eighth chapter of Genesis.

Bathsheba, the mother of Solomon, was a woman whom David seduced from her husband Uriah. The full story can be found in 2 Samuel chapters 11 and 12.

The stories of women who had notorious backgrounds, influencing the life and future of the nation were entries that most writers would have wanted to keep hidden. The message contained in Jesus' Family Tree shows us the very essence of the gospel that God in Jesus Christ breaks down all the barriers that have separated men from God.

The barrier between Jew and Gentile is torn down.

The barrier between male and female is torn down.

Jesus' Family Tree *According to Luke*	*Jesus' Family Tree* *According to Luke*
Luke 3:23-38 23 Jesus, when he began his ministry, was about thirty years of age, being the son (as was supposed) of Joseph, the son of Heli, 24 the son of Matthat, the son of Levi, the son of Melchi, the son of Jan'na-i, the son of Joseph, 25 the son of Mattathi'as, the son of Amos, the son of Nahum, the son of Esli, the son of Nag'ga-i, 26 the son of Ma'ath, the son of Mattathi'as, the son of Sem'e-in, the son of Josech, the son of Joda, 27 the son of Jo-an'an, the son of Rhesa, the son of Zerub'babel, the son of She-al'ti-el, the son of Neri, 28 the son of Melchi, the son of Addi, the son of Cosam, the son of Elma'dam, the son of Er, 29 the son of Joshua, the son of Elie'zer, the son of Jorim, the son of Matthat, the son of Levi, 30 the son of Simeon, the son of Judah, the son of Joseph, the son of Jonam, the son of Eli'akim,	**Comment** **Luke 3:23-38** Luke establishes the ancestry of Jesus' family tree beginning with Joseph and ending with God. Luke is the only one who tells us that Jesus was about thirty years old when he began his ministry (v. 23).

³¹ the son of Me'le-a, the son of Menna, the son of Mat'tatha, the son of Nathan, the son of David, ³² the son of Jesse, the son of Obed, the son of Bo'az, the son of Sala, the son of Nahshon, ³³ the son of Ammin'adab, the son of Admin, the son of Arni, the son of Hezron, the son of Perez, the son of Judah, ³⁴ the son of Jacob, the son of Isaac, the son of Abraham, the son of Terah, the son of Nahor, ³⁵ the son of Serug, the son of Re'u, the son of Peleg, the son of Eber, the son of Shelah, ³⁶ the son of Ca-'nan, the son of Arphax'ad, the son of Shem, the son of Noah, the son of Lamech, ³⁷ the son of Methuselah, the son of Enoch, the son of Jared, the son of Maha'lale-el, the son of Ca-'nan, ³⁸ the son of Enos, the son of Seth, the son of Adam, the son of God.

Chapter 2

Herod and His Boys

CARPENTER'S SHOP

Luke quickly introduces us to one of the most villainous men in history, Herod the Great (Luke 1:5a). They were as unsavory a bunch of people that we will meet in the pages of the New Testament. "One problem we have when we read the New Testament is that there are simply too many Herods in it! (One would be too many!) In the first century before Christ a man named Antipater had a son named Herod who made himself 'King of the Jews.' Around the year 47 B.C. he (Herod the Great) became the territorial ruler of Galilee and around 37 B.C. he became King of all Judea, including the Galilee, Batanea, and the Decapolis. Now, Herod was not a true Jew, but an Idumean, and therefore not entitled to be king. He became king by might, rather than king by right. He was not naturally a Jew, but the offspring of parents who had been forcibly converted to Judaism. We usually refer to him as 'Herod the Great.' I call him 'Herod the Paranoid.'" (Dr. Donald Strobe)

"Herod had ten wives. We know of at least fifteen children, of whom ten were sons. One of his ten wives, his favorite, named Miriamne, had a better claim to the throne than he did because she was of the Hasmonean line. So he had her murdered. He then had his two sons by Miriamne, Alexander and Aristobulus, who had a better claim to the throne than he did, murdered also. This prompted Caesar Augustus to say of him, 'In Herod's palace I would rather be his pig than his prince.' (Actually, he made a play on Greek words here. In the Greek, *'hus'* means pig, and *'huios'* means son. I have kept the alliterative play on words, using 'pig' and 'prince.') Herod didn't kill pigs ... in deference to Jewish kosher laws. Herod had three sons named Herod, and one of the sons he had murdered had a son named Herod, who had a son named Hero. We meet all of these 'Herods' at one time or another in the New Testament, so you can see how easy it is to become confused. That is why I say that there are just too many Herods in the New Testament!" (Dr. Donald Strobe, used with permission.)

BIRTH OF JOHN THE BAPTIST	BIRTH OF JOHN THE BAPTIST
<u>***Zechariah, John the Baptist, father visited by the angel***</u>	<u>***Zechariah, John the Baptist, father visited by the angel***</u>
Luke 1:5a-7	Luke 1:5a-7
5 In the days of Herod, king of Judea, there was a priest named Zechari'ah, of the division of Abi'jah; and he had a wife of the daughters of Aaron, and her name was Elizabeth. 6 And they were both righteous before God, walking in all the commandments and ordinances of the Lord	**Comment** Every direct descendent of Aaron was automatically a priest. There were so many Priests, they were divided into twenty-four divisions. Except for the major Holy days the

blameless. 7 But they had no child, because Elizabeth was barren, and both were advanced in years.

priest would only serve two, one-week terms each year.

A childless wife was a great embarrassment to the husband and even more so to a priest. Barrenness was a justifiable reason for divorce for any member of the priesthood.

Zechariah sees the angel

Luke 1:8-23

8 Now while he was serving as priest before God when his division was on duty, 9 according to the custom of the priesthood, it fell to him by lot to enter the temple of the Lord and burn incense. 10 And the whole multitude of the people were praying outside at the hour of incense. 11 And there appeared to him an angel of the Lord standing on the right side of the altar of incense. 12 And Zechari'ah was troubled when he saw him, and fear fell upon him. 13 But the angel said to him, "Do not be afraid, Zechari'ah, for your prayer is heard, and your wife Elizabeth will bear you a son, and you shall call his name John. 14 And you will have joy and gladness, and many will rejoice at his birth; 15 for he will be great before the

Zechariah sees the angel

Luke 1:8-23

Comment

Zechariah's job was to burn incense in the Temple. As he entered Temple he was startled by the presence of the angel Gabriel. Gabriel cheerfully tells him not to be afraid, then begins to deliver his message, "Your prayer is heard … Elizabeth will bare you a son, and you will call him John." This was a totally unexpected moment. Zechariah had prayed for years for a son. Now, he no longer believed it could happen even though he still continued to pray.

Zechariah's lack of faith burst forth as he, without realizing it, questioned God's power to make it happen, because he and

Lord, and he shall drink no wine nor strong drink, and he will be filled with the Holy Spirit, even from his mother's womb. 16 And he will turn many of the sons of Israel to the Lord their God, 17 and he will go before him in the spirit and power of Eli'jah, to turn the hearts of the fathers to the children, and the disobedient to the wisdom of the just, to make ready for the Lord a people prepared." 18 And Zechari'ah said to the angel, "How shall I know this? For I am an old man, and my wife is advanced in years." 19 And the angel answered him, "I am Gabriel, who stand in the presence of God; and I was sent to speak to you, and to bring you this good news. 20 And behold, you will be silent and unable to speak until the day that these things come to pass, because you did not believe my words, which will be fulfilled in their time." 21 And the people were waiting for Zechari'ah, and they wondered at his delay in the temple. 22 And when he came out, he could not speak to them, and they perceived that he had seen a vision in the temple; and he made signs to them and remained dumb. 23 And when his time of service was ended, he went to his home.

Elizabeth were old and well past the time of childbearing. The penalty for his faith failure was limited in duration. He would be unable to speak until after the boy was born.

Elizabeth conceived **Luke 1:24-25** 24 After these days his wife Elizabeth conceived, and for five months she hid herself, saying, 25 "Thus the Lord has done to me in the days when he looked on me, to take away my reproach among men."	***Elizabeth conceived*** **Luke 1:24-25** **Comment** God was not deterred by the questions of his chosen servant. Zechariah returned home unable to speak a word. When Elizabeth conceived, she remained hidden in her home until Mary came and revealed that she too was pregnant.
The announcement of Jesus' Birth **Luke 1:26** 26 In the sixth month the angel Gabriel was sent from God to a city of Galilee named Nazareth,	***The announcement of Jesus' Birth*** **Luke 1:26** **Comment** I have long pondered what the "sixth month" really refers to. Was it the sixth month of the year? Was it that Elizabeth (in Hebrew, *Elisheva*) was six months pregnant? This is truly a difficult question to answer. It is especially difficult when you add in the factor that it ultimately has a bearing on the dating of Jesus' birth.

Another related question to the above, speaks to the accuracy of December 25 being the "real" date of Jesus' birth. Scarcely any information is provided by the Bible.

My Israeli friend and guide, David Aaron, and I have had many discussions concerning the Bible. He had this to say about the "sixth month." He interprets it this way, "If Jesus was six months younger than John the Baptist and he was born in December that would put the meeting of Mary and her cousin Elizabeth six months prior, possibly in the Hebrew months of Sivan or Tamuz. That is in the month of June."

Thus, the only conclusion I can draw from the report of Luke and the tradition of December 25 being the date of Jesus' birth is that it is the best we can do. Hopefully we discover more information some day in the future.

It is noteworthy that Nazareth is not mentioned in the O.T.

Nazareth is located on the southern slope of a mountain ridge that runs north into

Lebanon. Nazareth is about fourteen miles from the Sea of Galilee and about six miles west from Mount Tabor. The main road connecting Egypt and the interior of Asia lay close to Nazareth as it made its way northward to Damascus.

Nazareth was the home of Joseph and Mary (Luke 2:39) and here the angel announced to the Virgin the birth of the Messiah.

Hail, O favored one

Luke 1:27-28

Hail, O favored one

Luke 1:27-28

27 to a virgin betrothed to a man whose name was Joseph, of the house of David; and the virgin's name was Mary. 28 And he came to her and said, "Hail, O favored one, the Lord is with you!"

Comment

Tradition (not the New Testament) tells us that Mary was drawing water from the only water supply in Nazareth when Gabriel spoke to her.

Mary could never have dreamed what it would mean to be the "favored one" as the mother of the Son of God. Truly her heart would be repeatedly pulled, torn and broken.

Mary, the Well, and Nazareth

Mary's Well is one of the authentic sites in the Holy Land. There is no doubt that Jesus came here with his mother to draw water. Today, the women and children of Nazareth still come to the well.

The stream gushes out of the mountain and runs through a conduit to a public fountain.

The Greek Orthodox claim the Annunciation took place while the Virgin Mary was drawing water from the fountain and built their church over it.

The original name of this location is unknown to us. However, the old settlement dates back into the Bronze Age and was apparently deserted in the year 733 B.C., when Tiglath-Pileser III, the Assyrian conqueror, invaded Galilee. He forced most of the Israelites into exile in Assyria. He then created the Assyrian province of Megiddo, replacing the Israelites with people from other conquered territories.

Excavations indicate that Nazareth was uninhabited during the Persian and early Hellenistic times (8th – 2nd century B.C.). The lack of any Assyrian, Persian and early Hellenistic artifacts support this assumption. The site was later resettled by a group of the Davidic Natzorean, immigrants from the Babylonian exile.

She was greatly troubled	*She was greatly troubled*
Luke 1:29-30a ^{29} But she was greatly troubled at the saying, and considered in her mind what sort of greeting this might be. ^{30} And the angel said to her, "Do not be afraid,	**Luke 1:29-30a** **Comment** Time would establish the validity of her fears. There was no way she could have anticipated the gravity of God's gift.

You have found favor with God	***You have found favor with God***
Luke 1:30b-34	**Luke 1:30b-34**
Mary, for you have found favor with God. 31 And behold, you will conceive in your womb and bear a son, and you shall call his name Jesus. 32 He will be great, and will be called the Son of the Most High; and the Lord God will give to him the throne of his father David, 33 and he will reign over the house of Jacob for ever; and of his kingdom there will be no end." 34 And Mary said to the angel, "How shall this be, since I have no husband?"	**Comment** Mary did not doubt but was curious as to how God would bring all this to fruition.
The child will be called Holy	***The child will be called Holy***
Luke 1:35	**Luke 1:35**
35 And the angel said to her, "The Holy Spirit will come upon you, and the power of the Most High will overshadow you; therefore the child to be born will be called holy, the Son of God.	**Comment** This will be the unique Son of God.
The angel Gabriel tells Mary that Elizabeth is pregnant	***The angel Gabriel tells Mary that Elizabeth is pregnant***
Luke 1:36-38	**Luke 1:36-38**
36 And behold, your kinswoman Elizabeth in her old age has also	**Comments**

conceived a son; and this is the sixth month with her who was called barren. 37 For with God nothing will be impossible." 38 And Mary said, "Behold, I am the handmaid of the Lord; let it be to me according to your word." And the angel departed from her.

Gabriel revealed astounding, wonderful news to Mary.

It was already the sixth month of Elizabeth's pregnancy.

Truly nothing is impossible for God.

Mary Visits Elizabeth

Luke 1:39-56
39 In those days Mary arose and went with haste into the hill country, to a city of Judah, 40 and she entered the house of Zechari'ah and greeted Elizabeth. 41 And when Elizabeth heard the greeting of Mary, the babe leaped in her womb; and Elizabeth was filled with the Holy Spirit 42 and she exclaimed with a loud cry, "Blessed are you among women, and blessed is the fruit of your womb! 43 And why is this granted me, that the mother of my Lord should come to me? 44 For behold, when the voice of your greeting came to my ears, the babe in my womb leaped for joy. 45 And blessed is she who believed that there would be a fulfilment of what was spoken to her from the Lord." 46 And Mary said, "My soul magnifies the Lord, 47 and my spirit rejoices in

Mary Visits Elizabeth

Luke 1:39-56

Comment

This is an independent statement of Luke.

The angel had disclosed to Mary that her cousin, Elizabeth, was expecting a child in her old age. Mary went at once to visit her. Elizabeth's home was in the hill country, meaning this was not a town or even a small village, it was rather what we would call living in a rural setting. Upon arrival, Mary joyfully greeted Elizabeth.

At their meeting, the baby in Elizabeth's womb made a dramatic move that she explained as though he had leaped for joy. At the Holy Spirit's prompting, Elizabeth

God my Savior, 48 for he has regarded the low estate of his handmaiden. For behold, henceforth all generations will call me blessed; 49 for he who is mighty has done great things for me, and holy is his name. 50 And his mercy is on those who fear him from generation to generation. 51 He has shown strength with his arm, he has scattered the proud in the imagination of their hearts, 52 he has put down the mighty from their thrones, and exalted those of low degree; 53 he has filled the hungry with good things, and the rich he has sent empty away. 54 He has helped his servant Israel, in remembrance of his mercy, 55 as he spoke to our fathers, to Abraham and to his posterity for ever." 56 And Mary remained with her about three months, and returned to her home.

pronounced a blessing upon Mary, calling her blessed among women.

Elizabeth then asked Mary why she had come. To this inquiry, Mary began to say, what has become known as the "Magnificat." She began to praise God, to magnify His presence among them. Mary's words were intended to make God more visible to people everywhere. In a sense the word "magnify" would perform the action of using a magnifying glass to make something larger to be seen better. She rejoiced, because within her God had taken decisive action to send forth His son into the human world.

Mary referred to herself as the handmaiden of the Lord. This word carries the meaning of a female slave. Mary rejoiced in her bewilderment that God has selected her, one of such lowly status, to be honored with such a great responsibility. She understood that what God was doing through her would bless people of every race, color, and creed and in turn they would call her blessed for evermore.

	Not only was Mary blessed, but all who fear God, would be blessed. Here the word *fear* means to reverence God and to be obedient to Him. God's act lifted the poor and humble to levels beyond the status of the strong, proud, mighty, even that of Kings and Queens.
	Here is an announcement that would warm the hearts of the lowly and downcast. It would at the same moment send tremors of fear through the rich. God was in the process of fulfilling his promises to Abraham and to the forefathers of Israel that their savior was coming.
	Mary remained with Elizabeth for about three months. This was long enough for the first signs of her pregnancy to begin to appear.
Birth of John the Baptist	**_Birth of John the Baptist_**
Luke 1:57-66	**Luke 1:57-66**
	Comment
57 Now the time came for Elizabeth to be delivered, and she gave birth to a son. 58 And her neighbors and kinsfolk heard that the Lord had shown great mercy to her, and they rejoiced with her. 59 And on the eighth	When John was born, neighbors and family wanted him named Zechariah after his father. Elizabeth said, "No." Zechariah

day they came to circumcise the child; and they would have named him Zechari'ah after his father, 60 but his mother said, "Not so; he shall be called John." 61 And they said to her, "None of your kindred is called by this name." 62 And they made signs to his father, inquiring what he would have him called. 63 And he asked for a writing tablet, and wrote, "His name is John." And they all marveled. 64 And immediately his mouth was opened and his tongue loosed, and he spoke, blessing God. 65 And fear came on all their neighbors. And all these things were talked about through all the hill country of Judea; 66 and all who heard them laid them up in their hearts, saying, "What then will this child be?" For the hand of the Lord was with him.	was given a writing tablet to write his name for the child, he confirmed John as the name for his son. Immediately, Zechariah regained his speech and blessed God.
Zechariah breaks his silence	***Zechariah breaks his silence***
Luke 1:67-80	Luke 1:67-80
	Comment
67 And his father Zechari'ah was filled with the Holy Spirit, and prophesied, saying, 68 "Blessed be the Lord God of Israel, for he has visited and redeemed his people, 69 and has raised up a horn of salvation for us in the house of his servant David,	Zechariah with his ability to speak restored and being filled with the Holy Spirit began to prophesy saying, "Blessed be the Lord God of Israel," He

⁷⁰ as he spoke by the mouth of his holy prophets from of old, ⁷¹ that we should be saved from our enemies, and from the hand of all who hate us; ⁷² to perform the mercy promised to our fathers, and to remember his holy covenant, ⁷³ the oath which he swore to our father Abraham, ⁷⁴ to grant us that we, being delivered from the hand of our enemies, might serve him without fear, ⁷⁵ in holiness and righteousness before him all the days of our life. ⁷⁶ And you, child, will be called the prophet of the Most High; for you will go before the Lord to prepare his ways, ⁷⁷ to give knowledge of salvation to his people in the forgiveness of their sins, ⁷⁸ through the tender mercy of our God, when the day shall dawn upon us from on high ⁷⁹ to give light to those who sit in darkness and in the shadow of death, to guide our feet into the way of peace." ⁸⁰ And the child grew and became strong in spirit, and he was in the wilderness till the day of his manifestation to Israel.	has visited and redeemed His people. From the house of David as God promised through the prophets will come the Blessed One. Through him we will be saved from our enemies and all who hate us. As free men we will serve Him without fear. Zechariah held and expressed the common view of Messiah; he too was looking for a Priestly Warrior. "And you, John, will be called the prophet of the Most High; for you will go before the Lord to prepare his ways. You will give knowledge of salvation and call his people to repentance from their sins and to receive forgiveness and salvation. The Blessed One will give light to those who sit in darkness and guide our feet into the way of peace." John grew in body and spirit. Living in the wilderness may imply that he was raised by members of the Essenes. When he ventured forth it was to prepare the way of the Lord. Word quickly spread and everyone became fearful because they knew that the hand of God was upon this child.

Chapter 3

A MANGER

The Birth of Jesus The Christ	*The Birth of Jesus The Christ*
	Comment
	It should be noted that neither Mark nor John record any information concerning the birth of Jesus.
In the beginning was the Word	*In the beginning was the Word*
John 1:1-5 ¹ In the beginning was the Word, and the Word was with God, and	**John 1:1-5** **Comment**

the Word was God. 2 He was in the beginning with God; 3 all things were made through him, and without him was not anything made that was made. 4 In him was life, and the life was the light of men. 5 The light shines in the darkness, and the darkness has not overcome it…

John establishes the Divinity of Jesus calling him the True Light.

The only True Light

John 1:9-13

9 The true light that enlightens every man was coming into the world. 10 He was in the world, and the world was made through him, yet the world knew him not. 11 He came to his own home, and his own people received him not. 12 But to all who received him, who believed in his name, he gave power to become children of God; 13 who were born, not of blood nor of the will of the flesh nor of the will of man, but of God.

The only True Light

John 1:9-13

Comment

This passage refers to Believers' second birth in Jesus the Christ. Jesus has come to the whole world not just to Nazareth.

Jesus first lived with the people of Nazareth and none had the faintest idea that he was the son of God.

As one of the old Spiritual songs says it, "We didn't know who you was…" Neither did the people of his time with the exception of a small handful who followed him for the rest of their lives. Slowly over time more and more individuals were touched by him and knew he was the Messiah.

	These followers were the product of the second birth which comes by the Holy Spirit to those who truly believe.
And the Word Became Flesh	***And the Word Became Flesh***
John 1:14-18	**John 1:14-18**
14 And the Word became flesh and dwelt among us, full of grace and truth; we have beheld his glory, glory as of the only Son from the Father. 15 He (*John*) bore witness to him, and cried, "This was he of whom I said, 'He who comes after me ranks before me, for he was before me.'" 16 And from his fulness have we all received, grace upon grace. 17 For the law was given through Moses; grace and truth came through Jesus Christ. 18 No one has ever seen God; the only Son, who is in the bosom of the Father, he has made him known.	**Comment** John gives a theological statement of the birth of Jesus. He also states that he, John the Apostle, and John the Baptist are both witnesses to the living Christ.
Jesus is the Son of God	***Jesus is the Son of God***
Mark 1:1 1 The beginning of the gospel of Jesus Christ, the Son of God.	**Mark 1:1** **Comment** Mark opens his account of the Gospel of Jesus with this affirmation.

Evidences that Jesus was Unique

Here are a few evidences that Jesus was not like anyone before or after him.

- Jesus chose to live among the poor and was also born to the poor.

- His closest friends were fishermen, tax collectors, zealots, and quite an assortment of other sinners.

- He touched the sick, lame, and the lepers.

- He professed, "I am the light … Way … resurrection", and more.
- He spoke of God as his personal father.

- He challenged the rich, the religious orthodox, and the Roman Governor.

Garry Wills writes, "He is not like us, that he has higher rights and powers, that he has authority as arbitrary as God's in the book of Job… He is the divine mystery walking among men."[1]

Give thanks for Matthew and Luke

Only Matthew and Luke tell us the events preceding the birth of Jesus. I cannot imagine the Christmas story without these magnificent moments in the event of God coming to be with us.

---

1 *What Jesus Meant,* pp. xvi-xvii.

Joseph resolved to divorce her quietly

Matthew 1:18-19
18 Now the birth of Jesus Christ took place in this way. When his mother Mary had been betrothed to Joseph, before they came together she was found to be with child of the Holy Spirit; 19 and her husband Joseph, being a just man and unwilling to put her to shame, resolved to divorce her quietly.

Joseph, son of David, do not fear

Matthew 1:20-25
20 But as he considered this, behold, an angel of the Lord appeared to him in a dream, saying, "Joseph, son of David, do not fear to take Mary your wife, for that which is conceived in her is of the Holy Spirit; 21 she will bear a son, and you shall call his name Jesus, for he will save his people from their sins." 22 All this took place to fulfill what the Lord had spoken by the prophet: 23 "Behold, a virgin shall conceive and bear a son, and his name shall be called Emmanuel" (which means, God with us)

Joseph resolved to divorce her quietly

Matthew 1:18-19

Comment

When Mary left to visit Elizabeth she was slim and trim. She returned home looking very pregnant. Joseph knew this was not his child. Can we even begin to imagine how he felt? Joseph believed Mary had betrayed him and his heart is broken.

Joseph, son of David, do not fear

Matthew 1:20-25

Comment

This is an independent passage found only in Matthew.

Joseph went to sleep that night with a very troubled mind. His anguish reached the breaking point as he considered quietly divorcing Mary to protect her from being stoned for having a child out of wedlock. Relief finally came as an angel of the Lord revealed the plan of God. Now with full peace Joseph

[Isa.7:14]. 24 When Joseph woke from sleep, he did as the angel of the Lord commanded him; he took his wife, 25 but knew her not until she had borne a son; and he called his name Jesus.	went to Mary to consol her.
Decree of Caesar Augustus	***Decree of Caesar Augustus***
Luke 2:1 1 In those days a decree went out from Caesar Augustus that all the world should be enrolled.	**Luke 2:1** **Comment** Only Luke gives us the information found in chapter 2 of his Gospel. God includes a pagan Emperor, Caesar Augustus, in His plan to have His Son born in Bethlehem.

The Holy Land

It will serve us well to learn a few things about the Holy Land so that we may better understand the power of the Gospels.

The Holy Land possesses many features but the two most significant are: (1) It is the place and to a special people that the Almighty Creator God chose to reveal Himself through His Son Jesus the Christ. (2) It is the land bridge of three continents, Africa, Asia, and Europe.

A Land of Milk and Honey

When God appeared to Moses at the burning bush, He said, "I have come down to deliver Israel out of the hands of the Egyptians, and to bring them up out of that land to a good and broad land, a land flowing with *milk and honey*" (Exod. 3:1-8, emphasis added).

"Flowing with milk and honey" was a proverbial expression meaning that Canaan was fruitful and productive.

It was "a land of wheat and barley, of grapes and fig trees, a land of olive trees and honey, a land in which [Israel was promised] you will eat bread without scarcity, in which you will lack nothing, a land whose stones are iron, and out of whose hills you can dig copper" (Deut. 8:7-9).

The Land Between

Palestine is the land bridge between the continents of Asia and Africa. Rulers of both continents wanted to possess the Holy Land to control its trade routes. Palestine, therefore, was frequently invaded and became subject to foreign rulers. As George Adam Smith explained, the land now called Israel was "between two of the oldest homes of the human race [which] made her a passage for the earliest intercourse and exchanges of civilization. There is probably no older road in all the world than that which can still be used by caravans from the Euphrates to the Nile, through Damascus, Galilee, Esdraelon, Jezreell, the Maritime Plain, and Gaza."[2]

The Holy Land is small in size (14,000 sq. miles); however, it has played an inordinate role in human history. Here lay the ruins of the world's most ancient civilizations. In this land the prophets and Christ spoke immortal teachings and gave divine laws, to direct the course of humanity toward justice, peace and brotherly love. Here were birthed the three monotheistic faiths.

Perhaps the best description of the Holy Land I have encountered comes from my friend Dr. Donald B. Strobe, who said of his work, "Take it and share."

"If you look at a map of Israel, you can divide up the country into four quarters in the following manner:

---
2 Smith, p. 32.

"Draw a vertical line which passes downward from Mt. Hermon in the North, touches the western tip of the Sea of Galilee, goes down through Samaria, Shechem, Bethel, Jerusalem, Hebron, and Debir to Beersheba. Now you have divided the country into the western and eastern halves.

"The western side is affected by the wind and the rains from Europe. The eastern side is affected by the great Arabian Desert. Temperatures in Kuwait for example can climb to 150 degrees Fahrenheit. As the hot air rises, it creates a vacuum. This vacuum sucks in the weather patterns from Europe, which hit the western coastline of Israel. The clouds then run into the great Syrian-African rift, crack up, cross the line of the valley, regroup, and drop the end of their rain on the mountains to the immediate east side of the Jordan Valley. Thus while the coastline is extremely fertile, the eastern side of the Holy Land is barren, like a desert.

"Now, draw a line horizontally across the country, through Jerusalem. The left-hand side of that line should just touch the tip of the Sinai Peninsula, while the right-hand side touches the top of the Dead Sea. Everything to the north of that line is affected by the wind and rains from Europe.

"Everything below that line is affected by the Sahara desert.
"In addition, everything here is affected by the great Syrian-African rift, the deepest scar on the earth's surface, which goes from Turkey in the North to Mozambique in the South. Beginning at Mt. Hermon, 9,348 feet, you have a vast drop in height to the Sea of Galilee which is 700 feet below sea level, then you follow the Jordan River down through the valley until it empties into the Dead Sea which is 1,300 feet below sea level. Nowhere else on earth do you have such vast differences in elevation in such a small distance.

"The rules for the weather patterns in this country are as follows: high is wet and cold, low is dry and warm. That is why different cities only a few miles apart can have vastly different weather characteristics.

"The division of the country between the eastern and western halves has a great meaning for students of the Bible. Along the western coastline you have farmers. Where you farm, you have nectar, where you have nectar, you have bees you have honey.

"The people on the eastern side are not farmers: they are Bedouins, nomads, who wander the land with their sheep and their goats. The sheep and goats provide wool and milk and cheese. And so we have the 'land of milk and honey' which is mentioned in Deuteronomy 8 and 11. The phrase 'land of milk and honey' refers to two very different ways of living upon the land. The 'honey' people (farmers) are builders. They settle on the land and cultivate it for their uses. The 'milk' people are herdsmen. They want to use the land for grazing of their animals. Much of the Hebrew Bible can be understood as wars between the people who live on the eastern side and those who live on the western side.

"In addition, we must remember that the 'honey' side of the land was often occupied by foreigners. Israel is the land bridge between three continents Asia, Africa, and Europe. An important highway runs right down the middle of that land bridge called the 'Via Maris,' the 'Way of the Sea.' The problem is that if you live in the middle of a highway, you are likely to get run over! Only during a very few years in its history was Israel strong enough to control the western side of the country.

"In the 1800 years from Abraham to Jesus, this land knew only 150 years of peace. New Testament scholar N.T. Wright notes that during the past four thousand years, armies have marched into and through this land on average every forty-four years![3]

"From the West came the enemies of this land: Philistines, Phoenicians, Romans, Greeks, Byzantines, the Crusaders, and the Turks (who were really a western influence. Ataturk, of Turkey, made his country over and using the western alphabet and clothing ... This may give

---

3 N.T. Wright. *The New Testament and the People of God.* (Minneapolis: Fortress Press, 1992), Introduction.

us a clue as to why the author of the Book of Revelation says in chapter 21 that in the final reckoning end-time of history, there will be 'no more sea.' John may have written this way for two reasons: (1.) he was exiled by the emperor Domitian on the island of Patmos in the middle of the Aegean Sea, far away from friends and family, in a barren, inhospitable place, where he got mighty tired of listening to the roar and crash of the waves all day and all night. (2.) Jews in ancient times were never sailors. They feared the sea. Their enemies came from there. And they believed that a giant sea creature, more frightening than the Loch Ness monster lived in the depths of the sea. The monster's name was 'Leviathan.' (Cf. Job 3:8; 41:1; Ps. 74:14; 104:26; Isa. 27:1.) In fact, one way of reading Psalm 74:14 is to understand that the writer is describing the great messianic Banquet at the end-time when God has put all of His enemies under His feet, and God's people find themselves seated at a Great Dinner table where the main course is 'baked Leviathan!' So: from the West came the enemies of the people of this land.

"From the East came the 'ites': the Ammonites, the Moabites, the Edomites, the Perizites, and, most importantly for our study, the Israelites. Historian Arnold Toynbee once pondered the question as to why none of the great prophets came from the western or 'honey' side of the land, where the living was relatively easy. Instead, they came from the eastern side, the barren desert, where life was hard and they had to rely completely upon God for their sustenance. Perhaps there is something about the silences of the desert which encourages contemplation and a closer relationship with the Eternal God. It certainly gives those of us who live in the comfort of the West something to think about. Amidst the noise and confusion of the concrete canyons of our great cities, is it possible that we might miss the voice of God speaking to us altogether?"[4]

---

4 Dr. Donald B. Strobe, Lectures delivered in Jerusalem 2000. Used with permission.

The first enrollment

Luke 2:2-5
2 This was the first enrollment, when Quirin'i-us was governor of Syria. 3 And all went to be enrolled, each to his own city. 4 And Joseph also went up from Galilee, from the city of Nazareth, to Judea, to the city of David, which is called Bethlehem, because he was of the house and lineage of David, 5 to be enrolled with Mary, his betrothed, who was with child.

Swaddling cloths

Luke 2:6-7
6 And while they were there, the time came for her to be delivered. 7 And she gave birth to her first-born son and wrapped him in swaddling cloths, and laid him in a manger. because there was no place for them in the inn.

The first enrollment

Luke 2:2-5

Comment

By giving us certain facts scholars have been able to accurately determine the date of this event. It is the first enrollment. Quirin'i-us is governor of Syria. Many ancient records are still available for research.

Swaddling cloths

Luke 2:6-7

Comment

Swaddling cloths were long strips of cloth used to wrap a new born infant. We might call this an infant's baby clothes.

The manger was a large carved stone basin used to hold water or food for the animals.

The inn would have been very different from where we stay when we travel in Israel. It would likely consist of a dwelling for the owner with a wall around the property with rooms built along the inside of the wall for sleeping quarters. A stable would be provided for the animals. Meals would have been prepared over open camp fires by the various travelers or their servants.

Shepherds

Luke 2:8-14

8 And in that region there were shepherds out in the field, keeping watch over their flock by night. 9 And an angel of the Lord appeared to them, and the glory of the Lord shone around them, and they were filled with fear. 10 And the angel said to them, "Be not afraid; for behold, I bring you good news of a great joy which will come to all the people; 11 for to you is born this day in the city of David a Savior, who is Christ the Lord. 12 And this will be a sign for you: you will find a babe wrapped in swaddling cloths and lying in a manger." 13 And suddenly there was with the angel a multitude of the heavenly host praising God and saying, 14 "Glory to God in the highest, and on earth peace among men with whom he is pleased!"

Shepherds

Luke 2:8-14

Comment

Shepherds were very low on the social scale. Theirs was a seven days a week, twelve months a year job, making it impossible for them to be in worship, keep the Sabbath, or observe the ritual laws of washing hands, etc. The shepherds are another example of God selecting the least and the last for great opportunity.

Luke does not give us a description of the angel. Much later, artists would give us their impression of the angelic appearance. There was definitely something about him that troubled Zechariah, Mary, and now the shepherds. Which was it that troubled them; his appearance or his message? Why else would he say, "Do not be afraid?"

The multitude that join the angel were "Praising God" but who decided they were singing Christmas hymns?

When the angels went away

When the angels went away

Luke 2:15-20

15 When the angels went away from them into heaven, the shepherds said to one another, "Let us go over to Bethlehem and see this thing that has happened, which the Lord has made known to us." 16 And they went with haste, and found Mary and Joseph, and the babe lying in a manger. 17 And when they saw it they made known the saying which had been told them concerning this child; 18 and all who heard it wondered at what the shepherds told them. 19 But Mary kept all these things, pondering them in her heart. 20 And the shepherds returned, glorifying and praising God for all they had heard and seen, as it had been told them.

Luke 2:15-20

Comment

Bethlehem is located five miles south of Jerusalem on a rocky hill 2,600 feet above sea-level.

The shepherds wasted no time in investigating what the angel said. They went and found the Holy family. They explained why they had come by recounting what they had experienced.

Were there more present than Joseph and Mary when the shepherds came? Verse eighteen clearly says, "All" raising the possibility others were there too.

Bethlehem

Bethlehem's roots go back to the very remote times of the Patriarchs. It was mentioned in the Bible in connection with the death of Rachel. *[16] Then they journeyed from Bethel; and when they were still some distance from Ephrath, Rachel travailed, and she had hard labor. [17] And when she was in her hard labor, the midwife said to her, "Fear not; for now you will have another son." [18] And as her soul was departing (for she died), she called his name Ben-o'ni; but his father called his name Benjamin. [19] So Rachel died, and she was buried on the way to Ephrath (that is, Bethlehem),* (Gen. 35:16-18).

The next major player in the history of Bethlehem was Ruth, whose story is rich and compelling.

Ruth

[1] In the days when the judges ruled there was a famine in the land, and a certain man of Bethlehem in Judah went to sojourn in the country of Moab, he and his wife and his two sons. [2] The name of the man was Elim'elech and the name of his wife Na'omi, and the names of his two sons were Mahlon and Chilion; they were Eph'rathites from Bethlehem in Judah. They went into the country of Moab and remained there. [3] But Elim'elech, the husband of Na'omi, died, and she was left with her two sons. [4] These took Moabite wives; the name of the one was Orpah and the name of the other Ruth (Ruth 1:1-4).

David

[1] The LORD said to Samuel, "How long will you grieve over Saul, seeing I have rejected him from being king over Israel? Fill your horn with oil, and go; I will send you to Jesse the Bethlehemite, for I have provided for myself a king among his sons" (1 Sam. 16:1-2).

Prophecy

[2] But you, O Bethlehem Eph'rathah, who are little to be among the clans of Judah, from you shall come forth for me one who is to be ruler in Israel, whose origin is from of old, from ancient days (Mic. 5:2).

After centuries of waiting, the time finally came when the words of the prophets came true.

Jesus is circumcised **Luke 2:21** 21 And at the end of eight days, when he was circumcised, he was called Jesus, the name given by the angel before he was conceived in the womb.	***Jesus is circumcised*** Luke 2:21 **Comment** How did the ancients know that blood begins to coagulate on the seventh day after birth? Circumcision was the sign of the covenant between God and Abraham.
Mary's purification **Luke 2:22-24** 22 And when the time came for their purification according to the law of Moses, they brought him up to Jerusalem to present him to the Lord 23 (as it is written in the law of the Lord, "Every male that opens the womb shall be called holy to the Lord") 24 and to offer a sacrifice according to what is said in the law of the Lord, "a pair of turtledoves, or two young pigeons."	***Mary's purification*** Luke 2:22-24 **Comment** After a walk of at least two hours, they arrived at the Temple. At that time, thousands of laborers were working on the restoration and enlargement of the Temple compound and its buildings, which Herod the Great had started in the year 18 B.C. Now, in the twelfth year (the year 6 B.C.) the work on the sanctuary, which had been the first to be enlarged, was already finished.

Another precept required the mother to purify herself after each birth in a ritual bath (Mikveh), to become ritually pure again. As devout Jews, Joseph and Mary observed these rules forty days after the birth.

Simeon

Luke 2:25-35

Simeon

Luke 2:25-35

Comment

25 Now there was a man in Jerusalem, whose name was Simeon, and this man was righteous and devout, looking for the consolation of Israel, and the Holy Spirit was upon him. 26 And it had been revealed to him by the Holy Spirit that he should not see death before he had seen the Lord's Christ. 27 And inspired by the Spirit he came into the temple; and when the parents brought in the child Jesus, to do for him according to the custom law, 28 he took him up in his arms and blessed God and said, 29 "Lord, now lettest thou thy servant depart in peace, according to thy word; 30 for mine eyes have seen thy salvation 31 which thou hast prepared in the presence of all peoples, 32 a light for revelation to the Gentiles, and for glory to thy people Israel."

After Joseph had offered a sacrifice of a pair of doves for the purification of Mary's motherhood, they were approached by two old pious Jews, who came out of a corner: Simeon and Anna. They belonged to the "Devout of Israel," who were waiting and yearning for the arrival of the Messianic salvation. The Greek expression "the devout" used for Simeon, according to many was a backhand way to speak of the Hassid or Essene. His entire behavior, his gift to prophesy, his fervor seemed to imply this. This formulation expresses exactly the Messianic hope of the devout in Qumran. The words of old Simeon aroused unforgettable hopes and deep

33 And his father and his mother marveled at what was said about him; 34 and Simeon blessed them and said to Mary his mother, "Behold, this child is set for the fall and rising of many in Israel, and for a sign that is spoken against 35 (and a sword will pierce through your own soul also), that thoughts out of many hearts may be revealed."

anxiety in Mary that never left her.

Anna

Luke 2:36-40
36 And there was a prophetess, Anna, the daughter of Phan'u-el, of the tribe of Asher; she was of a great age, having lived with her husband seven years from her virginity, 37 and as a widow till she was eighty-four. She did not depart from the temple, worshiping with fasting and prayer night and day. 38 And coming up at that very hour she gave thanks to God, and spoke of him to all who were looking for the redemption of Jerusalem.

39 And when they had performed everything according to the law of the Lord, they returned into Galilee, to their own city, Nazareth. 40 And the child grew and became strong, filled with

Anna

Luke 2:36-40

Comment

Just for fun, calculate the numbers Luke gives to account for Anna's age.

- Married at age 12
- Married for 7 years
- Widow for 65 years
- Total= 84

Luke differs from Matthew saying, "They returned ... to their own city, Nazareth."

Matthew tells us they went to Egypt to escape Herod.

wisdom; and the favor of God was upon him.

Wise Men

Matthew 2:1-6

1 Now when Jesus was born in Bethlehem of Judea in the days of Herod the king, behold, wise men from the East came to Jerusalem, saying, 2 "Where is he who has been born king of the Jews?

For we have seen his star in the East, and have come to worship him." 3 When Herod the king heard this, he was troubled, and all Jerusalem with him; 4 and assembling all the chief priests and scribes of the people, he inquired of them where the Christ was to be born.

5 They told him, "In Bethlehem of Judea; for so it is written by the prophet: 6 'And you, O Bethlehem, in the land of Judah, are by no means least among the rulers of Judah; for from you shall come a ruler who will govern my people Israel.'"

Wise Men

Matthew 2:1-6

Comment

The wise men from the east went to the palace of Herod the King. Where else would the wise men have thought the infant heir would be born?

These wise men had no doubt the star would lead them to the next King of Israel. Herod truly believed the men knew something he did not know and became greatly troubled upon hearing them.

The exact quote of verse two is as follows.

"But you, O Bethlehem Eph'rathah, who are little to be among the clans of Judah, from you shall come forth for me one who is to be ruler in Israel, whose origin is from of old, from ancient days." Micah 5:2

Herod is alarmed

Matthew 2:7-12

7 Then Herod summoned the wise men secretly and ascertained from them what time the star appeared; 8 and he sent them to Bethlehem, saying, "Go and search diligently for the child, and when you have found him bring me word, that I too may come and worship him." 9 When they had heard the king they went their way; and lo, the star which they had seen in the East went before them, till it came to rest over the place where the child was. 10 When they saw the star, they rejoiced exceedingly with great joy; 11 and going into the house they saw the child with Mary, his mother, and they fell down and worshiped him. Then, opening their treasures, they offered him gifts, gold and frankincense and myrrh. 12 And being warned in a dream not to return to Herod, they departed to their own country by another way.

Herod is alarmed

Matthew 2:7-12

Comment

Herod wanted to talk with them privately. He did not want word of a possible challenger having been born who might have a legitimate claim to his crown being talked about openly.

This statement reveals the absolute depravity of Herod. The furthest thing from his mind was worshipping such a potential threat! What did he care if a few lies made it possible to achieve his aims? Herod was thinking, "Go find him for me and I will take care of it from there!"

Had the light of the star vanished when they determined they knew where it was going to lead them? As they emerged from Herod's palace they were fully aware of their error. Once more placing their trust in God for guidance they rejoiced at seeing the star.

Upon finding the heir apparent to the throne the wise men offered their gifts brought from

	the east. Gold we understand, it is a source of currency in every financial system in the world. But what do we know about frankincense and myrrh? Below is an enlargement on what they are and why they were given as gifts. Their route home would not include another visit to Jerusalem. Being warned in a dream they exited at once to escape the treachery of King Herod. At no time does Matthew name these wise men from the east.

Frankincense and Myrrh

The way that people collect the sap is similar to the way people collect rubber-tree sap or pine-tree sap. Cutting the tree's bark causes the sap to ooze out of the cut. The sap used to create both frankincense and myrrh comes slowly and is allowed to dry on the tree. The hardened sap is collected and used as frankincense and myrrh.

Why frankincense? What is myrrh? In fact, these resins and their essential oils were priceless medicines, worth their weight in gold to the Egyptians and Greeks, and were used to treat everything from skin disorders to viral infections, from cancer to depression and more.

Frankincense is tapped from the very scraggly but hardy *Boswellia* tree by scraping the bark and allowing the exuded resins to bleed out and harden. These hardened resins are called tears. There are numerous species and varieties of frankincense trees, each producing a slightly different type of resin. Differences in soil and climate create even more diversity of the resin, even within the same species.

Frankincense trees are also considered unusual for their ability to grow in environments so unforgiving that they sometimes seem to grow directly out of solid rock. The means of initial attachment to the stone is not known but is accomplished by a bulbous disk-like swelling of the trunk. This disk-like growth at the base of the tree prevents it from being torn away from the rock during the violent storms that frequent the region they grow in. This feature is slight or absent in trees grown in rocky soil or gravel. The tears from these hardy survivors are considered superior due to their more fragrant aroma.

Frankincense is edible and often used in various traditional medicines in Asia for digestion and healthy skin. Edible frankincense must be pure for internal consumption, meaning it should be translucent, with no black or brown impurities. It is often light yellow with a (very) slight greenish tint. It is often chewed like gum, but it is stickier because it is a resin.

Indian frankincense (Boswellia serrata) has been used for hundreds of years for treating arthritis. Burning frankincense repels mosquitoes and thus helps protect people and animals from mosquito-borne illnesses, such as malaria.

Myrrh also has been used in the treatment of amenorrhea, dysmenorrhea, menopause, and uterine tumors, as its "blood-moving" properties can purge stagnant blood out of the uterus.

In folk tradition it was helpful to cure muscular pains and in rheumatic plasters it has also been used to treat bleeding disorders and wounds in traditional china. Called *mo yao* in China, it has been used since at least 600 B.C. Primarily as a wound herb and blood stimulant.[5]

---

[5] Information taken from Wikipedia.

Joseph's dream	***Joseph's dream***
Matthew 2:13-15	**Matthew 2:13-15**
13 Now when they [*the wise men*] had departed, behold, an angel of the Lord appeared to Joseph in a dream and said, "Rise, take the child and his mother, and flee to Egypt, and remain there till I tell you; for Herod is about to search for the child, to destroy him." 14 And he rose and took the child and his mother by night, and departed to Egypt, 15 and remained there until the death of Herod. This was to fulfill what the Lord had spoken by the prophet, "Out of Egypt have I called my son."	**Comment** An angel appeared to Joseph in a dream telling him what Herod planned. Joseph was told what to do before hearing why. This is a very hard lesson for the young. *When Israel was a child, I loved him, and out of Egypt I called my son. Hosea 11:1* As a father, Joseph, took serious the word of God, he took positive action!
Herod orders death to the children	***Herod orders death to the children***
Matthew 2:16-18	**Matthew 2:16-18**
16 Then Herod, when he saw that he had been tricked by the wise men, was in a furious rage, and he sent and killed all the male children in Bethlehem and in all that region who were two years old or under, according to the time which he had ascertained from the wise men. 17 Then was fulfilled what was spoken by the prophet Jeremiah:	**Comment** Herod murdered his favorite wife, Miriam, and several of his sons, so the death of hundreds of infants would mean nothing to him. Before King Herod the great died, he ordered the jailing of 1000 of the leading citizens of

18 "A voice was heard in Ramah, wailing and loud lamentation, Rachel weeping for her children; she refused to be consoled, because they were no more."

Israel. He ordered all of these to be executed upon notification of his death. Herod wanted to assure that there would be mourning in Israel at the time of his death.

Death of Herod The Great

Matthew 2:19-20
19 But when Herod died, behold, an angel of the Lord appeared in a dream to Joseph in Egypt, saying, 20 "Rise, take the child and his mother, and go to the land of Israel, for those who sought the child's life are dead."

Death of Herod The Great

Matthew 2:19-20

Comment

The death of Herod the Great opened the way for the return of Jesus to Nazareth.

Archelaus becomes ruler of Judea

Matthew 2:21-23
21 And he rose and took the child and his mother, and went to the land of Israel. 22 But when he heard that Archelaus reigned over Judea in place of his father Herod, he was afraid to go there, and being warned in a dream he withdrew to the district of Galilee. 23 And he went and dwelt in a city called Nazareth, that what was spoken by the prophets might be fulfilled, "He shall be called a Nazarene." *[This exact quote can't be found]*.

Archelaus becomes ruler of Judea

Matthew 2:21-23

Comment

Matthew chapter 2 is unique.

Quickly Joseph led his family back to his homeland. Hearing that Archelaus, son of Herod the Great, now ruled Judea he was afraid the risk was too great to settle within its borders. He made the decision to go to Nazareth in the Galilee to make their new start.

Matthew chapter 2 is unique—
No other Gospel records this information

"When Herod the Great died the Romans decided to place both Judea and Samaria under the rule of one of his sons by the name of Archaelus, who was something of a carbon copy of his father, with the same disregard for the life and property of everyone except his own, (he's not gonna last long); he couldn't keep the peace, he could not collect the taxes, and so they removed him about 6 A.D. Then the Romans decided not to replace him with another member of the family, but to install a Roman administrator. [These are all a matter of records. When the Romans did it they wrote it down. So these administrators are all known.] The first 4 you don't need to know and probably have no occasion to remember, but the 5th one you know, his name is Pontius Pilate. Thus political history washes across the Christian faith. This fact places Pilate in Jerusalem at the time of Jesus arrest, trial, and execution."[6]

Jesus at age twelve	*Jesus at age twelve*
Luke 2:41-43	**Luke 2:41-43**
41 Now his parents went to Jerusalem every year at the feast of the Passover. 42 And when he was twelve years old, they went up according to custom; 43 and when the feast was ended, as they were returning, the boy Jesus stayed behind in Jerusalem. His parents did not know it,	**Comment** Joseph and Mary went every year to the Passover. Did Jesus go before he was twelve years of age? Why did Luke tell his readers Jesus was twelve years old? This would be the age for his Bar Mitzvah. This was the time of passage when a boy became a man.

---

6 Donald Strobe.

According to the noted scholar, William Barclay, "The law required that every adult male Jew who lived within twenty miles of Jerusalem must attend the Passover. In point of fact, it was the aim of every Jew in the world at least once in a lifetime to attend the feast. A Jewish boy became a man when he was twelve years of age. Then he became a son of the law and had to take the obligations of the law upon him."

At this point Jesus made the decision to stay in Jerusalem. Mary and Joseph assumed he was with some part of the family and felt no reason to check.

Comment

Luke 2:44-45

Luke 2:44-45
44 but supposing him to be in the company they went a day's journey, and they sought him among their kinsfolk and acquaintances; 45 and when they did not find him, they returned to Jerusalem, seeking him.

Do you remember the feelings you had when your kids were late coming in from a date, etc?

Comment

Luke 2:46-47

Luke 2:46-47
46 After three days they found him in the temple, sitting among the teachers, listening to them and asking them questions;

Luke 2:46 begins the account of Jesus separating himself from his family.

47 and all who heard him were amazed at his understanding and his answers.

The family started for Nazareth, only to find at the end of the day that Jesus was not with them. They returned to Jerusalem to begin a search to find their son. It took three days before they finally locate him in the temple and to their amazement he is sitting among the teachers. It is interesting to note that sitting was the posture of the Rabbi when he was teaching. Jesus was sitting with the Rabbis listening and asking questions. The rabbis were amazed at his understanding and the answers he gave. Obviously, they were asking him questions and he was asking them questions.

Comment

Luke 2:48-52

Luke 2:48-52

48 And when they saw him they were astonished; and his mother said to him, "Son, why have you treated us so? Behold, your father and I have been looking for you anxiously." 49 And he said to them, "How is it that you sought me? Did you not know that I must be in my Father's house?" 50 And they did not understand the saying which he spoke to them. 51 And he went down with them and came to Nazareth, and was obedient to them; and his mother kept all these things in

We need to look closely at this exchange between Mary, Joseph, and Jesus. Jesus says in essence, after they complained that he has mistreated them, "Why didn't you look for me in my father's house in the first place?"

Jesus then joined them and returned to Nazareth. He fulfilled the role of elder son until the time came for him to leave Nazareth and begin his ministry.

her heart. 52 And Jesus increased in wisdom and in stature, and in favor with God and man.	

By staying behind

By staying behind without informing them, Jesus provides us with early evidence of the independence of his thoughts and actions that were to become hallmarks of his life.

We are still amazed at his teaching and wisdom. He still refuses to conform to our conventions. He comes to us on his terms (only). We can only come to him on his terms!

I find it very interesting that while the rabbis were present and heard the entire exchange there was no negative response on their part when Jesus claimed his relationship of son to father with God. Later the orthodox would want him dead for this very point.

Chapter 4

The Beginning

THE WILDERNESS

John's Ministry Defined	**John's Ministry Defined**
<u>*Dating of John's appearance in the wilderness*</u>	<u>*Dating of John's appearance in the wilderness*</u>
Luke 3:1 ¹ In the fifteenth year of the reign of Tiber'i-us Caesar, Pontius Pilate being governor of Judea, and Herod being tetrarch of Galilee, and his brother Philip tetrarch of the region of Iturae'a and Trachoni'tis, and Lysa'ni as tetrarch of Abile'ne,	**Luke 3:1** **Comment** Trachoni'tis: The Greek name of this rugged region on the east side of the Jordan River (Luke 3:1); was one of the five Roman provinces that were divided into

	districts. It was in the tetrarchy of Philip.
	Iturae'a: A district in the northeast of Palestine, forming, along with the adjacent territory of Trachonitis, the tetrarchy of Philip
	Lysa'ni: Tetrarch of Abilene.
	Abile'ne: district thirty- miles from Damascus.
	Luke 3:1 establishes a date on the timeline for these occurrences. The Romans decided to put the Galilee under the rule of Herod Antipas, one of the sons of Herod the great. Remember this name, because this man is important. He's a constant force and factor in everything that Jesus does in Galilee. Remember, Herod Antipas' job is to keep the peace and pay the taxes.

Geopolitical regions

In order to understand the geopolitical regions in Jesus' day, it is helpful to imagine the face of a clock. From 6:00 a.m. to 12 noon is the area on the western side of the Jordan River which is "our side" (Biblically speaking), the Jewish side, under the control of Herod Antipas, whom Jesus called "that fox" (Luke 13:32) and Pontius Pilate. Around the year 20 A.D., Herod Antipas moved the capital of the Galilee from

Sepphoris to Tiberias, but there is no record that Jesus ever entered that Roman town.

From 12 noon to 3:00 p.m. is the territory under the control of Herod Philip. This was an area made up of Greeks and assimilated Jews, that is, Jews who had taken a lot of Greek culture into their lives. Herod Philip noted that his father had built a magnificent city on the Great Sea called Caesarea, naming it after the Roman ruler, so he built a second Caesarea, and called it Caesarea Philippi. This area becomes important when we remember that it was there Jesus gave his final exam to his students, according to Matthew, chapter 16.

High-priesthood	*High-priesthood*
Luke 3:2a 2 in the high-priesthood of Annas and Ca'iaphas,	**Luke 3:2a** **Comment** The high priesthood of Annas and Caiaphas is listed as singular, while this was a father-in-law and son-in-law that both served in the office on an alternating basis during the life of Jesus.
His name was John	*His name was John*
John 1:6-8 6 There was a man sent from God, whose name was John. 7 He came for testimony, to bear witness to the light, that all might believe through him. [Jesus]. 8 He was not the light, but came to bear witness to the light	**John 1:6-8** **Comment** The Gospel of John makes it unmistakably clear that John the Baptist was not the Christ.

| | John was sent from God. It is significant that God's plan for John's life is clearly spelled out. He will testify as an eyewitness to the identity of Jesus being truly the son of God. His goal is that "all" might believe that Jesus is the true and only son of God.

John is not the light he is a reflection of the light. He will be the beacon to draw many to the light itself. |
|---|---|
| <u>*John's mission is to prepare the way for Jesus*</u>

Mark 1:2-3;
Matthew 3:3;
Luke 3:4-6 | <u>*John's mission is to prepare the way for Jesus*</u>

Mark 1:2-3;
Matthew 3:3;
Luke 3:4-6 |
| **Mark 1:2-3**
2 As it is written in Isaiah the prophet, "Behold, I send my messenger before thy face, who shall prepare thy way; 3 the voice of one crying in the wilderness: Prepare the way of the Lord, make his paths straight"

Matthew 3:3
3 For this is he who was spoken of by the prophet Isaiah when he said, "The voice of one crying in the wilderness: Prepare the way of the Lord, make his paths straight." | **Comment**

John is God's messenger. Mark's word "messenger" and Luke's word "angel" are the same Greek word. John emerges out of the wilderness (the word means desert, desolate, solitary or wasteland).

Here the reference is from Isaiah and literally tells us what happened when Kings went to visit their realm. They demanded the roads be straight and smooth. |

Luke 3:4-6

4 As it is written in the book of the words of Isaiah the prophet, "The voice of one crying in the wilderness: Prepare the way of the Lord, make his paths straight. 5 Every valley shall be filled, and every mountain and hill shall be brought low, and the crooked shall be made straight, and the rough ways shall be made smooth; 6 and all flesh shall see the salvation of God."

Vast numbers of slaves would be dispatched ahead of time to straighten out the roads and to make them smooth so the King would be made comfortable while traveling.

John comes preaching

**Mark 1:4-5;
Matthew 3:1-2;
Luke 3:2b-3**

John comes preaching

**Mark 1:4-5;
Matthew 3:1-2;
Luke 3:2b-3**

Mark 1:4-5

4 John the baptizer appeared in the wilderness, preaching a baptism of repentance for the forgiveness of sins. 5 And there went out to him all the country of Judea, and all the people of Jerusalem; and they were baptized by him in the river Jordan, confessing their sins.

Matthew 3:1-2

1 In those days came John the Baptist, preaching in the wilderness of Judea, 2 "Repent, for the kingdom of heaven is at hand."

Comment

We might say that John the Baptist was the original hellfire and brimstone preacher.

The wilderness of Palestine is far different from the wilderness most Americans envision.

John's parish bounds were from the lush banks of the Jordan River to the desolate waste of the burning sands of this wilderness.

Luke 3:2b-3	
the word of God came to John the son of Zechari'ah in the wilderness; ³ and he went into all the region about the Jordan, preaching a baptism of repentance for the forgiveness of sins.	

The Kingdom of Heaven

The Kingdom of Heaven is a favorite comment of Matthew and implies that the rule of God is about to become evident in the world. Other gospel writers use the term Kingdom of God.

If we approach this passage in a literal sense, it would seem that suddenly out of nowhere John appeared. This is hardly the case. John's personality and appearance would never have allowed him to be inconspicuous. His very presence commanded attention.

He spent his formative years under the influence of Essene theology. John's message was straight forward: people need to repent of their sins. He was painfully aware of the sinfulness that was integrated into everyday life. He saw in the lives of those around him the need for them to turn away from their lifestyle and seek God's will. John believed that it was necessary to repent, and to ask for forgiveness.

When we are told that all the country of Judea and all the people of Jerusalem came to him, without a doubt this is hyperbolic language. Jerusalem was a highly populated city for its day, and obviously there were many who turned out to see, hear, and greet John the Baptist. Judea was a large territory including Jerusalem, and land further to the south.

It is interesting to note that while these converts came to the River Jordan to be baptized they also confessed their sins. Open confession has become almost nonexistent within Christian society today.

John's appearance

**Mark1:6;
Matthew 3:4-6**

Mark 1:6

6 Now John was clothed with camel's hair, and had a leather girdle around his waist, and ate locusts and wild honey.

Matthew 3:4-6

4 Now John wore a garment of camel's hair, and a leather girdle around his waist; and his food was locusts and wild honey. 5 Then went out to him Jerusalem and all Judea and all the region about the Jordan, 6 and they were baptized by him in the river Jordan, confessing their sins.

"I am not the Christ."

John 1:19-23

19 And this is the testimony of John, when the Jews sent priests and Levites from Jerusalem to ask him, "Who are you?" 20 He confessed, he did not deny, but confessed, "I am not the Christ." 21 And they asked him, "What then? Are you Elijah?" He said, "I am not." "Are you the prophet?" And he answered, "No." 22 They said to him then, "Who are you?

John's appearance

**Mark1:6;
Matthew 3:4-6**

Comment

John made a dramatic first impression. He wore a camel's hair tunic, bound at the waist by a leather girdle, made on the order of a pair of men's briefs. His food was locusts and wild honey. The locust tree is common to upper Judea and the Galilee. It produces a pod that when boiled has a likeness to bread. Locust and honey are not found in the wilderness of Judea or southward toward the Dead Sea.

"I am not the Christ."

John 1:19-23

Comment

The Jews sent Priests and Levites from their H.Q. (Jerusalem) to question John. "Who are you?" they asked.

John confessed, he did not deny, "I am not the Christ."

Let us have an answer for those who sent us. What do you say about yourself?" ²³ He said, "I am the voice of one crying in the wilderness, 'Make straight the way of the Lord,' as the prophet Isaiah said."	Then they queried, "Are you Elijah?" "Not on your Life." So they continued, "What about the Prophet?" The Prophet was foretold by Moses. *"The LORD your God will raise up for you a prophet like me from among you, from your brethren—him you shall heed— Deuteronomy 18:15* John replied, "Wrong again." With great frustration they asked their final question, "Then just who are you?" John unequivocally told them, "I am not the Christ I am not worthy to untie his sandals. I have come to make straight the path as Isaiah said.'"
<u>**Bethany beyond the Jordan**</u> **John 1:24-28** ²⁴ Now they had been sent from the Pharisees. ²⁵ They asked him, "Then why are you baptizing, if you are neither the Christ, nor	<u>**Bethany beyond the Jordan**</u> **John 1:24-28** **Comment** John answered their question,

Elijah, nor the prophet?" ²⁶ John answered them, "I baptize with water; but among you stands one whom you do not know, ²⁷ even he who comes after me, the thong of whose sandal I am not worthy to untie." ²⁸ This took place in Bethany beyond the Jordan, where John was baptizing.	"I baptize with water;" They probably wanted to jump in and say something like, "But you claim your baptism leads to the forgiveness of sin." John forged on and made a statement that surely stunned them into silence for the moment, "There is one coming after me that makes me look like a weakling by comparison."

BETHANY BEYOND THE JORDAN

The area almost directly across the Jordan River from Jericho has been identified for nearly 2,000 years as the place where Jesus was baptized by John the Baptist. The site called (Arabic: ***el-Maghtas***) is located on the Jordanian side of the river. Excavations only began there in 1996, following Jordan's peace treaty with Israel in 1994. The site had been unapproachable due to its position along a disputed border and was saturated with thousands of land mines. It took two years to clear the mines from the area. In 1996, archaeologists were able to begin excavating Wadi Kharrar. Their findings have led many scholars to conclude that this is the biblical "Bethany beyond the Jordan." Their work is seen as one of the most important discoveries in recent years for biblical archaeology.

Arguments for the Jordanian site rather that the Batanea site.

John was preaching in the wilderness at a location that was accessible to large numbers of people. Bethany beyond the Jordan was located on one of the major trade routes known as The King's Highway. Travelers, merchants, military, and common folks moved back and forth on this thoroughfare. Seeing and hearing John preach was the stuff of lively conversation.

Bethany beyond the Jordan was easily visible from Jericho. The road leading from Jericho to Jerusalem was heavily used and dangerous, (The Jericho Road is best remembered by the story of the Good Samaritan). News of John raised the concerns of the Pharisees to the extent they sent a delegation to check him out. They were greeted with a salutation of condemnation, "Who warned you brood of vipers …" (Matt. 3:7-10 and Luke 3:7-9).

Jesus traveled from Nazareth to the Jordan River to be baptized by his cousin John the Baptist (Mark 1:9 and Matt. 3:13). Following Jesus' baptism the Spirit drove him into the wilderness to be tempted by Satan (Mark 1:9-13; Matt. 4:1-2; Luke 4:1-13). The quickest access to the wilderness was the barren hills behind Jericho.

An alternate site for Bethany beyond the Jordan

An alternate location for John's ministry has been proposed by Pixner and Riesner. Their view is based on the independent conclusion of several scholars that, in light of variations of spelling in the first century, Bethany should be understood as Batanea. The location then would have been in the region of the Yarmuk River, which drained the Lower Golan (Bashan) area east of the Sea of Galilee. This, of course, would place John's baptism "beyond Jordan."

This location of Bethany in the north would support the sequence of days John mentions (John 1:19-2:12). A Batanea location would have placed Jesus closer to Bethsaida, the home of Peter, Andrew and Philip who met Jesus where John was baptizing. Also, this location would have been nearer to Capernaum, the home of John, who, with Andrew, met privately with Jesus.

What conclusion may we draw from these two positions?

The Pixner/Riesner position is based on the following:

1. They believe the word Bethany was misspelled and should read Batanea.

2. Placing the site in the north makes it more convenient to match the future disciples Peter, Andrew, and Philip with their home town of Bethsaida and a journey to Capernaum. Both towns were located on the northern edge of the Sea of Galilee. (John 1:19-2:12)

Archaeology and Bethany beyond the Jordan:

1. The correct spelling of Bethany is not contested by the majority of scholars.
2. Bethany beyond the Jordan clearly delineates this town from the home town of Lazarus and his sisters.
3. The events of John 1:19-2:12 are not eight sequential days.
    a) John 1:19, The Pharisees send priest and Levites to question John. This could have taken place at either location.
    b) John 1:29, John proclaims, "Behold the Lamb of God."
    c) John 1:35, Two of John's disciples follow Jesus.
    d) John 1:43, Jesus decides to go to Galilee.
    e) John 2:1-11, The miracle at Cana.
    f) John 2:12, Jesus goes to Capernaum.

Matthew and Luke report the Temptations of Jesus as taking place immediately after John baptized him. He was then in the wilderness for forty days. Taken literally or figuratively forty days is a long time.

The comparison of scriptural passages coupled with the work of the archaeologist make me very confident that the site of Jesus' baptism was near Jericho at the Jordan River rather than in Batanea.

He is mightier than me

Mark 1:7-8

7 And he preached, saying, "After me comes he who is mightier than I, the thong of whose sandals I am not worthy to stoop down and untie. 8 I have baptized you with water; but he will baptize you with the Holy Spirit."

You brood of vipers

**Matthew 3:7-10;
Luke 3:7-9**

Matthew 3:7-10

7 But when he saw many of the Pharisees and Sad'ducees coming for baptism, he said to them, "You brood of vipers!

He is mightier than me

Mark 1:7-8

Comment

This message was simple and straightforward. All of you are sinners and now it is time for you to repent. To repent meant to turn around and go the opposite way that is to stop what you are presently doing and accept a new direction, a new way of living.

There was an outpouring of positive response to John's message as people came from the city of Jerusalem and the surrounding area of Judea, and all along the Jordan River, and even gentiles from the Decapolis came to hear this powerful speaker.

You brood of vipers

**Matthew 3:7-10;
Luke 3:7-9**

Comment

Matthew and Luke report the same message but they address it to different audiences.

Who warned you to flee from the wrath to come? 8 Bear fruit that befits repentance, 9 and do not presume to say to yourselves, 'We have Abraham as our father'; for I tell you, God is able from these stones to raise up children to Abraham. 10 Even now the axe is laid to the root of the trees; every tree therefore that does not bear good fruit is cut down and thrown into the fire.

Look closely at verse seven, it bristles with hostility. John's greeting was similar to a whip lash, another way of John saying it is, "Who told you to get your act together, are you ready to repent of your sham of false religiosity?"

They countered immediately, "Who are you, and by what authority do you preach and baptize?"

John ignores their question about authority.

Luke 3:7-9
7 He said therefore to the multitudes that came out to be baptized by him, "You brood of vipers! Who warned you to flee from the wrath to come? 8 Bear fruits that befit repentance, and do not begin to say to yourselves, 'We have Abraham as our father'; for I tell you, God is able from these stones to raise up children to Abraham. 9 Even now the axe is laid to the root of the trees; every tree therefore that does not bear good fruit is cut down and thrown into the fire."

Luke 3:7-9

Comment

Luke carries the idea of the multitudes that come out to John to another level. John greeted them by saying, "You brood of vipers who warned you?" John was a no-nonsense preacher. As we say today, he cut immediately to the chase.

In all likelihood, the ones who warned them were those who had heard John's message. John quickly turned to the most important aspect of repentance. If there is true repentance the fruit of their lives should bear witness to it. If they continue to live as before, has repentance actually occurred?

The people of Israel looked to Abraham as their father. They lived vicariously on his faith in God. They believed that because they were his ancestors that his relationship to God would carry them through.

John made it very clear if God wanted more children of Abraham he could raise them up from the very stones upon which they walked. John saw the future as being almost present, as he said the ax was already laid to the root of the tree. This conveyed the meaning that every life that does not bear spiritual fruit would be cut down. As frightening as that concept was, John expanded it to say those that were cut down would be thrown into the fire. The people fully understood you cannot afford to let a barren tree take up space from a fruitful one!

John believed and preached that to love God is a joy and to disregard God is absolute folly.

THREE TORAH SCHOOLS

The following should help to explain some of the differences among the religious positions of the time.

At the time of Jesus all three religious movements were recognized forms of Jewish life. All three recognized the Torah as supreme law, but each group had its own interpretation of how the law should be observed. Of these three religious movements, only the school of the Pharisees has survived among the Jewish people until today and is the foundation of rabbinic Judaism.

The most significant was the school of the PHARISEES. They originally belonged to the Hasidic movement, but later separated from them and developed their own set of beliefs concerning the Torah. They maintained that the collection of their Oral Ancestral Tradition went back to Moses himself. Their central concern was to safeguard observance of the Divine Law by creating a multitude of secondary laws that formed a hedge around the Torah. They regarded the Writings of the Prophets as the word of God too. They believed in the resurrection of the dead at the end of time.

During the first part of the second century B.C., the Hellenistic rulers of Antiochia (Seleucids) began to interfere in the religious policy of Israel, and the observance of Jewish laws was punished as an offense, among them the group of the Hassidim, fled to the hills (1 Macc. 2:42). Initially, they supported the uprising of the Maccabees against the Syrians (2 Macc. 14:6), but when Jonathan, the brother of Judas the Maccabee, from the lower ranking priestly line of the Hasmoneans, was enthroned as high priest and king, they denied him recognition. Others separated themselves [Hebrew: perushl] and formed the group of the Perushim [Pharisees]. This group, which consisted mainly of non-priests, gradually became the influential Torah School of the Pharisees (Josephus, ANTIQUITIES XIII 171).

The SADDUCEES were politically the most influential. They were composed largely of the priestly aristocracy. They regarded only the five Books of Moses as the Word of God. They rejected the Books of the Prophets. They also rejected belief in the resurrection of the dead. They held that God rewarded the just in this life.

The ESSENES were a deeply religious movement having come into being under the leadership of the "Teacher of Righteousness", who withdrew from the Temple service into the desert around the middle of the second century B.C. They regarded the Maccabean (Hasmonean) high priests, who invested themselves with royal powers, as usurpers, and their sacrificial offerings in the Temple as illegitimate. To purify themselves from guilt they no longer offered sacrifices but purified themselves in ritual baths. Judging from the Copper Scroll they had three monastic centers, called "kokhlit", one at Secacah (the ruins of Qumran) another on the southwestern hill of Jerusalem (present-day Zion) and a third in "the Land of Damascus" (in the corner formed by the rivers Yarmuk and Rukkad (in modern southern Syria). [Father Pixner].

Both Philo and Flavius Josephus, tell us unmarried as well as married Essenes were to be found in most towns and villages of the country. It is possible that John the Baptist belonged to this movement, but left it to pursue his own mission. (The Natzorean clan might possibly have been influenced by them.)

As we shall see later, there are reasons to believe that Jesus' family was influenced by the Essenes. In addition, Mary was related to Elizabeth, daughter and wife of priests. Zechariah and John the Baptist were both priests (cf. Luke 1:5).

Baptize with water Matthew 3:11-12; Luke 3:15-17	***Baptize with water*** Matthew 3:11-12; Luke 3:15-17
Matthew 3:11-12 11 "I baptize you with water for repentance, but he who is	**Comment** The Greek word we translate

coming after me is mightier than I, whose sandals I am not worthy to carry; he will baptize you with the Holy Spirit and with fire. 12 His winnowing fork is in his hand, and he will clear his threshing floor and gather his wheat into the granary, but the chaff he will burn with unquenchable fire."

mightier, means, a strong mighty man, strong in both body and mind, one who has strength of soul to sustain the attacks of Satan.

The Greek word we translate *worthy* means, sufficient in ability.

When John said that he was not worthy to carry the sandals of Jesus he was attempting to describe in graphic terms the high position in which he held Jesus as compared to himself. This would resonate with the people who comprised his audience.

John said that Jesus would baptize with the Holy Spirit and with fire. In this context the word fire can be thought of as a gift of power from God.

Luke 3:15-17
15 As the people were in expectation, and all men questioned in their hearts concerning John, whether perhaps he were the Christ, 16 John answered them all, "I baptize you with water; but he who is mightier than I is coming, the thong of whose sandals I am not worthy to untie; he will baptize you with the Holy Spirit

Luke 3:15-17

Comment

As people listened to John preach they wondered in their hearts if he in fact was the Christ. Perceiving this, or possibly being questioned about it, John gave a specific and emphatic answer. John stated that he came to baptize

and with fire. ^{17} His winnowing fork is in his hand, to clear his threshing floor, and to gather the wheat into his granary, but the chaff he will burn with unquenchable fire."	with water but the one who is coming behind him, the Christ, will baptize with the Holy Spirit and with fire. John said, "As strong and formidable as I may appear he is mightier than me. He is so far above me I am not even worthy to untie his sandals or to wash his feet." John used an illustration his audience would clearly understand, he pictured the Christ coming with his winnowing fork in his hand. (This winnowing fork would resemble a pitchfork in a farmer's tool shed. The fork was used to toss the stalks of grain into the air and let the force of the wind blow away the lighter husk and stalk allowing the kernels of grain to fall to the floor.) John emphasized a further well-known point; the chaff was always destroyed by fire. John further said those who do not choose to live up to God's claim on their life will also be burnt up but in an unquenchable fire.

What then shall we do?

Luke 3:10-14

¹⁰ And the multitudes asked him, "What then shall we do?" ¹¹ And he answered them, "He who has two coats, let him share with him who has none; and he who has food, let him do likewise." ¹² Tax collectors also came to be baptized, and said to him, "Teacher, what shall we do?" ¹³ And he said to them, "Collect no more than is appointed you." ¹⁴ Soldiers also asked him, "And we, what shall we do?" And he said to them, "Rob no one by violence or by false accusation, and be content with your wages."

What then shall we do?

Luke 3:10-14

Comment

As the multitudes listened they begin to wonder and ask, "What shall we do?" John was explicit in his answer. His answer gave a clear glimpse of everyday life during the time of Jesus.

"What you should do is very simple," John said, "if you have two coats share one of them. If you have food to eat share it with those who do not."

Tax collectors were among his hearers and he told them not to collect more than was right. (In chapter 7 we will look at the tax collecting system in more detail). Many soldiers came to hear John and were struck by the power and directness of his words and asked the same question and John gave a strikingly clear answer. He said, "Do not rob anyone by violence or by false accusations. Be content with your wage and do not extort from innocent people."

John's preaching was relevant

People today frequently talk about the lack of relevance preaching has for their lives. Without question John's preaching was relevant to the people who heard him. One can only wonder how uncomfortable congregations today would be in truly hearing what should be done to bear fruits of the Spirit in their lives.

Chapter 5

Jesus Begins His Ministry

THE JORDAN RIVER

Baptism of Jesus	*Baptism of Jesus*
Mark 1:9; Matthew 3:13	Mark 1:9; Matthew 3:13
Mark 1:9 9 In those days Jesus came from Nazareth of Galilee and was baptized by John in the Jordan. **Matthew 3:13** 13 Then Jesus came from Galilee to the Jordan to John, to be baptized by him.	**Comment** In what days? This can best be explained by quoting Luke 3:23, "Jesus, when he began his ministry, was about thirty years of age,"

Jesus departed Nazareth

Jesus departed Nazareth, intending to be baptized by his cousin, John. From Nazareth Jesus would have followed a valley known as the Valley of the wind and the doves. This valley is about twenty-two miles long and comes out on the Sea of Galilee near the city of Capernaum. Once on the shoreline he would have followed its banks until he crossed the Jordan River. Here he would have turned south toward Jericho and Bethany beyond the Jordan. Prior to the last thirty to forty years, when scholars spoke of Bethany they were referring to the city on the Mount of Olives by that name which was the home of Lazarus and his two sisters, Martha and Mary.

The Jordan River begins at the base of Mt. Hermon and plunges steadily downward until its waters mingle with those of Lake Galilee. (The name Jordan means "the descender.") By the time it empties into the lake it has dropped from a height of some 4,000 feet above sea level to a depth of around 700 feet below sea level.

From the Sea of Galilee, the Jordan River wends its way downward for some 65 miles as the crow flies, or 135 miles as the river wends, to the Dead Sea 1,300 feet below sea level. There is no other place on the face of the earth where you will find such a vast difference in such a small geographical area.

Three stages in the development of baptism:

- Stage one: Baptism of oneself was performed in running (living) water, in order to gain ritual purity, as practiced by the Essenes or in a Mikveh when no natural running water was available.

The Mikveh is a specific type of bath designed for the purpose of ritual immersion. The word *mikveh*, as used in the Hebrew Bible, literally means a "collection" generally, a collection of water.

Several biblical regulations specify that full immersion in water is required to regain ritual purity after ritually impure incidents have occurred. Most forms of impurity could be nullified through immersion in any natural collection of water. Some however require "living water," such as springs or groundwater wells. Living water has the further advantage of being able to purify even while flowing as opposed to rainwater which must be stationary in order to purify. The *mikveh* is designed to simplify this requirement, by providing a bathing facility that remains in ritual contact with a natural source of water.[7]

- Stage two: Plunging one into running water by a Baptizer as a sign of conversion and repentance in preparation for the kingdom of God.

- Stage three: Christian baptism in the form of immersion, pouring, or sprinkling as an effective sign of entry into God's kingdom.

John was reluctant to baptize Jesus	*John was reluctant to baptize Jesus*
Matthew 3:14-15	**Matthew 3:14-15**
14 John would have prevented him, saying, "I need to be baptized by you, and do you come to me?" 15 But Jesus answered him, "Let it be so now; for thus it is fitting for us to fulfil all righteousness." Then he consented.	**Comment** John was very uncomfortable with Jesus' request for baptism. He realized that if one needed to be baptized it was himself not Jesus. Jesus assured him they were doing the right thing. Jesus' baptism was not for the forgiveness of sin.

---

7 Wikipedia, the free encyclopedia.

### *Behold, the Lamb of God*	### *Behold, the Lamb of God*
John 1:29-34 29 The next day he *(John)* saw Jesus coming toward him, and said, "Behold, the Lamb of God, who takes away the sin of the world! 30 This is he of whom I said,' After me comes a man who ranks before me, for he was before me.' 31 I myself did not know him; but for this I came baptizing with water, that he might be revealed to Israel." 32 And John bore witness, "I saw the Spirit descend as a dove from heaven, and it remained on him. 33 I myself did not know him; but he who sent me to baptize with water said to me, 'He on whom you see the Spirit descend and remain, this is he who baptizes with the Holy Spirit.' 34 And I have seen and have borne witness that this is the Son of God."	**John 1:29-34** **Comment** John's version is quite different from the other Evangelists. John the Baptist acknowledged Jesus as above him in every way. He also said that he did not know his cousin, Jesus, was the Messiah until after the baptism was completed. This was when John saw the Spirit descend upon Jesus and remain upon him. God had previously told John to watch for this occurrence. This would be the sign by which John would recognize the Christ.
### *Jesus emerges from the water*	### *Jesus emerges from the water*
Mark 1:10-11; Matthew 3:16-17; Luke 3:21-22	**Mark 1:10-11; Matthew 3:16-17; Luke 3:21-22**
Mark 1:10-11 10 And when he came up out of the water, immediately he saw the heavens opened and the Spirit	**Comment** Luke tells us that all the people

descending upon him like a dove; 11 and a voice came from heaven, "Thou art my beloved Son; with thee I am well pleased."

Matthew 3:16-17
16 And when Jesus was baptized, he went up immediately from the water, and behold, the heavens were opened and he saw the Spirit of God descending like a dove, and alighting on him; 17 and lo, a voice from heaven, saying, "This is my beloved Son, with whom I am well pleased."

Luke 3:21-22
21 Now when all the people were baptized, and when Jesus also had been baptized and was praying, the heaven was opened, 22 and the Holy Spirit descended upon him in bodily form, as a dove, and a voice came from heaven, "Thou art my beloved Son; with thee I am well pleased."

He also tells us that Jesus was praying and then the heavens opened.

When Jesus came up out of the water, indicating that he had been immersed. The spirit of God came upon him in the form or likeness of a dove. At the same moment a voice was heard from God saying, "Thou art my beloved son with thee I am well pleased."

The moment of destiny for Jesus had come. The Spirit of God led him into the desert, where a radical and far-reaching change came over him.

It is more than coincidental that Jesus came to his cousin John to receive baptism. As we will soon see, Jesus' early ministry was heavily influenced by John who fits the description of an Essene prophet preacher.

*<u>The Spirit drives/leads,
Jesus into the wilderness</u>*

Mark 1:12-13;
Matthew 4:1-2;
Luke 4:1-2

*<u>The Spirit drives/leads,
Jesus into the wilderness</u>*

Mark 1:12-13;
Matthew 4:1-2;
Luke 4:1-2

Mark 1:12-13

Comment

12 The Spirit immediately drove him out into the wilderness. 13 And he was in the wilderness forty days, tempted by Satan; and he was with the wild beasts; and the angels ministered to him.

Matthew 4:1-2
1 Then Jesus was led up by the Spirit into the wilderness to be tempted by the devil. 2 And he fasted forty days and forty nights, and afterward he was hungry.

Luke 4:1-2
1 And Jesus, full of the Holy Spirit, returned from the Jordan, and was led by the Spirit 2 for forty days in the wilderness, tempted by the devil. And he ate nothing in those days; and when they were ended, he was hungry.

It was the Spirit of God that drove Jesus into the wilderness.

Before making my first visit to The Holy Land, the word "wilderness" signified to me the land that confronted the Pilgrims as they landed in Massachusetts, tall trees and almost impassable undergrowth.

The writers of Scripture know nothing of such geography. To them the wilderness means desert, desolation, a place where virtually nothing grows. It is a region populated by goats, sheep, camels, scorpions and Nomads. And it is always hot. It was into this environment that the Spirit drove Jesus.

Mark tells us that he stayed there for forty days. When the Bible uses forty days, or forty years, it is talking about a long time not how many calendar days or weeks it involves. Jesus had very specific reasons for his sojourn into the desert for that long period of time. He went to think, pray, meditate, and let God speak to him, as he put the final issues of his ministry together.

Mark makes no mention of the Temptations.

There are two kinds of temptations

- Gratification: relates to one's basic needs; food when you're hungry, clothes to wear when you are naked, and shelter.

- Affirmation: relates to those things one receives from others; applause, homage, and adoration.

The first temptation: ***to turn stones into bread is*** ***A temptation for Gratification***	*The first temptation:* ***to turn stones into bread is*** ***A temptation for Gratification***
Matthew 4:3-4; **Luke 4:3-4**	**Matthew 4:3-4;** **Luke 4:3-4**
Matthew 4:3-4 3 And the tempter came and said to him, "If you are the Son of God, command these stones to become loaves of bread." 4 But he answered, "It is written, 'Man shall not live by bread alone, but by every word that proceeds from the mouth of God.'" **Luke 4:3-4** 3 The devil said to him, "If you are the Son of God, command this stone to become bread." 4 And Jesus answered him, "It is written, 'Man shall not live by bread alone.'"	**Comment** As Jesus prepared to leave the wilderness he realized how extremely hungry he was. Satan appeared and said, "If you're so hungry just change some of these stones into bread, you can do it 'If' you are the son of God." Every temptation begins with "If". Isn't this also the opening word of the temptations we face? For the vast majority of the population hunger was a constant condition. Jesus said, "I am not so hungry as to defy my Father who has told us that man shall not live by bread alone" (Deut. 8:3).

	Jesus made it abundantly clear that anyone who simply feeds the masses will lose their allegiance when their bellies become empty. Jesus came for more than that.
<u>Satan's second temptation is also A Temptation of Affirmation</u>	**<u>Satan's second temptation is also A Temptation of Affirmation</u>**
Matthew 4:5-7; Luke 4:9-12	**Matthew 4:5-7; Luke 4:9-12**
Matthew 4:5-7 5 Then the devil took him to the holy city, and set him on the pinnacle of the temple, 6 and said to him, "If you are the Son of God, throw yourself down; for it is written, 'He will give his angels charge of you,' and 'On their hands they will bear you up, lest you strike your foot against a stone.'" 7 Jesus said to him, "Again it is written, 'You shall not tempt the Lord your God.'" **Luke 4:9-12** 9 And he took him to Jerusalem, and set him on the pinnacle of the temple, and said to him, "If you are the Son of God, throw yourself down from here; 10 for it is written, 'He will give his angels charge of you, to guard	**Comment** Remember the word affirmation in part means, "A positive declaration or assertion." Satan tried to entice Jesus to attract the attention of the masses by using this spectacular event. For his second temptation, the devil took Jesus to the Temple in Jerusalem to the highest of the pinnacles and said to him, "Jump, you do not need to be afraid, if you're the son of God." Satan referred to Psalms 91:11-12, "For he will give his angels charge of you to guard you in all your ways. On their hands they will bear you up, lest you dash your foot against a stone. Jesus replied, "I will not tempt God."

will bear you up, lest you strike your foot against a stone.'" 12 And Jesus answered him, "It is said, 'You shall not tempt the Lord your God.'"

to Deuteronomy 6:16, "You shall not put the LORD your God to the test, as you tested him at Messah." In essence, Jesus said you may dazzle the crowd with spectacular events, but you do not win their hearts. No amount of miracles will win the allegiance of the heart.

This is the Second Temptation of Affirmation

**Matthew 4:8-11;
Luke 4:5-8**

Matthew 4:8-11
8 Again, the devil took him to a very high mountain, and showed him all the kingdoms of the world and the glory of them; 9 and he said to him, "All these I will give you, if you will fall down and worship me." 10 Then Jesus said to him, "Begone, Satan! for it is written, 'You shall worship the Lord your God and him only shall you serve.'" 11 Then the devil left him, and behold, angels came and ministered to him.

Luke 4:5-8
5 And the devil took him up, and showed him all the kingdoms of the world in a moment of time, 6 and said to him, "To you I will give all this authority and their

This is the Second Temptation of Affirmation

**Matthew 4:8-11;
Luke 4:5-8**

Comment

The highest place Matthew could imagine was the top of a mountain, so he said that was where the devil took Jesus.

Satan said to Jesus, "Why go to all this trouble. You are trying to win these people I will simply give them to you."

Luke says, "The devil took him up." Until modern times man had no conception of how you could see more than a few miles in any direction. Today we see pictures taken from satellites that make visible half the earth at a single glimpse. Thus, the third temptation becomes more

glory; for it has been delivered to me, and I give it to whom I will. 7 If you, then, will worship me, it shall all be yours." 8 And Jesus answered him, "It is written, 'You shall worship the Lord your God, and him only shall you serve.'"

understandable to this and subsequent generations.

"Everything you see belongs to me. I can do with them as I please," said Satan.

The world is the kingdom of Satan! Jesus did not dispute his claim! (Jesus spoke often of the coming Kingdom of God.)

Satan's prime objective was to entice Jesus to bow down and worship him, just one time! Jesus understood the full implication of what worshiping Satan meant. It would be tantamount to renouncing God and this Jesus would not do. Then Jesus orders Satan to be gone.

The most chilling, revealing, single verse in the New Testament!

Luke 4:13

13 And when the devil had ended every temptation, he departed from him until an opportune time.

The most chilling, revealing, single verse in the New Testament!

Luke 4:13

Comment

Here is one of the most critical/ chilling verses in the Bible. Satan told Jesus that he was not finished, and he would be back when his chances seem better!

This is an independent statement of Luke.

The decisions for Jesus' ministry were now finalized.

Israel's history had been littered with would-be Messiahs. Their agenda had always been the political overthrow of the dominating countries. Jesus had a new agenda. His objective was the reformation of the religious community of Israel. He fully understood that this would be a more formidable adversary to change.

The remainder of Jesus' ministry revolved around his attempts to revitalize Israel's basic faith in God. He would confront the religious authorities on many levels. This is seen in his healings, his teachings, and confrontations with scribes, Pharisees, Herodians, and even the chief priest.

Jesus returns to Galilee	***Jesus returns to Galilee***
Luke 4:14-15	**Luke 4:14-15**
14 And Jesus returned in the power of the Spirit into Galilee, and a report concerning him went out through all the surrounding country. 15 And he taught in their synagogues, being glorified by all.	**Comment** The comment *Jesus returned to Galilee*, means Jesus was not fleeing from Herod Antipas but was moving directly into his territory. Herod Antipas ruled Galilee and was the arch enemy of Jesus. The Pharisees served as eyes and ears for Herod no matter where Jesus went. What does it mean Jesus was glorified by the people as he spoke in their synagogue? It means most of those who heard were captivated by his words and impacted by the power of his message.

Jesus visits Capernaum

Mathew 4:13-16
13 and leaving Nazareth he went and dwelt in Caper'na-um by the sea, in the territory of Zeb'ulun and Naph'tali, 14 that what was spoken by the prophet Isaiah might be fulfilled: 15 "The land of Zeb'ulun and the land of Naph'tali, toward the sea, across the Jordan, Galilee of the Gentiles— 16 the people who sat in darkness have seen a great light, and for those who sat in the region and shadow of death light has dawned."

Jesus visits Capernaum

Matthew 4:13-16

Comment

This is an independent statement of Matthew.

Galilee of the Gentiles refers to the ninth chapter of Isaiah, written at the close of the eight century B.C., the prophet refers to this area as "Galilee of the Nations" or "Galilee of the Gentiles." The majority of this population consisted of non-Hebrews, and continued to be so for many centuries, unlike Judah in the south. Under the short lived rule of the Hasmoneans, Galilee was annexed into the larger Jewish state, and efforts were made to Judaize the heterogeneous population. But this effort proved to be unsuccessful. Thus, in Galilee Jesus would have come in contact with Gentiles from many parts of the world.

Sounds like John the Baptist

Matthew 4:17
17 From that time Jesus began to preach, saying, "Repent, for the kingdom of heaven is at hand."

Sounds like John the Baptist

Matthew 4:17

Comment

	This statement is a carbon copy of John the Baptist. If we could hear both men speak these words, then we might gage some difference in their tone or body language. Perhaps Jesus may have sounded more imperative while John may have sounded more judgmental.
Follow me **Mark 1:16-20; Matthew 4:18-22; Luke 5:1-11**	*Follow me* **Mark 1:16-20; Matthew 4:18-22; Luke 5:1-11**
Mark 1:16-20 16 And passing along by the Sea of Galilee, he saw Simon and Andrew the brother of Simon casting a net in the sea; for they were fishermen. 17 And Jesus said to them, "Follow me and I will make you become fishers of men." 18 And immediately they left their nets and followed him. 19 And going on a little farther, he saw James the son of Zeb'edee and John his brother, who were in their boat mending the nets. 20 And immediately he called them; and they left their father Zeb'edee in the boat with the hired servants, and followed him.	**Comment** At the outset, Jesus told these future members of the Inner circle little about Himself. He told them what they will become, "Fishers of men." They probably had no idea what Jesus was talking about. Certainly no idea of what the next few years held in store for them.

Matthew 4:18-22

18 As he walked by the Sea of Galilee, he saw two brothers, Simon who is called Peter and Andrew his brother, casting a net into the sea; for they were fishermen. 19 And he said to them, "Follow me, and I will make you fishers of men." 20 Immediately they left their nets and followed him. 21 And going on from there he saw two other brothers, James the son of Zeb'edee and John his brother, in the boat with Zeb'edee their father, mending their nets, and he called them. 22 Immediately they left the boat and their father, and followed him.

Luke 5:1-11

1 While the people pressed upon him to hear the word of God, he was standing by the lake of Gennes'aret. 2 And he saw two boats by the lake; but the fishermen had gone out of them and were washing their nets. 3 Getting into one of the boats, which was Simon's, he asked him to put out a little from the land. And he sat down and taught the people from the boat. 4 And when he had ceased speaking, he said to Simon, "Put out into the deep and let down your nets for a catch." 5 And Simon answered,

Luke 5:1-11

Comment

Gennesaret is another name for the Sea of Galilee. As Jesus walked along the shore a crowd soon collected, people wanted to see and hear him. Peter's boat was pulled on the shore, lying empty, Jesus asked to use it. Then sitting in the bow, he began to preach. When he finished his discourse he asked Peter to put out into the lake and do some fishing.

"Master, we toiled all night and took nothing! But at your word I will let down the nets." 6 And when they had done this, they enclosed a great shoal of fish; and as their nets were breaking, 7 they beckoned to their partners in the other boat to come and help them. And they came and filled both the boats, so that they began to sink. 8 But when Simon Peter saw it, he fell down at Jesus' knees, saying, "Depart from me, for I am a sinful man, O Lord." 9 For he was astonished, and all that were with him, at the catch of fish which they had taken; 10 and so also were James and John, sons of Zeb'edee, who were partners with Simon. And Jesus said to Simon, "Do not be afraid; henceforth you will be catching men." 11 And when they had brought their boats to land, they left everything and followed him.	Peter was astounded, mainly because Jesus had done such a magnificent job of teaching and preaching, but suddenly he transformed from evangelist to fishermen telling Peter to put out further in the lake and drop his nets. Peter attempted quietly and carefully to dissuade Jesus from such a decision. Peter went on to tell Jesus that he had fished all night and caught nothing. Fishing on the Sea of Galilee is done at night and Peter and his men were experienced fishermen. Since they had caught nothing during the dark they had no reason to believe fish would be caught in the sunlight. Jesus would not be deterred and compelled Peter saying, "Put down your net." Peter exhibited great faith as he let down the net. To his utter amazement the net was filled with a bountiful catch far exceeding his wildest dream. After the catch Peter looked at Jesus and said, "Lord, please go away from me because I'm a sinner and I'm scared to be so close to you."

Jesus and disciples visit Capernaum

Mark 1:21-28; Luke 4:31-37

Mark 1:21-28

21 And they went into Caper'na-um; and immediately on the sabbath he entered the synagogue and taught. 22 And they were astonished at his teaching, for he taught them as one who had authority, and not as the scribes. 23 And immediately there was in their synagogue a man with an unclean spirit; 24 and he cried out, "What have you to do with us, Jesus of Nazareth? Have you come to destroy us? I know who you are, the Holy One of God." 25 But Jesus rebuked him, saying, "Be silent, and come out of him!" 26 And the unclean spirit, convulsing him and crying with a loud voice, came out of him. 27 And they were all amazed, so that they questioned among themselves, saying, "What is this? A new teaching! With authority he commands even the unclean spirits, and they obey him." 28 And at once his fame spread everywhere throughout all the surrounding region of Galilee

Jesus and disciples visit Capernaum

Mark 1:21-28; Luke 4:31-37

Comment

Matthew does not include this incident in his report. The accounts given by Mark and Luke are almost identical.

The setting was Capernaum, the major city in its region. This event took place on the Sabbath.

Jesus went to the synagogue intending to teach, he was a regular attendee at public worship. Jesus was teacher while John the Baptist was a Preacher/Evangelist.

At the conclusion of his teaching he encountered a man with an unclean spirit. Unclean was a social/religious taboo related mainly to health issues.

Most of us would be unclean according to the code.
16 And the LORD said to Moses, 17 "Say to Aaron, None of your descendants throughout their generations who has a blemish may approach to offer the bread

Luke 4:31-37
31 And he went down to Caper'na-um, a city of Galilee. And he was teaching them on the sabbath; 32 and they were astonished at his teaching, for his word was with authority. 33 And in the synagogue there was a man who had the spirit of an unclean demon; and he cried out with a loud voice, 34 "Ah! What have you to do with us, Jesus of Nazareth? Have you come to destroy us? I know who you are, the Holy One of God." 35 But Jesus rebuked him, saying, "Be silent, and come out of him!" And when the demon had thrown him down in the midst, he came out of him, having done him no harm. 36 And they were all amazed and said to one another, "What is this word? For with authority and power he commands the unclean spirits, and they come out." 37 And reports of him went out into every place in the surrounding region.

of his God. 18 For no one who has a blemish shall draw near, a man blind or lame, or one who has a mutilated face or a limb too long, 19 or a man who has an injured foot or an injured hand, 20 or a hunchback, or a dwarf, or a man with a defect in his sight or an itching disease or scabs or crushed testicles;
Leviticus 21:16-20

Those who witnessed the event were thunderstruck. They were completely bewildered by the authority of Jesus who made even unclean spirits obey.

Careful reading of this and other such passages leads me to believe that the conversations between Jesus and the unclean spirits were audible only to Jesus and the unclean spirit. The on-lookers heard what Jesus said but were not privy to the comments of the unclean spirit.

The unclean spirit identified Jesus as the son of God. Without question each knew the other. There was no question as to who was the more powerful! Jesus gave two commands. Be silent and come out of him! The unclean spirit obeyed but vented his defiance by convulsing the man.

We do not know the nature of the unclean spirit. We can surmise the conduct of the man was less than what society deemed appropriate. The man had obviously under gone a transformation. The on-lookers were overwhelmed by what they had witnessed.

Is it any wonder Jesus' fame would spread?

Home of Simon Peter

Mark 1:29-31;
Matthew 8:14-15;
Luke 4:38-39

Home of Simon Peter

Mark 1:29-31;
Matthew 8:14-15;
Luke 4:38-39

Mark 1:29-31
29 And immediately he left the synagogue, and entered the house of Simon and Andrew, with James and John. 30 Now Simon's mother-in-law lay sick with a fever, and immediately they told him of her. 31 And he came and took her by the hand and lifted her up, and the fever left her; and she served them.

Matthew 8:14-15
14 And when Jesus entered Peter's house, he saw his mother-in-law lying sick with a fever; 15 he touched her hand, and the

Comment

After leaving the synagogue Jesus entered the house of Simon and Andrew. Only Mark includes Andrew as a resident of the house. All three writers tell us that it was Simon's mother-in-law who was sick with a fever.

The people present in the home told Jesus of her illness. He went to her, took her by the hand, lifted her up and the fever was gone. She was then well enough to serve them.

fever left her, and she rose and served him.

Luke 4:38-39
38 And he arose and left the synagogue, and entered Simon's house. Now Simon's mother-in-law was ill with a high fever, and they besought him for her. 39 And he stood over her and rebuked the fever, and it left her; and immediately she rose and served them.

Only Mark mentions that James and John accompanied them.

Luke gives us the most concise statement concerning this event. He tells us that Jesus went to the home of Simon where his mother-in-law was ill with a high fever.

It is the residents who seek Jesus' help for her. Jesus went to her and stood over her, rebuked the fever, and it left her. She then got up and served them. Luke says nothing about Jesus touching her.

Sabbath Sundown

**Mark 1:32-34;
Matthew 8:16-17;
Luke 4:40-41**

Sabbath Sundown

**Mark 1:32-34;
Matthew 8:16-17;
Luke 4:40-41**

Mark 1:32-34
32 That evening, at sundown, they brought to him all who were sick or possessed with demons. 33 And the whole city was gathered together about the door. 34 And he healed many who were sick with various diseases, and cast out many demons; and he would not permit the demons to speak, because they knew him.

Comment

When the sun went down the townspeople brought to Jesus all the sick and demon possessed. The city gathered at Simon's house. Jesus healed many [emphasis upon many]. This could imply that Jesus did not heal everyone who was brought to him.

Matthew 8:16-17
16 That evening they brought to him many who were possessed with demons; and he cast out the spirits with a word, and healed all who were sick. 17 This was to fulfil what was spoken by the prophet Isaiah, "He took our infirmities and bore our diseases."

Luke 4:40-41
40 Now when the sun was setting, all those who had any that were sick with various diseases brought them to him; and he laid his hands on every one of them and healed them. 41 And demons also came out of many, crying, "You are the Son of God!" But he rebuked them, and would not allow them to speak, because they knew that he was the Christ.

Jesus denied the demons the opportunity to speak. This means Jesus had power greater than the power of the demons. Jesus being able to command them meant that he was mightier even than Satan. Jesus chose not to be recognized publicly by an evil source.

Matthew goes on to say that this was to fulfill the prophecy of the Prophet Isaiah, "He took our infirmities and bore our diseases" (Isa. 53:4).

With the setting sun Sabbath came to a close.

Luke alone says that Jesus laid his hands on every one of them and healed them. Jesus was never afraid to make physical contact with those who suffered illness, possession, or deformity.

Luke says that when the demons came out they shouted, "You are the son of God," but Jesus hushed them and would not allow them to identify him.

The next morning

Mark 1:35-39;
Luke 4:42-44

The next morning

Mark 1:35-39;
Luke 4:42-44

Mark 1:35-39 35 And in the morning, a great while before day, he rose and went out to a lonely place, and there he prayed. 36 And Simon and those who were with him pursued him, 37 and they found him and said to him, "Every one is searching for you." 38 And he said to them, "Let us go on to the next towns, that I may preach there also; for that is why I came out." 39 And he went throughout all Galilee, preaching in their synagogues and casting out demons. **Luke 4:42-44** 42 And when it was day he departed and went into a lonely place. And the people sought him and came to him, and would have kept him from leaving them; 43 but he said to them, "I must preach the good news of the kingdom of God to the other cities also; for I was sent for this purpose." 44 And he was preaching in the synagogues of Judea.	**Comment** There are several slight deviations between the accounts of Mark and Luke. Mark tells us that Jesus went out early in the morning before daylight, while Luke says he departed after daylight. Mark says that Peter led the group to find Jesus. Luke says it was the group themselves who found Jesus. The important thing is, while the people wanted to keep Jesus for themselves, he told them his mission was to go to all the places where people lived to proclaim the good news. Mark says Jesus had to go through all of Galilee preaching and healing. While Luke says that Jesus went to all the synagogues in Judea, to preach. Since Jesus was already in Galilee it stands to reason that he would preach there first. He would then have moved south, in order to enter Judea, where he continued to preach.
<u>Would be Disciples</u> **Matthew 8:18-22** 18 Now when Jesus saw great	*<u>Would be Disciples</u>* **Matthew 8:18-22**

crowds around him, he gave orders to go over to the other side. ¹⁹ And a scribe came up and said to him, 'Teacher, I will follow you wherever you go." ²⁰ And Jesus said to him, "Foxes have holes, and birds of the air have nests; but the Son of man has nowhere to lay his head." ²¹ Another of the disciples said to him, "Lord, let me first go and bury my father." ²² But Jesus said to him, "Follow me, and leave the dead to bury their own dead."	**Comment** Among the people who followed Jesus closely, were the want-to-be disciples. Matthew quotes Jesus telling one would-be disciple, "I do not have a house or a place to lay my head. Is that something you are willing to accept?" It is of particular note that Jesus made no effort to run after the man or to lessen his demands in order to make him a follower. This scribe was among the mass of "disciples" better described as "the followers", who were unwilling to make the commitment of the "Inner-Circle" who gave up everything to follow Jesus. No scribe is named as part of this committed group.
Wedding at Cana **John 2:1-5** ¹ On the third day there was a marriage at Cana in Galilee, and the mother of Jesus was there; ² Jesus also was invited to the marriage, with his disciples. ³ When the wine failed, the mother of Jesus said to him, "They have no wine.' ⁴ And Jesus said to her,	***Wedding at Cana*** **John 2:1-5** **Comment** Who was getting married? We don't know because we are not told. Who invited Jesus? Again, we do not know. The writer, John, did not feel it important to

Jesus and the Gospel Timeline 91

"O woman, what have you to do with me? My hour has not yet come." ⁵ His mother said to the servants, "Do whatever he tells you."

So what was important? They ran out of wine! Was it because they had more guests than expected? Or could it have been they did not have enough wine to begin with?

A great truth is revealed here, "The problem is never as important as the solution!" Mary became aware of the problem, and knew who would find the solution. She went to her son, Jesus, and explained the situation. Jesus responded in less than a pleasant tone, "Woman why come to me?" He explained his question by saying, "I didn't plan to announce my public ministry by turning water into wine!"

Reading between the lines we hear Mary tell the servants, "Never mind what he said to me just do whatever he tells you."

<u>*Six stone jars*</u>

John 2:6-11
⁶ Now six stone jars were standing there, for the Jewish rites of purification, each holding twenty or thirty gallons. ⁷ Jesus said to them, "Fill the jars with water." And they filled them up

<u>*Six stone jars*</u>

John 2:6-11

Comment

Standing nearby were six very large stone jars. They were

to the brim. 8 He said to them, "Now draw some out, and take it to the steward of the feast." So they took it. 9 When the steward of the feast tasted the water now become wine, and did not know where it came from (though the servants who had drawn the water knew), the steward of the feast called the bridegroom 10 and said to him, "Every man serves the good wine first; and when men have drunk freely, then the poor wine; but you have kept the good wine until now." 11 This, the first of his signs, Jesus did at Cana in Galilee, and manifested his glory; and his disciples believed in him.

especially large in order to provide a sufficient supply of water to perform the Jewish ritual of purification. "Purification" was for the purpose of washing away sin and contamination.

As Mary walked away, Jesus looked at the confused servants and said, "Okay, fill the jars to the brim with water." When the jars were full Jesus said, "Draw out a sample and let the steward of the feast taste it."

When the steward tasted it he was amazed, this was perhaps the best wine to ever touch his lips. He immediately called for the bridegroom and congratulated him for such a novel approach by saving the best wine for last.

Jesus used the elements at hand to celebrate the future, water and wine. Water would be for baptism and wine would be in remembrance of Jesus' shed blood.

I guess the philosophy of saving the best wine till last was more practical than accidental, "They will become tipsy and not notice the difference nor be able to drink as much."

<u>120 to 180 gallons of wine!</u>

Why did Jesus do his first miracle at the wedding at Cana of Galilee? The miracle itself seems to be an absolute over reaction. Wouldn't a few bottles of wine have done just as well? Why six stone jars with a capacity of twenty to thirty gallons each?

Using the following formula:
      20 x 6 = 120 gallons
      30 x 6 = 180 gallons
Jesus provided enough wine to get the whole town drunk!

There is however, a much deeper meaning to this miracle, we aren't just fixed by Jesus we are transformed by him. Jesus was there and he met their needs.

Chapter 6

From Cana to Capernaum	***From Cana to Capernaum***
John 2:12 12 After this he went down to Caper'na-um, with his mother and his brothers and his disciples; and there they stayed for a few days.	**John 2:12** **Comment** After the miracle at Cana, Jesus with His family and new disciples went to visit Capernaum. This interlude gave these special people a little time to become better acquainted.
Passover is at hand	***Passover is at hand***
John 2:13 13 The Passover of the Jews was at hand, and Jesus went up to Jerusalem.	**John 2:13** **Comment** This is Jesus' first recorded visit to Jerusalem after his baptism. The most significant of all Holy Days for the Jews is Passover.

Elements for the sacrificial rites of the Temple

Oxen, sheep and doves, were necessary elements for the sacrificial rites of the Temple. People who came from outside Jerusalem for example, from Galilee and beyond, brought money with them to buy animals for the sacrifices. It was more convenient to buy the animals on the spot rather than risk emaciating them on the long journey and risk the Priest rejecting them as an offering. For those on pilgrimage it was also customary to exchange Roman coins, on which the Emperor's likeness was imprinted, for Jewish coins that were void of any likeness, to offer as Temple gifts.

__Jesus cleanses the Temple__	*__Jesus cleanses the Temple__*
John 2:14-17 14 In the temple he found those who were selling oxen and sheep and pigeons, and the money-changers at their business. 15 And making a whip of cords, he drove them all, with the sheep and oxen, out of the temple; and he poured out the coins of the money-changers and overturned their tables. 16 And he told those who sold the pigeons, "Take these things away; you shall not make my Father's house a house of trade." 17 His disciples remembered that it was written, "Zeal for thy house will consume me."	**John 2:14-17** **Comment** John places Jesus' cleansing of the Temple during this initial visit to Jerusalem following his baptism. Jesus was deeply upset by the abuses of the vendors within the Temple area. He made a whip from cords and drove all the vendors from the Temple. By this action the people of Jerusalem would long remember this man from the Galilee. A major expectation of the Messiah's coming included the cleansing of the Temple and return to its rightful place as the house of God. The quote in verse seventeen comes from Psalms 69:9.

What sign have you for doing this?

John 2:18-22
18 The Jews then said to him, "What sign have you to show us for doing this?" 19 Jesus answered them, "Destroy this temple, and in three days I will raise it up." 20 The Jews then said, "It has taken forty-six years to build this temple, and will you raise it up in three days?" 21 But he spoke of the temple of his body. 22 When therefore he was raised from the dead, his disciples remembered that he had said this; and they believed the scripture and the word which Jesus had spoken.

What sign have you for doing this?

John 2:18-22

Comment

The religious authorities demanded Jesus' justification for the act. He gave this surprising answer, *"Destroy this Temple and I will raise it again in three days."* Jesus' meaning was not understood. Only after his resurrection would the disciples comprehend he had spoken of the Temple of his body.

To help us date this Passover event, a remark made by an unknown individual is of critical significance, "It has taken forty-six years to build this Temple!"

Herod the Great started construction of the new Temple in 18 B.C. (18 BC + 28 AD = 46 years).

Mark tells us Jesus cleansed the Temple during Holy Week

Many believed because of the signs Jesus performed

John 2:23-25
23 Now when he was in Jerusalem at the Passover feast,

Many believed because of the signs Jesus performed

John 2:23-25

Comment

many believed in his name when they saw the signs which he did; ^{24} but Jesus did not trust himself to them, ^{25} because he knew all men and needed no one to bear witness of man; for he himself knew what was in man.

Father Pixner holds the "many" who believed in Jesus during this stay, came from among the Essenes. Even their enthusiasm for him, the purifier of the Temple, did not convince Jesus to reveal himself to them. Perhaps Jesus saw these extremely zealous followers as an obstacle rather than a help to his more inclusive approach.

Jesus meets Nicodemus

John 3:1-15

^{1} Now there was a man of the Pharisees, named Nicode'mus, a ruler of the Jews. ^{2} This man came to Jesus by night and said to him, "Rabbi, we know that you are a teacher come from God; for no one can do these signs that you do, unless God is with him." ^{3} Jesus answered him, "Truly, truly, I say to you, unless one is born anew, he cannot see the kingdom of God." ^{4} Nicode'mus said to him, "How can a man be born when he is old? Can he enter a second time into his mother's womb and be born?" ^{5} Jesus answered, "Truly, truly, I say to you, unless one is born of water and the Spirit, he cannot enter the kingdom of God. ^{6} That which is born of the flesh is flesh, and

Jesus meets Nicodemus

John 3:1-15

Comment

Jesus received a nocturnal visitor by the name of Nicodemus. He was a ruler of Israel, meaning he was a member of the Sanhedrin, or the religious high court, (Supreme Court).

Why did he come at night? We do not know because Scripture is silent on the point. However, we can choose from many possible answers. Here are two of the most reasonable possibilities.

1. Jesus was a very busy man and Nicodemus did not want to

that which is born of the Spirit is spirit. 7 Do not marvel that I said to you, 'You must be born anew.' 8 The wind blows where it wills, and you hear the sound of it, but you do not know whence it comes or whither it goes; so it is with every one who is born of the Spirit." 9 Nicode'mus said to him, "How can this be?" 10 Jesus answered him, "Are you a teacher of Israel, and yet you do not understand this?

11 Truly, truly, I say to you, we speak of what we know, and bear witness to what we have seen; but you do not receive our testimony. 12 If I have told you earthly things and you do not believe, how can you believe if I tell you heavenly things? 13 No one has ascended into heaven but he who descended from heaven, the Son of man. 14 And as Moses lifted up the serpent in the wilderness, so must the Son of man be lifted up, 15 that whoever believes in him may have eternal life."

interrupt his daily routine and he wanted time to speak at length and in private.

2. Nicodemus was anxious about being seen or identified with Jesus at this moment.

Their conversation was far more revealing than Nicodemus could possibly have expected. Nicodemus thought in literal terms while Jesus spoke in spiritual terms. Jesus said everyone must enter the Kingdom of God through new birth. Nicodemus knew about physical birth but spiritual birth was a subject he has never encountered before.

Having entered into a new realm of spirituality, Jesus confronted Nicodemus, saying, "If you are to be a teacher in Israel, a ruler, a leader, you must learn what it means to enter into the Kingdom of God."

God so loved the world

John 3:16-21

16 For God so loved the world that he gave his only Son, that whoever believes in him should

God so loved the world

John 3:16-21

Comment

not perish but have eternal life. ¹⁷ For God sent the Son into the world, not to condemn the world, but that the world might be saved through him.

¹⁸ He who believes in him is not condemned; he who does not believe is condemned already, because he has not believed in the name of the only Son of God. ¹⁹ And this is the judgment, that the light has come into the world, and men loved darkness rather than light, because their deeds were evil. ²⁰ For every one who does evil hates the light, and does not come to the light, lest his deeds should be exposed. ²¹ But he who does what is true comes to the light, that it may be clearly seen that his deeds have been wrought in God.

Clearly Jesus had not come to condemn the world. He came to save it. He had not come to destroy mankind he had come to save mankind.

The sound of Jesus' words are reminiscent of the Essene vocabulary. The contrast between darkness and light was one of their major themes. The Essenes considered themselves as sons of light.

This may be an occasion where Jesus felt to use the approach of the Essenes would be more effective with a Pharisee than any other theological position he might choose.

Jesus and John are both baptizing in the same area

John 3:22-24
²² *After this* Jesus and his disciples went into the land of Judea; there he remained with them and baptized. ²³ John also was baptizing at Ae'non near Salim, because there was much water there; and people came and were baptized. ²⁴ For John

Jesus and John are both baptizing in the same area

John 3:22-24

Comment

With the Passover feast concluded, Jesus took his disciples into the province of Judea. John tells us that Jesus baptized believers during this

had not yet been put in prison. (emphasis added)	period of his ministry. John later said Jesus did not actually baptize anyone.
	This happened before John the Baptist was imprisoned.
John's disciples have a dispute with the Jews about purifying	***John's disciples have a dispute with the Jews about purifying***
John 3:25	**John 3:25**
25 Now a discussion arose between John's disciples and a Jew over purifying.	**Comment**
	John says a "discussion arose," this is a polite way of saying a serious argument about a controversial matter took place.
	This discussion involved John's disciples, and the Jews. The term Jews meant the people belonging to the Jewish nation. These were people who were Jewish by birth, origin, and religion.
	The issue was purification. More precisely, it concerned whether the ritual was being observed or ignored. The ritual was administered by washing. Quite possibly the controversy was over whether or not John's disciples washed their hands

John's worried disciples

John 3:26-30

26 And they came to John, and said to him, "Rabbi, he who was with you beyond the Jordan, to whom you bore witness, here he is, baptizing, and all are going to him." 27 John answered, "No one can receive anything except what is given him from heaven. 28 You yourselves bear me witness, that I said, I am not the Christ, but I have been sent before him. 29 He who has the bride is the bridegroom; the friend of the bridegroom, who stands and hears him, rejoices greatly at the bridegroom's voice; therefore this joy of mine is now full. 30 He must increase, but I must decrease."

---

before eating. A second major aspect of the Purification laws concerned women after childbirth. Whatever the reason, it sparked an argument between John's disciples and the people of John's congregation.

John's worried disciples

John 3:26-30

Comment

There is a total disconnect between verses twenty-five and twenty-six. The former speaks to controversy the latter speaks to jealousy.

In verse twenty-six, we are told John's disciples are concerned about the growing fame of Jesus. They said boldly he is baptizing, and perhaps the thing they are most concerned about is those converts are not following John but Jesus.

Verses twenty-nine and thirty are a simple parable John used to express his joy and commitment to Jesus. He likens Jesus to a bridegroom and himself to the best man. The best man is overjoyed at the good fortune of his friend, the bridegroom. As John says his joy is now full because he has personally been in the presence of the Son of God.

He who believes in the Son has eternal life

John 3:31-36

31 He who comes from above is above all; he who is of the earth belongs to the earth, and of the earth he speaks; he who comes from heaven is above all. 32 He bears witness to what he has seen and heard, yet no one receives his testimony; 33 he who receives his testimony sets his seal to this, that God is true. 34 For he whom God has sent utters the words of God, for it is not by measure that he gives the Spirit; 35 the Father loves the Son, and has given all things into his hand. 36 He who believes in the Son has eternal life; he who does not obey the Son shall not see life, but the wrath of God rests upon him.

He who believes in the Son has eternal life

John 3:31-36

Comment

John continues with statements that are steeped in thought and theology and should be pondered with deliberation and prayer.

He uses the analogy that those of us who are from the earth, those of us who are earthly humans, speak of the things that we see and hear. John goes on to make sure his disciples understand God's seal of approval is upon Jesus and he came from the presence of the father to speak of things that are beyond this world. The sadness is few received Jesus' testimony.

There is a powerful word in verse thirty-six that should cause us to give serious thought to what we believe and why we believe it. John said if we believe in the Son we have eternal life. On the other side of the coin he said if we do not obey the Son we will not have life but will receive the wrath of God.

Accepting or rejecting Jesus Christ as Savior is the decision or option of the individual hearer and that choice has eternal consequences.

Pharisees pose a real problem

John 4:1-3

1 Now when the Lord knew that the Pharisees had heard that Jesus was making and baptizing more disciples than John 2 (although Jesus himself did not baptize, but only his disciples), 3 he left Judea and departed again to Galilee.

Pharisees pose a real problem

John 4:1-3

Comment

In these three verses we encounter four distinct propositions.

1. We are told the Pharisees have heard about Jesus making disciples and baptizing.

2. The number of Jesus' followers is now exceeding that of John's.

3. When Jesus became aware that the Pharisees knew of his success he realized the growing danger to his followers. He was also concerned about John's

	personal reaction of becoming over shadowed.

4. Jesus decided the best course of action was for him to leave Judea and return to Galilee. |
| ***Jesus passed through Samaria*** | ***Jesus passed through Samaria*** |
| **John 4:4-6**
4 He had to pass through Samar'ia. 5 So he came to a city of Samar'ia, called Sy'char, near the field that Jacob gave to his son Joseph. 6 Jacob's well was there, and so Jesus, wearied as he was with his journey, sat down beside the well. It was about the sixth hour. | **John 4:4-6**

Comment

Leaving Judea Jesus puts separation between himself and John the Baptist. It is interesting that John says Jesus "had" to pass through Samaria. It was customary and expected that a Jew would not put his foot on Samaritan soil.

A Jewish traveler going from Judea to Galilee would have continued north until he reached the Samarian border. At that point, he would have turned east and traveled to the Jordan River, crossed it and headed north again until he had cleared Samaria. Then he would have turned west and once more crossed the River Jordan to enter Galilee. |

Circuitous route

This circuitous route was the outgrowth of the animosities that existed between the Jewish and Samarian people. The ill will started several hundred years earlier when Judea was defeated by the Assyrian armies and many of the survivors were carried into captivity and resettled with other conquered people. A remnant of survivors were left in their homeland of Samaria, while captives of other nations were resettled among them. With the passage of time intermarriage became a way of life.

After many years, those survivors sent North regained their freedom and returned to their homeland of Israel. When these returnees learned of the mixed blood resulting from the intermarriage with other races, they had no tolerance for the people of Samaria. Vivid evidence of this condition is revealed in the book of Nehemiah as Nehemiah tells the people of Samaria to not come close to the rebuilding of the city of Jerusalem but to go back to their homeland. Jesus deliberately breaks this taboo.

The Samarian Woman	*The Samarian Woman*
John 4:7-42	**John 4:7-42**
7 There came a woman of Samar'ia to draw water. Jesus said to her, "Give me a drink." 8 For his disciples had gone away into the city to buy food. 9 The Samaritan woman said to him, "How is it that you, a Jew, ask a drink of me, a woman of Samar'ia?" For Jews have no dealings with Samaritans. 10 Jesus answered her, "If you knew the gift of God, and who it is that is saying to you, 'Give me a drink,' you would have	**Comment** John gives the exact location where this conversation took place. Sychar, the town mentioned in the narrative, is believed by some scholars to probably be another name for the town of Shechem, a town in Samaria, near the well of Jacob. Jesus arrived at Jacob's well near the noon hour tired and

asked him, and he would have given you living water." 11 The woman said to him, "Sir, you have nothing to draw with, and the well is deep; where do you get that living water? 12 Are you greater than our father Jacob, who gave us the well, and drank from it himself, and his sons, and his cattle?" 13 Jesus said to her, "Every one who drinks of this water will thirst again, 14 but whoever drinks of the water that I shall give him will never thirst; the water that I shall give him will become in him a spring of water welling up to eternal life." 15 The woman said to him, "Sir, give me this water, that I may not thirst, nor come here to draw."

16 Jesus said to her, "Go, call your husband, and come here." 17 The woman answered him, "I have no husband." Jesus said to her, "You are right in saying, 'I have no husband'; 18 for you have had five husbands, and he whom you now have is not your husband; this you said truly." 19 The woman said to him, "Sir, I perceive that you are a prophet. 20 Our fathers worshiped on this mountain; and you say that in Jerusalem is the place where men ought to worship." 21 Jesus said to her, "Woman, believe me, the

hungry. The disciples went into the city to attempt to buy food. We should not overlook the feelings and anxiety the disciples felt being on Samaritan territory and going to do business with them.

Soon a woman from the city came to draw water. Midday was not the customary time to draw water. Obviously this woman was different from the other mothers and wives of the community. Her timing indicates that she was not welcome among the town's womenfolk.

For Jesus to speak would cause deep concern for the woman. Jesus asked her for a drink of water. For him to make any request of her was exceedingly troublesome. Her response indicates that she understood the taboos and separation between Samaritans and Jews.

Jesus quickly moved the conversation to matters he wanted to bring to light. He told her she did not know who she was talking to, if she did, she would have asked him for "living water." She is unfamiliar with the term "living water."

hour is coming when neither on this mountain nor in Jerusalem will you worship the Father. 22 You worship what you do not know; we worship what we know, for salvation is from the Jews. 23 But the hour is coming, and now is, when the true worshipers will worship the Father in spirit and truth, for such the Father seeks to worship him. 24 God is spirit, and those who worship him must worship in spirit and truth." 25 The woman said to him, "I know that Messiah is coming (he who is called Christ); when he comes, he will show us all things." 26 Jesus said to her, "I who speak to you am he." 27 Just then his disciples came. They marveled that he was talking with a woman, but none said, "What do you wish?" or, "Why are you talking with her?" 28 So the woman left her water jar, and went away into the city, and said to the people, 29 "Come, see a man who told me all that I ever did. Can this be the Christ?" 30 They went out of the city and were coming to him.

31 Meanwhile the disciples besought him, saying, "Rabbi, eat." 32 But he said to them, "I have food to eat of which you do not know." 33 So the disciples said to one another, "Has any

Jesus said, when you drink the living water, "You will never thirst again." The woman quickly pointed out that the well was deep and obviously he did not have anything with which to draw water. She might have thought, okay Mr. Smart Guy, I'll play this game with you. "If I drink your living water does that mean I will never have to come to the well and draw water again?"

Jesus knew she was not yet ready to drink from his well. He abruptly changed the tone of the discussion by asking her to go and get her husband. In the following conversation Jesus revealed how much he knew about her. Much to her credit, she acknowledged the truth of his words.

Now it is the woman's turn to change the conversation. She suddenly realized she was in the presence of a prophet. Immediately she raised the question of where was the proper place to worship. Samaritans were refused the opportunity to worship at Jerusalem. Therefore, they selected Mount Gerizim* as their high place for worship.

one brought him food?" ³⁴ Jesus said to them, "My food is to do the will of him who sent me, and to accomplish his work. ³⁵ Do you not say, 'There are yet four months, then comes the harvest'? I tell you, lift up your eyes, and see how the fields are already white for harvest. ³⁶ He who reaps receives wages, and gathers fruit for eternal life, so that sower and reaper may rejoice together. ³⁷ For here the saying holds true, 'One sows and another reaps.' ³⁸ I sent you to reap that for which you did not labor; others have labored, and you have entered into their labor."

³⁹ Many Samaritans from that city believed in him because of the woman's testimony, "He told me all that I ever did." ⁴⁰ So when the Samaritans came to him, they asked him to stay with them; and he stayed there two days. ⁴¹ And many more believed because of his word. ⁴² They said to the woman, "It is no longer because of your words that we believe, for we have heard for ourselves, and we know that this is indeed the Savior of the world."

She earnestly wanted to hear the prophet's position. Jesus gave an unexpected reply. He told her the day had already come when God could be worshiped in many places, and not just in Jerusalem or on Mt. Gerizim.

Jesus revealed a great truth to the Samaritan woman, telling her that authentic worship was not a matter of location it was a matter of the heart and spirit. Again the woman's question takes a quantum leap. She acknowledged her belief in the coming Messiah, but before she can complete her question, Jesus says, "I am he." This is the first time that Jesus has publicly announced that he is the Messiah.

Abruptly the conversation ended as the disciples returned. They were confused and bewildered that Jesus was having a conversation with a woman, a Samaritan woman at that!

The woman took the opportunity to leave. She went straight back to town and told everyone that a prophet was in their midst. She gave the same invitation Jesus so frequently used, "come and see."

The essence of the story is that Jesus did not allow prejudice or convention to dictate his ministry and who he chose to bring it to.

I find it interesting that Jesus used the third person format of speech as he led into revealing who he really was.

* Samaritans still celebrate Passover on Mount Gerizim.

Herod Antipas has John Arrested

Mark 1:14-15; Luke 3:18-20

Mark 1:14-15

14 Now after John was arrested, Jesus came into Galilee, preaching the gospel of God, 15 and saying, "The time is fulfilled, and the kingdom of God is at hand; repent, and believe in the gospel."

Luke 3:18-20

18 So, with many other exhortations, he preached good news to the people. 19 But Herod the tetrarch, who had been reproved by him for Hero'di-as, his brother's wife, and for all the

Herod Antipas has John Arrested

Mark 1:14-15; Luke 3:18-20

Comment

Luke identifies him as Herod the Tetrarch, this Greek word means a governor of a forth part of a region. This fits perfectly with the division of the kingdom of Herod the great. Herod Antipas ruled the Galilee equaling something over a fourth of the kingdom. Herod Philip ruled over another section known as Batanea, which would have measured just under a fourth of his father's kingdom. The remaining southern half of the

evil things that Herod had done, 20 added this to them all, that he shut up John in prison.

remaining southern half of the kingdom was placed under the governorship of Pontius Pilate.

Reason for John's Arrest

Mark 6:17-20

17 For Herod had sent and seized John, and bound him in prison for the sake of Hero'di-as, his brother Philip's wife; because he had married her. 18 For John said to Herod, "It is not lawful for you to have your brother's wife." 19 And Hero'di-as had a grudge against him, and wanted to kill him. But she could not,

20 for Herod feared John, knowing that he was a righteous and holy man, and kept him safe. When he heard him, he was much perplexed; and yet he heard him gladly.

Reason for John's Arrest

Mark 6:17-20

Comment

Strong's Greek Dictionary defines bound as to bind, fasten with chains, to throw into chains.

John accused Herod Antipas of committing adultery with a woman he unlawfully called his wife.

Herod had seized John

Matthew 14:3-5

3 For Herod had seized John and bound him and put him in prison, for the sake of Hero'di-as, his brother Philip's wife; 4 because John said to him, "It is not lawful for you to have her." 5 And though

Herod had seized John

Matthew 14:3-5

Comment

Mark and Matthew referred to the principal character of this passage simply as Herod.

he wanted to put him to death, he feared the people, because they held him to be a prophet.	The arrest resulted from the unlawful act of Antipas stealing Herodias, the wife of his brother Philip.

Both Matthew and Mark state plainly that it was not lawful for Antipas to do this. Luke says that John "reproved" Herod. Is this simply a more damning or mild term for what John said as recorded by Mark and Matthew?

Luke further says that Antipas did many evil things; however, he doesn't elaborate on the nature of these unspecified evils. Only Luke tells us that Antipas wanted to put John the Baptist to death. The only reason Antipas did not execute John was because he was afraid the people might revolt against him. Luke tells us that the people accepted John as a prophet. |
| ***Jesus returns to Galilee***

Matthew 4:12;
John 4:43-45 | ***Jesus returns to Galilee***

Matthew 4:12;
John 4:43-45 |
| **Matthew 4:12**
12 Now when he heard that John had been arrested, he withdrew into Galilee; | **Comment**

Jesus remained among the Samaritans for two more days before leaving. It is very |

John 4:43-45 43 After the two days he departed to Galilee. 44 For Jesus himself testified that a prophet has no honor in his own country. 45 So when he came to Galilee, the Galileans welcomed him, having seen all that he had done in Jerusalem at the feast, for they too had gone to the feast.	important to notice that Jesus won acceptance among the Samaritans as he moved from the south heading north toward Galilee. He will later be rejected by these Samaritans as he moves south from Galilee, going back toward Jerusalem. Their rejection revealed their deep-seated hatred of the Jews. When he reached Galilee the Galileans who had witnessed Jesus' cleansing the Temple in Jerusalem greeted him warmly. Without doubt these Galileans were influenced by the Essene theology. They expected the Messiah to cleanse the Temple of all its corruption, and to replace the illegitimate priest with a legitimate priest from the tribe of Levi. When Jesus cleansed the Temple their hopes of the Messiah's return were stirred. With Jesus' return to Galilee they had the opportunity to inspect him thoroughly to determine if he possessed all the attributes of their expectations.

Jesus' fame spread	*Jesus' fame spread*
Matthew 4:23-25	**Matthew 4:23-25**
23 And he went about all Galilee, teaching in their synagogues and preaching the gospel of the kingdom and healing every disease and every infirmity among the people. 24 So his fame spread throughout all Syria, and they brought him all the sick, those afflicted with various diseases and pains, demoniacs, epileptics, and paralytics, and he healed them. 25 And great crowds followed him from Galilee and the Decap'olis and Jerusalem and Judea and from beyond the Jordan.	**Comments** Jesus' fame had already spread widely. He was known from Syria to Galilee, and in the cities of the Decapolis, in Judea, and the lands south and east of the Jordan River.

The Decapolis Described

This area was composed of pagan Gentile cities known as the "Decapolis," or "ten cities." These were cities where good Jewish boys and girls did not go. They had a lot of things which good Jews would find offensive: theaters, where most of the plays were about the pagan gods; and pigs, which were "unclean" according to the kosher laws of Leviticus.

The Galilee Described

The Galilee in Jesus' day, as today, is not a very large area, approximately twenty-five by thirty-five miles. Indeed, the entire land of the Bible is not now nor has it ever been very large. Some 95 percent of the biblical story takes place on a stage approximately 50 by 150 miles.[8]

---

[8] Dr. Donald Strobe.

Official's son is at point of death

John 4:46-54

46 So he came again to Cana in Galilee, where he had made the water wine. And at Caper'naum there was an official whose son was ill. 47 When he heard that Jesus had come from Judea to Galilee, he went and begged him to come down and heal his son, for he was at the point of death. 48 Jesus therefore said to him, "Unless you see signs and wonders you will not believe." 49 The official said to him, "Sir, come down before my child dies." 50 Jesus said to him, "Go; your son will live." The man believed the word that Jesus spoke to him and went his way. 51 As he was going down, his servants met him and told him that his son was living. 52 So he asked them the hour when he began to mend, and they said to him, "Yesterday at the seventh hour the fever left him." 53 The father knew that was the hour when Jesus had said to him, "Your son will live"; and he himself believed, and all his household. 54 This was now the second sign that Jesus did when he had come from Judea to Galilee.

Official's son is at point of death

John 4:46-54

Comment

This is an independent passage of John.

Jesus passed through Cana, continuing north.

This is another healing at Capernaum. This time the son of an official is near death. Jesus had returned from Judea.

Jesus' words to this father seem to imply that he was testing him to see if he just wanted to see a miracle or if he was a real believer. The man's answer clearly states his belief, "hurry before my son dies." Jesus speaks the most wonderful words this heartbroken father could possibly hear, "your son will live."

According to John this is the second miracle of Jesus.

Chapter 7

THE SYNAGOGUE AT CAPERNAUM

Jesus heals the Leper	*Jesus heals the Leper*
Mark 1:40-45; Matthew 8:1-4; Luke 5:12-16	Mark 1:40-45; Matthew 8:1-4; Luke 5:12-16
Mark 1:40-45 40 And a leper came to him beseeching him, and kneeling said to him, "If you will, you can make me clean." 41 Moved with pity, he stretched out his hand and touched him, and said to him, "I will; be clean." 42 And immediately the leprosy left him, and he was made clean.	**Comment** The location of this healing cannot be determined due to the differences reported by the writers. Mark—a leper came to Jesus. Matthew—Jesus had just come down the mountain. Luke—they were in one of the

⁴³ And he sternly charged him, and sent him away at once, ⁴⁴ and said to him, "See that you say nothing to any one; but go, show yourself to the priest, and offer for your cleansing what Moses commanded, for a proof to the people." ⁴⁵ But he went out and began to talk freely about it, and to spread the news, so that Jesus could no longer openly enter a town, but was out in the country; and people came to him from every quarter.

Matthew 8:1-4
¹ When he came down from the mountain, great crowds followed him; ² and behold, a leper came to him and knelt before him, saying, "Lord, if you will, you can make me clean." ³ And he stretched out his hand and touched him, saying, "I will; be clean." And immediately his leprosy was cleansed. ⁴ And Jesus said to him, "See that you say nothing to any one; but go, show yourself to the priest, and offer the gift that Moses commanded, for a proof to the people."

Luke 5:12-16
¹² While he was in one of the cities, there came a man full of leprosy; and when he saw Jesus, he fell on his face and besought him, "Lord, if you will, you

cities.

We can identify this as the same event however, because the leper said "If you will." Jesus was moved with compassion at this statement of faith and immediately he performed the miracle of healing.

It is important to note Jesus never hesitated to touch the leper. He commanded the cleansed leper to tell no one of his healing. Jesus gave this admonition only when he was in Galilee. Jesus knew his every move was being reported to Herod Antipas.

The cleansed leper told everyone of his good fortune. The word spread far and rapidly rendering Jesus no longer able to go quietly about his Ministry.

Jesus' reference to Moses is found in Leviticus 14:2-31.

can make me clean." 13 And he stretched out his hand, and touched him, saying, "I will; be clean." And immediately the leprosy left him. 14 And he charged him to tell no one; but "go and show yourself to the priest, and make an offering for your cleansing, as Moses commanded, for a proof to the people." 15 But so much the more the report went abroad concerning him; and great multitudes gathered to hear and to be healed of their infirmities. 16 But he withdrew to the wilderness and prayed.

Capernaum and the Centurion

**Matthew 8:5-13;
Luke 7:1-10**

Matthew 8:5-13
5 As he entered Caper'na-um, a centurion came forward to him, beseeching him 6 and saying, "Lord, my servant is lying paralyzed at home, in terrible distress." 7 And he said to him, "I will come and heal him." 8 But the centurion answered him, "Lord, I am not worthy to have you come under my roof; but only say the word, and my servant will be healed. 9 For I am a man under authority, with soldiers under

Capernaum and the Centurion

**Matthew 8:5-13;
Luke 7:1-10**

Comment

Mark does not record this event. Matthew and Luke are essentially the same.

Jesus preformed miracles for Jews and Gentiles. Among the Gentiles were the Centurion, the woman from Tyre, the leper from Samaria, and many others.

The Centurion was overjoyed to hear Jesus was coming to his

me; and I say to one, 'Go,' and he goes, and to another, 'Come,' and he comes, and to my slave, 'Do this,' and he does it." 10 When Jesus heard him, he marveled, and said to those who followed him, "Truly, I say to you, not even in Israel have I found such faith. 11 I tell you, many will come from east and west and sit at table with Abraham, Isaac, and Jacob in the kingdom of heaven, 12 while the sons of the kingdom will be thrown into the outer darkness; there men will weep and gnash their teeth." 13 And to the centurion Jesus said, "Go; be it done for you as you have believed." And the servant was healed at that very moment.

Luke 7:1-10
1 After he had ended all his sayings in the hearing of the people he entered Caper'na-um. 2 Now a centurion had a slave who was dear to him, who was sick and at the point of death. 3 When he heard of Jesus, he sent to him elders of the Jews, asking him to come and heal his slave. 4 And when they came to Jesus, they besought him earnestly, saying, "He is worthy to have you do this for him, 5 for he loves our nation, and he built us our synagogue." 6 And Jesus went with them.

home. Suddenly he remembered Jews did not enter the homes of Gentiles because of their Purification laws. Honored that Jesus was willing to respond he quickly changed his request saying if Jesus would just say the word he believed his servant would be healed. Jesus responded by praising the Centurion's depth of faith and healed his servant. The Centurion exhibited genuine respect for Jesus by removing his request that Jesus come to his home.

Luke has a different version of the Centurion's conversation with Jesus. He reports the Centurion first contacted the Elders of the Jewish community asking them to intercede with Jesus on behalf of his slave. The Elders make a truly astounding statement telling Jesus he is "Worthy!" Such praise is almost unbelievable, because most Romans were hated and despised by the Jews.

One version says the Centurion and Jesus met while the other says they never saw each other in person. Still the event is the same. Both accounts agree Jesus healed the servant without ever

When he was not far from the house, the centurion sent friends to him, saying to him, "Lord, do not trouble yourself, for I am not worthy to have you come under my roof; 7 therefore I did not presume to come to you. But say the word, and let my servant be healed. 8 For I am a man set under authority, with soldiers under me: and I say to one, 'Go,' and he goes; and to another, 'Come,' and he comes; and to my slave, 'Do this,' and he does it." 9 When Jesus heard this he marveled at him, and turned and said to the multitude that followed him, "I tell you, not even in Israel have I found such faith." 10 And when those who had been sent returned to the house, they found the slave well.

touching or seeing him. This reveals an overlooked dimension of Jesus' healing power.

A place called Nain

Luke 7:11-17
11 Soon afterward he went to a city called Na'in, and his disciples and a great crowd went with him. 12 As he drew near to the gate of the city, behold, a man who had died was being carried out, the only son of his mother, and she was a widow; and a large crowd from the city was with her. 13 And when the Lord saw

A place called Nain

Luke 7:11-17

Comment

This is an independent account by Luke.

The city of Nain is located on the west side of the valley of Armageddon across from Nazareth. As Jesus entered the

her, he had compassion on her and said to her, "Do not weep." ¹⁴ And he came and touched the bier, and the bearers stood still. And he said, "Young man, I say to you, arise." ¹⁵ And the dead man sat up, and began to speak. And he gave him to his mother. ¹⁶ Fear seized them all; and they glorified God, saying, "A great prophet has arisen among us!" and "God has visited his people!" ¹⁷ And this report concerning him spread through the whole of Judea and all the surrounding country.

city he saw a funeral procession making its way out of the city. According to the ancient law of the Jews no one was allowed to be buried within the city limits. Therefore we read, the man was being "carried out."

The corpse was a young man. He was the only son of a widow. Tears ran down the cheeks of the devastated mother. Jesus saw the mother's sorrow, fears, and future. He was moved by compassion and told the mother "Do not weep." Then Jesus laid his hand upon the bier and said, "Young man, I say to you arise." And he did!

The onlookers were shocked, amazed, and wowed! The magnitude of what they had witnessed began to slowly register with them. They said to one another, "A great prophet has visited us this day."

Word of this miracle spread quickly throughout the surrounding country. Even through all of Judea. (Judea was the arena of Orthodox Judaism.)

A major undercurrent in Jesus' ministry

This story reveals a major undercurrent in Jesus' ministry. Gentiles were hated by Jews. Jesus did not hesitate to cross the racial exclusiveness barrier. Thus, Jesus was saying the Messiah welcomes the sick, lame, unclean, disease ridden, and the foreigner. This was not a challenge to the Romans it was a challenge to the Temple authorities.

At Home (Nazareth)/Paralytic	*At Home (Nazareth)/Paralytic*
Mark 2:1-12; Matthew 9:1-8; Luke 5:17-26	Mark 2:1-12; Matthew 9:1-8; Luke 5:17-26
Mark 2:1-12 1 And when he returned to Caper'na-um after some days, it was reported that he was at home. 2 And many were gathered together, so that there was no longer room for them, not even about the door; and he was preaching the word to them. 3 And they came, bringing to him a paralytic carried by four men. 4 And when they could not get near him because of the crowd, they removed the roof above him; and when they had made an opening, they let down the pallet on which the paralytic lay. 5 And when Jesus saw their faith, he said to the paralytic, "My son, your sins are forgiven." 6 Now some of the scribes were sitting there, questioning in their hearts, 7 "Why does this man	**Comment** Where did this healing take place? A casual reading of this story leads one to assume the healing took place in Capernaum. Mark's story begins saying they had reached Capernaum but continues saying, "After some days, it was reported that he was at home." Home was still Nazareth at this point in Jesus' ministry. Jesus was inside a home preaching. A large crowd soon gathered outside, all of whom wanted to hear him. During the message a group of four men came carrying an improvised stretcher with a paralytic lying upon it. The crowd made no way for them to carry the man

speak thus? It is blasphemy! Who can forgive sins but God alone?" 8 And immediately Jesus, perceiving in his spirit that they thus questioned within themselves, said to them, "Why do you question thus in your hearts? 9 Which is easier, to say to the paralytic, 'Your sins are forgiven,' or to say, 'Rise, take up your pallet and walk'? 10 But that you may know that the Son of man has authority on earth to forgive sins"—he said to the paralytic" 11 "I say to you, rise, take up your pallet and go home." 12 And he rose, and immediately took up the pallet and went out before them all; so that they were all amazed and glorified God, saying, "We never saw anything like this!"

Matthew 9:1-8

1 And getting into a boat he crossed over and came to his own city. 2 And behold, they brought to him a paralytic, lying on his bed; and when Jesus saw their faith he said to the paralytic, "Take heart, my son; your sins are forgiven." 3 And behold, some of the scribes said to themselves, "This man is blaspheming." 4 But Jesus, knowing their thoughts, said, "Why do you think evil in your hearts? 5 For which is easier, to

into the presence of Jesus. Not to be deterred they devised a plan.

Mark tells us they removed the roof. Luke says they let him down through the tiles. Strong's Greek Dictionary **Number 2766** says, The phrase "through the roof", means through the door in the roof to which a ladder or stairway led up from the street (the Rabbis distinguish two ways of entering a house, "the way through the door" and "the way through the roof"). A third possible explanation is they actually removed a section of the roof and lowered their friend into Jesus' presence. This would have been a major undertaking due to the way roofs were constructed. Such roofs contained several layers of branched crisscrossing over each other to form a base upon which dirt was spread and allowed to set during the rainy times and dry during the heat. Ultimately, the roof became a solid part of the home's construction.

Jesus was so impressed by the faith and ingenuity of the four friends, he said to the paralytic your sins are forgiven.

say, 'Your sins are forgiven,' or to say, 'Rise and walk'? 6 But that you may know that the Son of man has authority on earth to forgive sins" —he then said to the paralytic, "Rise, take up your bed and go home." 7 And he rose and went home. 8 When the crowds saw it, they were afraid, and they glorified God, who had given such authority to men.

Luke 5:17-26
17 On one of those days, as he was teaching, there were Pharisees and teachers of the law sitting by, who had come from every village of Galilee and Judea and from Jerusalem; and the power of the Lord was with him to heal. 18 And behold, men were bringing on a bed a man who was paralyzed, and they sought to bring him in and lay him before Jesus; 19 but finding no way to bring him in, because of the crowd, they went up on the roof and let him down with his bed through the tiles into the midst before Jesus. 20 And when he saw their faith he said, "Man, your sins are forgiven you." 21 And the scribes and the Pharisees began to question, saying, "Who is this that speaks blasphemies? Who can forgive sins but God only?" 22 When Jesus perceived

All three Evangelists agree everyone present was amazed because they had never seen anything like this before.

There were Pharisees and scribes among those who heard and saw what happened. Their reaction was to say only God can forgive sin and this man is not God. Jesus let them know that he, the son of man, was given the power to forgive.

their questionings, he answered them, "Why do you question in your hearts? 23 Which is easier, to say, 'Your sins are forgiven you,' or to say, 'Rise and walk'? 24 But that you may know that the Son of man has authority on earth to forgive sins" —he said to the man who was paralyzed— "I say to you, rise, take up your bed and go home." 25 And immediately he rose before them, and took up that on which he lay, and went home, glorifying God. 26 And amazement seized them all, and they glorified God and were filled with awe, saying, "We have seen strange things today."

Jesus deliberately forgave the man

Mark and Matthew say that it was a scribe or scribes who spoke the word blasphemy! Luke includes the Pharisees in his list. All three Evangelists agree Jesus forgave the man deliberately to insure the scribes and Pharisees would understand his power.

Once more Jesus said, by way of his action, "I have the authority to forgive sin!" The Temple authorities present got the message loud and clear, here was a man to be reckoned with. The Temple authorities could not afford to have this itinerant backwoods preacher doing such things because it just might get out of hand.

What does the title "Son of Man" mean?

Son of man as referred to in the Old Testament

The phrase **"son of man"** is primarily used to denote humanity or self, it can be translated gender neutrally as offspring of Mankind, or Man's child.

In the O.T. the expression "son of man" is frequently used to denote simply "a man."

13 I saw in the night visions, and behold, with the clouds of heaven there came one like a son of man, (Son = man child, Man = human being and he came to the Ancient of Days (God) and was presented before him. (Dan. 7:13-14)

Matthew 24:30
30 then will appear the sign of the Son of man in heaven, and then all the tribes of the earth will mourn, and they will see the Son of man coming on the clouds of heaven with power and great glory;

Mark 13:24-27
24 "But in those days, after that tribulation, the sun will be darkened, and the moon will not give its light, **25** and the stars will be falling from heaven, and the powers in the heavens will be shaken. **26** And then they will see the Son of man coming in clouds with great power and glory. **27** And then he will send out the angels, and gather his elect from the four winds, from the ends of the earth to the ends of heaven.

Luke 21:27
27 And then they will see the Son of man coming in a cloud with power and great glory.

14 And to him was given dominion (sovereignty) and glory and kingdom, that all peoples, nations, and languages should serve him; his dominion is an everlasting dominion, which shall not pass away, and his kingdom one that shall not be destroyed. (Dan 7:13-14)

John 5:27
27 and has given him authority to execute judgment, because he is the Son of man.

Matthew 26:64-66
And the high priest said to him, "I adjure you by the living God, tell us if you are the Christ, the Son of God." **64** Jesus said to him, "You have said so. But I tell you, hereafter you will see the Son of man seated at the right hand of Power, and coming on the clouds of heaven." **65** Then the high priest tore his robes, and said, "He has uttered blasphemy. Why do we still need witnesses? You have now heard his blasphemy. **66** What is your judgment?" They answered, "He deserves death."

19 God is not man, that he should lie, or a son of man, that he should repent. Has he said, and will he not do it? Or has he spoken, and will he not fulfil it? (Num. 23:19)

4 what is man that thou art mindful of him, and the son of man that thou dost care for him? (Ps. 8:4)

17 But let thy hand be upon the man of thy right hand, the son of man whom thou hast made strong for thyself! (Ps. 80:17)

6 how much less man, who is a maggot, and the son of man, who is a worm!" (Job 25:6)

Strong defines "maggot, (Hebrew Number 7415) as worm, as cause and sign of decay."

Strong defines "worm, (Hebrew Number 8438) when the female of the scarlet worm species was ready to give birth to her young, she would attach her body to the trunk of a tree, fixing herself so firmly and permanently that she would never leave again. The eggs deposited beneath her body were thus protected until the larvae were hatched and able to enter their own life cycle. As the mother died, the crimson fluid stained her body and the surrounding wood. From the dead bodies of such female scarlet worms, the commercial scarlet dyes of antiquity were extracted."

What a picture this gives of Christ, dying on the tree, shedding His precious blood that He might bring many sons unto glory.

The expression *Son of Man* is found ninety times in the book of Ezekiel, where God uses the term for the prophet.

Gospel usage

The title, Son of Man, is used more than eighty times in the Gospels. While Jesus used the title when speaking of himself it was never used by anyone else in speaking of him.

Jesus used the Son of Man title to describe himself. Here are a few of those references. The italics are mine and used for the purpose of emphasis on the particular reference Jesus was making.

19 the *Son of man came eating and drinking*, and they say, 'Behold, a glutton and a drunkard, a friend of tax collectors and sinners!' Yet wisdom is justified by her deeds." (Matt. 11:19 and Luke 7:34)

31 And he began to teach them that the Son of man must *suffer* many things, and *be rejected* by the elders and the chief priests and the scribes, and be *killed*, and after three days *rise* again. (Mark 8:31)

34 and they will *mock* him, and spit upon him, and *scourge* him, and kill him; and after three days he will rise." (Mark 10:34)

21 *honor* and *dignity*, as *head and founder* of the kingdom of God, and *judge* of all men.
(Mark 14:21)

10 But that you may know that the Son of man has *authority* on earth to <u>forgive sins</u>"—he said to the paralytic— (Mark 2:10)

28 so the Son of man is *lord even of the sabbath*. (Mark 2:28)

41 The Son of man *will send* his angels, and they will *gather* out of his kingdom all causes of *sin and all evildoers*, (Matt. 13:41)

28 Truly, I say to you, there are some standing here who will not taste death before they *see* the Son of man coming in his kingdom." (Matt. 16:28)

28 Jesus said to them, "Truly, I say to you, in the new world, when the Son of man shall *sit on his glorious throne*, you who have followed me will also sit on twelve thrones, judging the twelve tribes of Israel. (Matt. 19:28)

Jesus used the title *Son of Man* to describe his role as servant and his role of divine authority. As the human side of the Son of Man, he would become the sacrificial lamb for the sins of all humanity.

The title Son of Man blends the heavenly and earthly aspects of Jesus the Christ. Because of his divine nature he has the God given authority to forgive sin. None of his followers immediately grasped what Jesus meant by this title, but with the passage of time they would understand that Jesus used it to claim authority, demonstrate power, and assume responsibilities no other man could.

<u>***Jesus invites a Tax Collector to follow***</u> Mark 2:13-14; Matthew 9:9; Luke 5:27-28	<u>***Jesus invites a Tax Collector to follow***</u> Mark 2:13-14; Matthew 9:9; Luke 5:27-28
Mark 2:13-14 13 He went out again beside the sea; and all the crowd gathered about him, and he taught them. 14 And as he passed on, he saw Levi the son of Alphaeus sitting at the tax office, and he said to him, "Follow me." And he rose and followed him.	**Comment** John does not give us an account of the calling of the tax collector Levi/Matthew. Because Matthew was a tax collector, he was considered a traitor to his people and a lackey of Rome. One wonders,

Matthew 9:9
⁹ As Jesus passed on from there, he saw a man called Matthew sitting at the tax office; and he said to him, "Follow me." And he rose and followed him.

Luke 5:27-28
²⁷ After this he went out, and saw a tax collector, named Levi, sitting at the tax office; and he said to him, "Follow me." ²⁸ And he left everything, and rose and followed him.

would John ever accept this one-time traitor as a full-fledged member of the Inner-Circle?

The introduction of a Tax Collector among Jesus' disciples must have had a colossal impact on everyone! Tax collectors were considered part of the same sack of garbage that contained the Romans. Jewish tax collectors were the worst of the filthy traitors because they were considered supporting the occupation! The Jews considered these taxes tribute they were forced to pay the enemy.

Matthew's response was to leave everything and follow Jesus. When we look at this word "everything" we must remember the society was made up of "the haves and the have-nots." The have-nots vastly outnumbered the haves. Matthew was a member of the "Haves." His position as a tax collector was very profitable. Saying yes to Jesus was also saying goodbye to a life of luxury.

This leads us to discuss the tax collecting system of Jesus' day.

Jesus' invitation to Matthew sent shock waves through the rest of His followers

Jesus bewildered his other followers by inviting this "filthy" tax collector to become part of their group! Peter, James, John, and Andrew were all fishermen and every fish they brought out of the Sea of Galilee was taxed! They had to pay the tax because Herod Antipas claimed the Sea of Galilee as his private lake and had a military force to back him up.

The tension was as obvious as lightning strikes on a stormy night. Why was Jesus doing this? He was inviting someone to join them that they would not in a million years have considered giving an invitation. In fact, they would have been more likely to stand in line for the opportunity to slit his throat. Clearly Matthew was the most unlikely individual they would have wanted as a traveling companion.

Obviously Jesus saw in Matthew qualities that were hidden to the eyes of the others. Remember, Jesus had many followers at this time. He had not yet made the final selection of the Inner-Circle (the twelve).

Again Jesus was sending a message to both the Romans and the Temple authorities that he had no intention of leading an armed revolt against Rome. Clearly he was saying his revolt was aimed at the corrupt actions of the religious leaders!

The Business of Tax Collecting

Modern tax structures differ largely from those of ancient Israel. The major differences are in the areas of who collects the tax and how much of the taxes will they keep for themselves. Today, in the United States, tax officials are elected at the local level, appointed at the state and federal levels. The amount of tax is derived from the cost of delivering services to the population as determined by the related elected official of the unit under question.

In ancient times the process was in no way democratic. Here is a very simplified but accurate example of how the taxing procedure was administered:

1. Rome required Herod the Great to remit say $1,000,000.

2. Herod would bill his Chief Tax Collector $2,000,000. Remember, Herod had to pay Rome and have enough to run his government and do everything he planned for the coming year.

3. The Chief Tax Collector in turn would apportion Herod's total to his various Tax Collectors plus an amount he considered a fair return on his investment, say another $1,000,000.

4. The last person in the chain was the local Tax Collector. He would be given a bill for his portion of the $3,000,000. He would now determine how much he would need for his expenses and profit to determine the amount he must raise during the coming year.

Perhaps the greatest difference in the whole Tax Business was when Rome sent Herod the tax bill ($1,000,000) they expected the full amount by return mail! So what did Herod expect from his Chief Tax Collector? You got it, he expected by return courier $2,000,000. Likewise the Chief Tax Collector expected the apportioned amount from his Tax Collectors by return courier. In this case he was looking for $ 3,000,000.

Since all taxes were required to be paid in full at the time they were assessed only very wealthy persons could afford to bid on the Tax collecting positions. These Tax collectors felt justified in adding to the amount charged them a sum large enough to insure having a successful bid the next tax season.

Celebration Meal **Mark 2:15-17;** **Matthew 9:10-13;** **Luke 5:29-32**	*Celebration Meal* **Mark 2:15-17;** **Matthew 9:10-13;** **Luke 5:29-32**
Mark 2:15-17 15 And as he sat at table in his house, many tax collectors and	**Comment** Mark tells us "Matthew" hosted a dinner for Jesus, and

sinners were sitting with Jesus and his disciples; for there were many who followed him. 16 And the scribes of the Pharisees, when they saw that he was eating with sinners and tax collectors, said to his disciples, "Why does he eat with tax collectors and sinners?" 17 And when Jesus heard it, he said to them, "Those who are well have no need of a physician, but those who are sick; I came not to call the righteous, but sinners."

Matthew 9:10-13
10 And as he sat at table in the house, behold, many tax collectors and sinners came and sat down with Jesus and his disciples. 11 And when the Pharisees saw this, they said to his disciples, "Why does your teacher eat with tax collectors and sinners?" 12 But when he heard it, he said, "Those who are well have no need of a physician, but those who are sick. 13 Go and learn what this means, 'I desire mercy, and not sacrifice.' For I came not to call the righteous, but sinners."

Luke 5:29-32
29 And Levi made him a great feast in his house; and there was a large company of tax collectors and others sitting at table with

his disciples, along with tax collectors, and assorted sinners. Such a large number of people attending the meal implied several things: 1) such a large number of people required a room suitable to accommodate them; 2) it tells us Matthew was a wealthy man.

The scribes and Pharisees were ever present. It is noteworthy that the scribes are definitively associated with the Pharisees, and the combination constituted the eyes and ears of Herod Antipas.

The meal had not progressed far when a challenge was issued to the disciples aimed at Jesus. Why does Jesus eat with tax collectors and sinners? Jesus heard the accusation and responded, healthy people do not need a doctor only the sick need a physician. Thus Jesus clearly delineated his reason for being on earth, "I came not to call the righteous but sinners."

The word mercy as used in Matthew 9:13 means, kindness or good will towards the miserable and the afflicted, with the desire to help them.

Luke names Levi as the host for the feast.

them. 30 And the Pharisees and their scribes murmured against his disciples, saying, "Why do you eat and drink with tax collectors and sinners?" 31 And Jesus answered them, "Those who are well have no need of a physician, but those who are sick; 32 I have not come to call the righteous, but sinners to repentance."

John's disciples question Jesus about fasting
John is now in prison

Mark 2:18-22;
Matthew 9:14-17;
Luke 5:33-39

John's disciples question Jesus about fasting
John is now in prison

Mark 2:18-22;
Matthew 9:14-17;
Luke 5:33-39

Mark 2:18-22

18 Now John's disciples and the Pharisees were fasting; and people came and said to him, "Why do John's disciples and the disciples of the Pharisees fast, but your disciples do not fast?" 19 And Jesus said to them, "Can the wedding guests fast while the bridegroom is with them? As long as they have the bridegroom with them, they cannot fast. 20 The days will come, when the bridegroom is taken away from them, and then they will fast in that day. 21 No one sews a piece

Comment

Mark says the "people" came and asked why Jesus' disciples did not observe fasting? They were confused by the differences in the conduct of the Pharisees and the disciples of Jesus. Matthew says John's disciples asked the question of "why?" Luke says "they" ask the questions.

Jesus answered their inquiries with a parable. Wedding guests would deeply offend the groom

of unshrunk cloth on an old garment; if he does, the patch tears away from it, the new from the old, and a worse tear is made. 22 And no one puts new wine into old wineskins; if he does, the wine will burst the skins, and the wine is lost, and so are the skins; but new wine is for fresh skins."

Matthew 9:14-17
14 Then the disciples of John came to him, saying, "Why do we and the Pharisees fast, but your disciples do not fast?" 15 And Jesus said to them, "Can the wedding guests mourn as long as the bridegroom is with them? The days will come, when the bridegroom is taken away from them, and then they will fast. 16 And no one puts a piece of unshrunk cloth on an old garment, for the patch tears away from the garment, and a worse tear is made. 17 Neither is new wine put into old wineskins; if it is, the skins burst, and the wine is spilled, and the skins are destroyed; but new wine is put into fresh wineskins, and so both are preserved."

Luke 5:33-39
33 And they said to him, "The

if they refused to eat with him. It would be an insult of unbelievable magnitude. All three Gospel writers agree with this position.

Jesus continued by telling them there would be enough opportunity for fasting after the bridegroom is taken away. The implication referred to his death, resurrection, and ascension. Although none present could possibly have made such an interpretation of the comment at that moment in time.

Then Jesus told them two additional short powerful parables.

The first concerned putting a patch on a garment. Mark and Matthew speak of un-shrunk cloth being applied to an old garment creating the potential of damage to the garment when the patch shrunk and burst its seams. Luke on the other hand implies that one would tear a new piece of cloth and use it as a patch on the old garment having the same end results.

The next parable was about putting new wine into old

disciples of John fast often and offer prayers, and so do the disciples of the Pharisees, but yours eat and drink." 34 And Jesus said to them, "Can you make wedding guests fast while the bridegroom is with them? 35 The days will come, when the bridegroom is taken away from them, and then they will fast in those days." 36 He told them a parable also: "No one tears a piece from a new garment and puts it upon an old garment; if he does, he will tear the new, and the piece from the new will not match the old. 37 And no one puts new wine into old wineskins; if he does, the new wine will burst the skins and it will be spilled, and the skins will be destroyed. 38 But new wine must be put into fresh wineskins. 39 And no one after drinking old wine desires new; for he says, 'The old is good.'"

wineskins. The point would have been immediately realized by Jesus' audience. All understood what would happen when you poured new wine into an old skin. The old inflexible skin would not be able to stretch and accommodate the fermentation process and thereby split and ruin the skin and waste the wine.

All three Gospel writers gave the same meaning to this parable. However, Luke's closing comment is pregnant with possible interpretation. Perhaps he could foresee how hard it would be for the Orthodox to embrace the new teaching of Jesus.

Grainfields

**Mark 2:23-28;
Matthew 12:1-8;
Luke 6:1-5**

Grainfields

**Mark 2:23-28;
Matthew 12:1-8;
Luke 6:1-5**

Mark 2:23-28
23 One sabbath he was going through the grainfields; and as

Comment

According to the orthodox Jews,

they made their way his disciples began to pluck heads of grain. 24 And the Pharisees said to him, "Look, why are they doing what is not lawful on the sabbath?" 25 And he said to them, "Have you never read what David did, when he was in need and was hungry, he and those who were with him: 26 how he entered the house of God, when Abi'athar was high priest, and ate the bread of the Presence, which it is not lawful for any but the priests to eat, and also gave it to those who were with him?" 27 And he said to them, "The sabbath was made for man, not man for the sabbath; 28 so the Son of man is lord even of the sabbath."

Matthew 12:1-8
1 At that time Jesus went through the grainfields on the sabbath; his disciples were hungry, and they began to pluck heads of grain and to eat. 2 But when the Pharisees saw it, they said to him, "Look, your disciples are doing what is not lawful to do on the sabbath." 3 He said to them, "Have you not read what David did, when he was hungry, and those who were with him: 4 how he entered the house of God and ate the bread of the Presence, which it was not lawful for him to eat nor for those who

the followers of Jesus were unclean because they did not perform the regular ablutions before meals, even when they were not dining in a formal setting.

The fact that God had created the Sabbath for the benefit of man was an unbelievably shocking concept to the Pharisees. They had never considered such a revolutionary thought.

Comment

Matthew 12:1-8

Walking beyond the prescribed distance was a violation of the Sabbath. Plucking the grain was considered as work, which was forbidden on the Sabbath. The Pharisees were quick to challenge Jesus over these breaches of the law. Just as quickly Jesus responded with two points for them to consider.

1. King David had taken the Bread of the Presence from the temple when his men

were with him, but only for the priests? 5 Or have you not read in the law how on the sabbath the priests in the temple profane the sabbath, and are guiltless? 6 I tell you, something greater than the temple is here. 7 And if you had known what this means, 'I desire mercy, and not sacrifice,' you would not have condemned the guiltless. 8 For the Son of man is lord of the sabbath."

Luke 6:1-5
1 On a sabbath, while he was going through the grainfields, his disciples plucked and ate some heads of grain, rubbing them in their hands. 2 But some of the Pharisees said, "Why are you doing what is not lawful to do on the sabbath?" 3 And Jesus answered, "Have you not read what David did when he was hungry, he and those who were with him: 4 how he entered the house of God, and took and ate the bread of the Presence, which it is not lawful for any but the priests to eat, and also gave it to those with him?" 5 And he said to them, "The Son of man is lord of the sabbath."

were starving. This bread was supposed to be eaten only by the temple priest. (1 Sam. 21:1-6)

1 Then came David to Nob to Ahim'elech the priest; and Ahim'elech came to meet David trembling, and said to him, "Why are you alone, and no one with you?" 2 And David said to Ahim'elech the priest, "The king has charged me with a matter, and said to me, 'Let no one know anything of the matter about which I send you, and with which I have charged you.' I have made an appointment with the young men for such and such a place. 3 Now then, what have you at hand? Give me five loaves of bread, or whatever is here." 4 And the priest answered David, "I have no common bread at hand, but there is holy bread; if only the young men have kept themselves from women." 5 And David answered the priest, "Of a truth women have been kept from us as always when I go on an expedition; the vessels of the young men are holy, even when it is a common journey; how much more today will their vessels be holy?" 6 So the priest gave him the holy bread; for there was no bread there but the

	bread of the Presence, which is removed from before the LORD, to be replaced by hot bread on the day it is taken away. Secondly, the Priest violated the law every time they performed a circumcision on the Sabbath day. Then to cinch his position Jesus quoted the Old Testament prophet Micah. *"What doth the LORD require of thee, but to do justly, and to love mercy, and to walk humbly with thy God?" Micah 6:8*
Jesus heals two blind men	***Jesus heals two blind men***
Matthew 9:27-31 27 And as Jesus passed on from there, two blind men followed him, crying aloud, "Have mercy on us, Son of David." 28 When he entered the house, the blind men came to him; and Jesus said to them, "Do you believe that I am able to do this?" They said to him, "Yes, Lord." 29 Then he touched their eyes, saying, "According to your faith be it done to you." 30 And their eyes were opened. And Jesus sternly charged them, "See that no one knows it." 31 But	**Matthew 9:27-31** **Comment** This is an independent story of Matthew. We are told two blind men addressed Jesus as the son of David. This was a way of saying they believed Jesus to be the Messiah, the promised one. Jesus asked if the men truly believed that he could heal

they went away and spread his fame through all that district.

them; without equivocation, they said "yes Lord."

Jesus touched their eyes to heal them, and in touching them he became unclean according to ritual law, because blind persons were considered unclean and no one should touch them.

Dumb Demoniac

Matthew 9:32-34
32 As they were going away, behold, a dumb demoniac was brought to him. 33 And when the demon had been cast out, the dumb man spoke; and the crowds marveled, saying, "Never was anything like this seen in Israel." 34 But the Pharisees said, "He casts out demons by the prince of demons.:

Dumb Demoniac

Matthew 9:32-34

Comment

The "dumb" man could not speak but had someone who cared enough to bring him to Jesus. Freed of the demon the man spoke proclaiming his healed condition. The on lookers marveled and praised God.
The Pharisees committed the unpardonable sin by saying Jesus healed by the power of Satan.

Jesus continues to preach in "all the cities"

Matthew 9:35-38
35 And Jesus went about all the cities and villages, teaching in their synagogues and preaching the gospel of the kingdom, and

Jesus continues to preach in "all the cities"

Matthew 9:35-38

Comment

Jesus' ministry continued

healing every disease and every infirmity. 36 When he saw the crowds, he had compassion for them, because they were harassed and helpless, like sheep without a shepherd. 37 Then he said to his disciples, "The harvest is plentiful, but the laborers are few; 38 pray therefore the Lord of the harvest to send out laborers into his harvest."	throughout the cities and villages of the entire area. Wherever a synagogue was located he went to preach and heal. As he gazed upon those who came to him they appeared to him as sheep without a shepherd. Speaking to the Inner-Circle He said the harvest is plentiful, but the laborers are few.

Chapter 8

Sabbath/healing/ withered hand + conflict

**Mark 3:1-6;
Matthew 12:9-14;
Luke 6:6-11**

Mark 3:1-6

1 Again he entered the synagogue, and a man was there who had a withered hand. 2 And they watched him, to see whether he would heal him on the sabbath, so that they might accuse him. 3 And he said to the man who had the withered hand, "Come here." 4 And he said to them, "Is it lawful on the sabbath to do good or to do harm, to save life or to kill?" But they were silent. 5 And he looked around at them with anger, grieved at their hardness of heart, and said to the man, "Stretch out your hand." He stretched it out, and his hand was restored. 6 The Pharisees went out, and immediately held counsel with the Hero'di-ans against him, how to destroy him.

Sabbath/healing/ withered hand + conflict

**Mark 3:1-6;
Matthew 12:9-14;
Luke 6:6-11**

Comment

Jesus entered the synagogue on the Sabbath day, which was his custom. Already in attendance was a man with a withered hand and a group of Pharisees from Jerusalem with orders to report Jesus' every word. Jesus knew what the Pharisees were thinking and that they cared nothing for the man or his deformity. Jesus understood everything but never let religious conformity stand in the way of doing God's will.

Jesus asked the man to stand up and come to him. Then he turned to the Pharisees and asked, "Is it better to heal or to do harm on the Sabbath?" The Pharisees failure to answer resulted in Jesus becoming

Matthew 12:9-14
⁹ And he went on from there, and entered their synagogue. ¹⁰ And behold, there was a man with a withered hand. And they asked him, "Is it lawful to heal on the sabbath?" so that they might accuse him. ¹¹ He said to them, "What man of you, if he has one sheep and it falls into a pit on the sabbath, will not lay hold of it and lift it out? ¹² Of how much more value is a man than a sheep! So it is lawful to do good on the sabbath." ¹³ Then he said to the man, "Stretch out your hand." And the man stretched it out, and it was restored, whole like the other. ¹⁴ But the Pharisees went out and took counsel against him, how to destroy him.

Luke 6:6-11
⁶ On another sabbath, when he entered the synagogue and taught, a man was there whose right hand was withered. ⁷ And the scribes and the Pharisees watched him, to see whether he would heal on the sabbath, so that they might find an accusation against him. ⁸ But he knew their thoughts, and he said to the man who had the withered hand, "Come and stand here." And he rose and stood there. ⁹ And Jesus said to them, "I ask

angry with them. He could not abide a closed mind or a cold heart and both marked the character of these Pharisees.

Jesus turned to the man and asked him to stretch out his hand. Luke said it was the right hand, and Jesus healed him. The Pharisees exited the synagogue feeling they had the information needed to take back to Jerusalem. Once out of the synagogue they contacted the Herodians, who were devoted followers of Herod Antipas, and together they began laying plans for the destruction of Jesus.

Matthew tells us it was the Pharisees who questioned Jesus about healing on the Sabbath.

Mark is the only one who said Jesus was angered by the attitude of the Pharisees.

Luke said the scribes with the Pharisees were filled with fury at Jesus' action.

you, is it lawful on the sabbath to do good or to do harm, to save life or to destroy it?" 10 And he looked around on them all, and said to him, "Stretch out your hand." And he did so, and his hand was restored. 11 But they were filled with fury and discussed with one another what they might do to Jesus.	

<u>The Herodians</u>

The Herodians' standard of living was directly tied to Herod Antipas. They were his ambassadors of support among the wealthy in Galilee. Staying on the friendly side of Herod Antipas was insurance for their future.

The Herodians were political by nature. The Pharisees were a combination of religious and political entanglements. The only bond these two groups shared was fear of Jesus and his power with the common people.

The old saying, "Strange bed fellows" is an apt description of the Pharisee-Herodian alliance.

Healings/do not tell anyone

**Mark 3:7-12;
Matthew 12:15-21;
Luke 6:17-19**

Mark 3:7-12

7 Jesus withdrew with his disciples to the sea, and a great multitude from Galilee followed; also from Judea 8 and Jerusalem and Idume'a and from beyond the Jordan and from about Tyre and Sidon a great multitude, hearing all that he did, came to him. 9 And he told his disciples to have a boat ready for him because of the crowd, lest they should crush him; 10 for he had healed many, so that all who had diseases pressed upon him to touch him. 11 And whenever the unclean spirits beheld him, they fell down before him and cried out, "You are the Son of God." 12 And he strictly ordered them not to make him known.

Matthew 12:15-21

15 Jesus, aware of this, withdrew from there. And many followed him, and he healed them all, 16 and ordered them not to make him known. 17 This was to fulfil what was spoken by the prophet Isaiah:
18 "Behold, my servant whom I have chosen,
   my beloved with whom my soul is well pleased.
I will put my Spirit upon him,

Healings/do not tell anyone

**Mark 3:7-12;
Matthew 12:15-21;
Luke 6:17-19**

Comment

Mark clearly establishes the popularity of Jesus throughout the land of Israel and the regions beyond its borders. The people of these areas converged upon Jesus somewhere on the shores of the Sea of Galilee, because they had heard Jesus was a great healer.

Jesus was concerned about crowd control, because there was none. To be prepared he ordered the disciples to have the boat ready for a speedy departure. His concerns were real as the crowd pushed and shoved trying to be the next one Jesus would touch and heal.

Matthew quotes Isaiah 42:1-4.

Isaiah was thinking of the Messiah establishing justice for the Gentiles. Jesus went far beyond justice and offered forgiveness and mercy. Isaiah's vision of the Messiah pictured a strong, quiet, gentle leader.

When Jesus and John the Baptist emerged on the scene they proclaimed the basic

and he shall proclaim justice to the Gentiles.
19 He will not wrangle or cry aloud,
  nor will any one hear his voice in the streets;
20 he will not break a bruised reed
  or quench a smoldering wick, till he brings justice to victory;
21 and in his name will the Gentiles hope."
 	
Luke 6:17-19
 	
17 And he came down with them and stood on a level place, with a great crowd of his disciples and a great multitude of people from all Judea and Jerusalem and the seacoast of Tyre and Sidon, who came to hear him and to be healed of their diseases; 18 and those who were troubled with unclean spirits were cured. 19 And all the crowd sought to touch him, for power came forth from him and healed them all.
	message of Isaiah, but their style of delivery was totally opposite to his concept. They were gentle and warm to those in need, to those who truly sought God. On the other hand, they brought strength to face opposing strength. They denounced the closed minded and all who distorted God and His message of love.

<u>*The unclean spirits*</u>

The unclean spirits knew Jesus and his power and purpose. They could not conceal themselves or deceive him. When he ordered them to be silent and not make him known only he heard them. He was without a doubt the only one who could see them. To better understand this concept, think of a person who has the flu. Everyone can see the person is ill but only those with a microscope can see the germs that are causing the illness.

Readers may wonder why at certain times Jesus instructed a person receiving healing to say nothing about it and at other times he gave no prohibition. The reason is predicated on the location of the event. Whenever Jesus was in Galilee, he instructed the recipient to say nothing about what had happened. The ruler of Galilee, Herod Antipas, was paranoid concerning Jesus. He was upset by the crowds following Jesus and the good reports concerning him. Herod feared Jesus as a threat to his position, but Jesus was not ready to give Herod cause to make trouble.

Naming the entire twelve at one time	*Naming the entire twelve at one time*
Mark 3:13-19a; Matthew 10:1-4; Luke 6:12-16	**Mark 3:13-19a; Matthew 10:1-4; Luke 6:12-16**
Mark 3:13-19a	**Comment**
13 And he went up on the mountain, and called to him those whom he desired; and they came to him. 14 And he appointed twelve, to be with him, and to be sent out to preach 15 and have authority to cast out demons: 16 Simon whom he surnamed Peter; 17 James the son of Zeb'edee and John the brother of James, whom he surnamed Bo-aner'ges, that is, sons of thunder; 18 Andrew, and Philip, and Bartholomew, and Matthew, and Thomas, and James the son of Alphaeus, and Thaddaeus, and Simon the Cananaean, 19a and Judas Iscariot, who betrayed him.	Mark gives us an entirely different setting for the calling of the Inner-Circle. Since he names Peter, Andrew, James, and John in the total list, it reinforces the position that the earlier call "follow me" was not to be considered enrollment in the Inner-Circle of twelve disciples who traveled and lived with Jesus. It is at this point in Jesus' ministry that he was satisfied he had the best of the best. Here he acknowledged them and their place in his traveling ministry. Jesus had separated himself

Matthew 10:1-4

1 And he called to him his twelve disciples and gave them authority over unclean spirits, to cast them out, and to heal every disease and every infirmity. 2 The names of the twelve apostles are these: first, Simon, who is called Peter, and Andrew his brother; James the son of Zeb'edee, and John his brother; 3 Philip and Bartholomew; Thomas and Matthew the tax collector; James the son of Alphaeus, and Thaddaeus; 4 Simon the Cananaean, and Judas Iscariot, who betrayed him.

Luke 6:12-16

12 In these days he went out to the mountain to pray; and all night he continued in prayer to God. 13 And when it was day, he called his disciples, and chose from them twelve, whom he named apostles; 14 Simon, whom he named Peter, and Andrew his brother, and James and John, and Philip, and Bartholomew, 15 and Matthew, and Thomas, and James the son of Alphaeus, and Simon who was called the Zealot, 16 and Judas the son of James, and Judas Iscariot, who became a traitor.

from John the Baptist in order to establish his independent ministry and began to form his own circle of followers. He called men from the working class, fishermen, unlearned men, and married men.

Luke refers to the selected twelve as "Apostles." The Greek word means, "A delegate, messenger, one sent forth with orders" (Strong's Greek Dictionary # 652).

"Disciple" means student

The word *Disciple* means student. Most moderns have narrowed the meaning to describe those twelve who traveled with Jesus throughout his ministry. A more careful reading of the Gospels reveals the use of the word disciple included thousands of people who listened and learned from Jesus but did not give up their regular life to itinerate with him. It is obvious there was a distinction between the mass of disciples and the twelve disciples. To retain this distinction, I refer to the twelve as the "Inner-Circle."

The Inner-Circle Man by Man

Jesus went out to the mountain to pray; and continued all night in prayer to God. And when it was day, he called his disciples, and from them he chose twelve, whom he named apostles; Simon, whom he named Peter, and Andrew his brother, James and John, Philip, Bartholomew, Matthew, Thomas, James the son of Alphaeus, Simon who was called the Zealot, Judas the son of James, and Judas Iscariot, who became a traitor.

#1 Peter

Simon Peter is the first named among the twelve selected to become the Inner-Circle of chosen disciples. Peter was born in the town of Bethsaida on the northern shore of the Sea of Galilee. Peter was married but there is no record of his wife's name or if they had any children. He and his brother, Andrew, were fishermen. At some point in time Peter moved to Capernaum, possibly when he married because the Gospel tells us that he lived in the home of his mother-in-law.

From the beginning, three members of the Inner-circle (Peter, James, and John) contended for the leadership role of second in command behind Jesus. Impetuosity was a major characteristic of Peter. Upon seeing Jesus walking on the water during a severe storm it was Peter who asked permission to get out of the boat and walk to Jesus. When Jesus asked the Inner-Circle, "Who do you say I am?" Only Peter said, "You are the Christ the Son of the Living God." Here Jesus changed his name to Peter (the rock). Shortly after this Jesus was explaining that he would soon die. Peter rebuked him for saying this. Jesus replied sharply, "Get behind me Satan." When Jesus was arrested in the garden it was Peter who drew his sword to defend him. Jesus sternly rebuked Peter telling him to put away the sword. It was this same Peter who crumbled under the weight of fear and denied knowing Jesus on three separate occasions.

After the resurrection Peter became a changed man and the true leader of what was to become known as Christianity. He became the leader of the apostles, after Jesus' ascension.

#2 Andrew

Andrew was the second disciple named by Jesus to the Inner-Circle. He was the brother of Simon Peter, and son of a man named Jonah (sometimes the name is rendered as John), and brother of Simon Peter. Like Peter he was born in Bethsaida on the north side of the Sea of Galilee. Andrew and his brother were partners in a fishing business with James and John.

Before Andrew met Jesus, he was a disciple of John the Baptist. He became convinced that Jesus was the Messiah and brought his brother Peter to meet Jesus. The brothers returned to their fishing, but later, Jesus saw them on the shores of the Sea of Galilee and said to them, "Follow me, and I will make you fishers of men." It was Andrew who inquired about the signs/miracles that would mark the end times. Andrew called attention to the boy with the loaves and fishes, when Jesus fed the 5,000 men not including women and children.

#3 James

James, the son of Zebedee and brother of John, was the third disciple Jesus inducted into the Inner-Circle. James, his father, and his brother were in the fishing business with Peter and Andrew. Jesus surnamed James and John Boanerges, which means "sons of thunder." James along with Peter and his brother John competed for the role of second in command behind Jesus. James was present at many of the important events recorded in the Gospels, including the restoration of the daughter of Jairus, the transfiguration, and the agony in Gethsemane. James was executed by King Herod Agrippa (Acts 12:1-2).

#4 John

John was the fourth disciple to be named to the Inner-Circle. John was the son of Zebedee and Salome. He and his brother James and their father Zebedee were Galilean fishermen. They were partners with Peter and Andrew. John, like Andrew, had been a disciple of John the Baptist. John is referred to as "beloved disciple" in the Gospel of John. We do not know the details of the connection but we do know that he was "known by the high priest" (John 18:15). Jesus entrusted him with the care of his mother Mary at the crucifixion (John 19:26). Being younger than Peter he outran him to the empty tomb (John 20:2-4).

After the resurrection, John emerged as one of the leaders of the early church. John later went to the city of Ephesus taking Mary with him. John enjoyed a long and fruitful ministry there before and after his exile to the island of Patmos. It is believed he wrote the Book of Revelation while exiled.

Five New Testament books, including the Gospel of John, The Revelation, and three Epistles, called John 1, John 2, John 3, are credited to him. Tradition says that John died at an old age.

#5 Philip

Philip was the fifth disciple enrolled into the Inner-Circle. Like Peter and Andrew he was from Bethsaida in Galilee. He was introduced to Jesus by his friend Nathanael (Bartholomew) who would also become a member of the Inner-Circle.

Before performing the miracle of feeding the multitude of people with a small amount of food, Jesus asked Philip, "How are we to buy bread, so that these people may eat?" Jesus was testing Philip, because he already knew that he would perform a miracle. The question must have shocked Philip. Later, a group of Greek Jews were in Jerusalem for Passover and asked Philip to introduce them to Jesus. During the Last Supper, Philip asked Jesus to show them the Father. Phillip was present at the prayer meeting in the upper room with the 120 after the ascension of Jesus.

#6 Bartholomew/Nathanael

Bartholomew (possibly also known as Nathanael) was the sixth disciple named to the Inner-Circle. The name Bartholomew does not appear in John's Gospel. Bartholomew may not have been the name most familiar to many people. Perhaps others knew him better as Nathanael. He was the son of Tolmai.

Philip tells Nathanael/Bartholomew, "We have found the Messiah! His name is Jesus, the Son of Joseph from Nazareth." Nathanael shouted, "Nazareth! Can anything good come from there?" Seeing them coming Jesus said, "Here comes an honest man, a true son of Israel." Nathanael asked, "How do you know what I am like?" Jesus replied, "I could see you under the fig tree before Philip found you." Nathanael then replied, "Sir you are the Son of God, the King of Israel."

#7 Matthew

Matthew was the seventh disciple commissioned into the Inner-Circle. He was also called Levi, son of Alphaeus (Mark 2:14). He was a hated tax collector before he was called by Jesus (Matt. 9:9). He is best known as the disciple who wrote the second oldest Gospel of the New Testament, (Mark is believed to be the oldest by date).

The Gospel of Matthew gives us the oldest detailed account of the ancestors of Jesus, (Luke also gives us an account of Jesus' ancestry). Matthew gives us insights into the events surrounding the birth of Jesus. His Gospel is the only source we have for the Sermon on the Mount. Many of the parables found in the Gospel are found nowhere else.

#8 Thomas

Thomas was the eighth disciple named to the Inner-Circle. There is considerable confusion, disagreement, and uncertainty as to the identity of Thomas. The Aramaic word for "Thomas" comes from the root-word for "twin." This led some to believe Thomas would be referred to as "Thomas Didmus" (Thomas the Twin). Some believe this may have been done to conceal Thomas' true identity; however, there is no evidence to support this position. Luke had no compulsion in any way to defer from calling him Thomas.

After Jesus raised Lazarus from the dead he announced that he was going to Jerusalem. The members of the Inner-Circle tried to dissuade Jesus from this dangerous decision. They had real grounds for trying to do so because of the avowed intentions of the authorities to kill him. Only Thomas expressed his awareness of the danger and his total commitment to follow Jesus regardless of where it led saying, "Let us also go, that we might die with him."

At the "Last Supper" Jesus said that he was going away and they knew where he was going. Philip expressed his confusion with Thomas joining in the conversation. After the resurrection the other members of the Inner-Circle were present when Jesus appeared to them. Being told that Jesus was alive, Thomas expressed his disbelief. When Jesus appeared to Thomas he exclaimed, "My Lord and my God!"

#9 James the son of Alphaeus

James, the son of Alphaeus, was the ninth disciple brought into the Inner-Circle. He is omitted in John's Gospel. Since the apostle Matthew was the son of a man named Alphaeus, some have thought that he and James were brothers. However, the two are never referred to as brothers, unlike Peter and Andrew, and James and John, who were consistently referred to as being brothers. Some believe his mother was one of the women who went to the tomb of Jesus, and found that it had been opened. James was also called "James the Less." He was among those who went to the upper room to pray after the Ascension of Jesus.

#10 Simon the Zealot

Simon the Zealot was the tenth man named to the Inner-Circle. He is the most obscure of the entire twelve. Beyond his name little is known about him. Simon was a very common name at the time. This is evidenced by the fact that the first man named was Simon Peter. To distinguish between these two the words "the Zealot" was added to his name. It is perhaps the only key we possess to develop further information about him. We may chose to think this identified him with the organization called the "Zealots." The Zealots were a violent anti-Roman wing of the Pharisees.

#11 Judas son of James

Luke refers to the eleventh member of the Inner-Circle as Judas, son of James. However, there is considerable confusion as to the accuracy of this name. Mark 3:18 (the earliest gospel) lists the name of Thaddaeus. Matthew 10:3 (the second gospel written) also contains the name Thaddeus. Luke 6:16 replaces the name Thaddaeus with the reference, "Judas son of James." And John 14:22 adds, "Judas (not Iscariot) said to him, "Lord, how is it that you will manifest yourself to us, and not to the world?" This comment was made in the "Upper Room."

The name Thaddaeus appears in Matthew's (10:3) list of the Inner-Circle stating, "And Lebbaeus, whose surname was Thaddaeus." This is placed in the list between James, son of Alphaeus, and Simon the Zealot. In Mark 3:18, Thaddaeus' name appears in the same placement. In Luke 6:16 the name Judas, son of James is listed among the Inner-Circle between Simon the Zealot and Judas Iscariot.

It is believed that Thaddaeus was also known as Judas, son of James but not to be confused with Judas Iscariot, the man who betrayed Jesus. In ancient times a person could have two or three different names such as a Greek-language name, a Hebrew name, and sometimes people were known primarily by their occupational title.

His given name was Judas but to distinguish him from the other Judas he was nicknamed Thaddaeus. According to Matthew's gospel his surname was Lebbaeus. Thus, from the evidence it is possible to think his full name may have been Judas Thaddaeus Lebbaeus.

Judas was a good name before Judas Iscariot tarnished it with his betrayal of Jesus. Possibly the remaining members of the Inner-Circle chose to use this nickname instead of his given name.

#12 Judas Iscariot

The twelfth and final selection to the Inner-Circle was Judas Iscariot. More Gospel information is available to us about Judas than any other disciple except Simon Peter. The four Evangelists tell us he betrayed Jesus. We are told he was the son of Simon Iscariot and that he came from the region "Kerioth" or Moab, (Amos 2:2). Judas was the treasurer for the Inner-Circle. John labeled Judas as a thief saying that he often dipped into the funds for his own personal use (John 12:3-6). John also accused Judas of having no real concern for the poor.

After Jesus and the Inner-Circle went to Jerusalem Satan entered Judas, (Luke 22:3). Judas approached the authorities offering to deliver Jesus into their hands. For the dastardly deed Judas was to receive thirty pieces of silver (Matt. 26:14-15).

During the Last Supper Jesus revealed Judas as his betrayer without calling his name (Matt. 26:25). Judas fulfilled his part of the bargain as he betrayed Jesus in the Garden of Gethsemane. Afterward, he received his blood money. After Jesus' arrest, Judas was seized with remorse.

Jesus knew the position both the Zealots and Publicans held in Hebrew society. They were bitter enemies. The tax collectors worked for the Romans, the Zealots fought the Romans. Without hesitation Jesus chose a disciple from both groups. We can only guess at the confrontations and conflict they brought into the small group of itinerate followers of Jesus.

John's version of the Calling

John 1:35-42

35 The next day again John was standing with two of his disciples; 36 and he looked at Jesus as he walked, and said, "Behold, the Lamb of God!" 37 The two disciples heard him say this, and they followed Jesus. 38 Jesus turned, and saw them following, and said to them, "What do you seek?" And they said to him, "Rabbi" (which means Teacher), "where are you staying?" 39 He said to them, "Come and see." They came and saw where he was staying; and they stayed with him that day, for it was about the tenth hour. 40 One of the two who heard John speak, and followed him, was Andrew, Simon Peter's brother. 41 He first found his brother Simon, and said to him, "We have found the Messiah" (which means Christ). 42 He brought him to Jesus. Jesus looked at him, and said, "So you are Simon the son of John? You shall be called Cephas" (which means Peter).

John's version of the Calling

John 1:35-42

Comment

John gives an independent narrative of the selection of the disciples. In fact, he never names a special group to this position. In the case of Andrew, who was a disciple of John the Baptist, and Simon, his brother, Jesus invited them to "Come and see." At the same time according to John, Jesus changed Simon's name to Peter. The other three Evangelists report the name change came at Caesera-Philippi when Peter confessed that Jesus was the Son of God. Neither does John name himself or his brother, James as disciples.

Follow me	*Follow me*
John 1:43-51	**John 1:43-51**
43 The next day Jesus decided to go to Galilee. And he found Philip and said to him, "Follow me." 44 Now Philip was from Beth-sa'ida, the city of Andrew and Peter. 45 Philip found Nathan'a-el, and said to him, "We have found him of whom Moses in the law and also the prophets wrote, Jesus of Nazareth, the son of Joseph." 46 Nathan'a-el said to him, "Can anything good come out of Nazareth?" Philip said to him, "Come and see." 47 Jesus saw Nathan'a-el coming to him, and said of him, "Behold, an Israelite indeed, in whom is no guile!" 48 Nathan'a-el said to him, "How do you know me?" Jesus answered him, "Before Philip called you, when you were under the fig tree, I saw you." 49 Nathan'a-el answered him, "Rabbi, you are the Son of God! You are the King of Israel!" 50 Jesus answered him, "Because I said to you, I saw you under the fig tree, do you believe? You shall see greater things than these." 51 And he said to him, "Truly, truly, I say to you, you will see heaven opened, and the angels of God ascending and descending upon the Son of man."	**Comment** The next day, Jesus went to Galilee and found Philip and invited him to, "Follow Me." Philip in turn found Nathaniel who was not impressed with anyone coming from Nazareth. Jesus wins him over on the spot. At this point John tells us no more concerning the Inner-Circle of disciples.

Two major scenarios

This passage contains two major scenarios that continued to emerge throughout the remainder of Jesus' earthly ministry. The first scenario was the constant demand on Jesus for healing the sick. He was so busy there was no time to eat or rest. When his family heard about it, they decided they must take matters into their own hands. If Jesus would not take care of his own basic health needs, they would take over and see to it that he did. They were greatly concerned over the rumors that Jesus was going mad, "He is beside himself."

The second scenario was the constant claim of the Jerusalem constabulary that Jesus used the power of the devil to accomplish his healings. Why would Satan undo his own handiwork? If Satan had become a doer of both evil and good his kingdom was doomed to self-destruct.

Jesus is accused of healing by the power of Beelzebul	*Jesus is accused of healing by the power of Beelzebul*
Mark 3:19b-27; Matthew 12:22-30; Luke 11:14-23	Mark 3:19b-27; Matthew 12:22-30; Luke 11:14-23
Mark 3:19b-27	**Comment**
Then he went home; 20 and the crowd came together again, so that they could not even eat. 21 And when his family heard it, they went out to seize him, for people were saying, "He is beside himself." 22 And the scribes who came down from Jerusalem said, "He is possessed by Be-el'zebul, and by the prince of demons he casts out the demons." 23 And he called them to him, and said	Thus, Jesus revealed his understanding of the power Satan possessed. Jesus told his listeners what they already understood and accepted, you cannot enter a strong man's home and take his property, unless you neutralize him first. Jesus established himself as the one who had entered the realm of evil and reclaimed it for God.

to them in parables, "How can Satan cast out Satan? 24 If a kingdom is divided against itself, that kingdom cannot stand. 25 And if a house is divided against itself, that house will not be able to stand. 26 And if Satan has risen up against himself and is divided, he cannot stand, but is coming to an end. 27 But no one can enter a strong man's house and plunder his goods, unless he first binds the strong man; then indeed he may plunder his house.

Matthew 12:22-30
22 Then a blind and dumb demoniac was brought to him, and he healed him, so that the dumb man spoke and saw. 23 And all the people were amazed, and said, "Can this be the Son of David?" 24 But when the Pharisees heard it they said, "It is only by Be-el'zebul, the prince of demons, that this man casts out demons." 25 Knowing their thoughts, he said to them, "Every kingdom divided against itself is laid waste, and no city or house divided against itself will stand; 26 and if Satan casts out Satan, he is divided against himself; how then will his kingdom stand? 27 And if I cast out demons by Be-el'zebul, by whom do your sons cast them out? Therefore they

Matthew says the man was both blind and dumb. Immediately after his healing, the man spoke clearly. When the audience heard his words they began to ask each other "Is this the son of David?" Matthew named the Pharisees as the ones who claimed Jesus had an evil spirit.

In his own defense, Jesus used two parables. His first parable stated a divided kingdom is destined to fall. Then he said to the Pharisees, if I am right "It means the kingdom of God has come to you and you have rejected it!" Seeing no favorable response, he continued with his second parable saying, if a strong man is to be robbed, you must first subdue him. Only then can you rob him.

shall be your judges. 28 But if it is by the Spirit of God that I cast out demons, then the kingdom of God has come upon you. 29 Or how can one enter a strong man's house and plunder his goods, unless he first binds the strong man? Then indeed he may plunder his house. 30 He who is not with me is against me, and he who does not gather with me scatters.

Luke 11:14-23
14 Now he was casting out a demon that was dumb; when the demon had gone out, the dumb man spoke, and the people marveled. 15 But some of them said, "He casts out demons by Be-el'zebul, the prince of demons"; 16 while others, to test him, sought from him a sign from heaven. 17 But he, knowing their thoughts, said to them, "Every kingdom divided against itself is laid waste, and a divided household falls. 18 And if Satan also is divided against himself, how will his kingdom stand? For you say that I cast out demons by Be-el'zebul. 19 And if I cast out demons by Be-el'zebul, by whom do your sons cast them out? Therefore they shall be your judges. 20 But if it is by the finger of God that I cast

out demons, then the kingdom of God has come upon you. 21 When a strong man, fully armed, guards his own palace, his goods are in peace; 22 but when one stronger than he assails him and overcomes him, he takes away his armor in which he trusted, and divides his spoil. 23 He who is not with me is against me, and he who does not gather with me scatters.

There is only one unforgivable sin

**Mark 3:28-30;
Matthew 12:31-32**

Mark 3:28-30
28 "Truly, I say to you, all sins will be forgiven the sons of men, and whatever blasphemies they utter; 29 but whoever blasphemes against the Holy Spirit never has forgiveness, but is guilty of an eternal sin"— 30 for they had said, "He has an unclean spirit."

Matthew 12:31-32
30 He who is not with me is against me, and he who does not gather with me scatters. 31 Therefore I tell you, every sin and blasphemy will be forgiven men, but the blasphemy against the Spirit will not be forgiven.

There is only one unforgivable sin

**Mark 3:28-30;
Matthew 12:31-32**

Comment

Blaspheme means to call the Spirit of God evil!

This is a good news bad news passage. The good news is man can be forgiven of his sins even against the Christ. The bad news is to sin against the Holy Spirit is unforgivable. Jesus' unnamed assailants have accused him of having an unclean spirit.

32 And whoever says a word against the Son of man will be forgiven; but whoever speaks against the Holy Spirit will not be forgiven, either in this age or in the age to come.

Who is my mother?

**Mark 3:31-35;
Matthew 12:46-50;
Luke 8:19-21**

Mark 3:31-35

31 And his mother and his brothers came; and standing outside they sent to him and called him. 32 And a crowd was sitting about him; and they said to him, "Your mother and your brothers are outside, asking for you." 33 And he replied, "Who are my mother and my brothers?" 34 And looking around on those who sat about him, he said, "Here are my mother and my brothers! 35 Whoever does the will of God is my brother, and sister, and mother."

Matthew 12:46-50

46 While he was still speaking to the people, behold, his mother and his brothers stood outside, asking to speak to him. 48 But he replied to the man who told

Who is my mother?

**Mark 3:31-35;
Matthew 12:46-50;
Luke 8:19-21**

Comment

This is another incident where Jesus and his family members had conflict. Most biblical readers would love to think Jesus never had any problems, especially with his own family.

Mary and her other sons had come to take Jesus home to Nazareth. The large crowd made it impossible for Mary to get close to her son. So someone was asked to go tell Jesus his mother wished to see him. Jesus sensed her intentions and knew that they were heartfelt and intended to be a help for him.

Without realizing it, Mary and her sons were attempting to place Jesus' ministry on hold not

him, "Who is my mother, and who are my brothers?" 49 And stretching out his hand toward his disciples, he said, "Here are my mother and my brothers! 50 For whoever does the will of my Father in heaven is my brother, and sister, and mother."

Luke 8:19-21
19 Then his mother and his brothers came to him, but they could not reach him for the crowd. 20 And he was told, "Your mother and your brothers are standing outside, desiring to see you." 21 But he said to them, "My mother and my brothers are those who hear the word of God and do it."

realizing his time was so short. To take Jesus from his mission would be playing into the hands of the evil one. Forgoing the pleasures of a family reunion Jesus forcefully expresses the need to continue serving God in the mission at hand.

Jesus' comments to his mother and brothers seems harsh, especially against the backdrop of the lavish praise for those who continue to follow in God's will, calling them his mother and his brothers.

Lamp under a bushel

**Mark 4:21-25;
Luke 8:16-18;
Luke 11:33-36**

Lamp under a bushel

**Mark 4:21-25;
Luke 8:16-18;
Luke 11:33-36**

Mark 4:21-25
21 And he said to them, "Is a lamp brought in to be put under a bushel, or under a bed, and not on a stand? 22 For there is nothing hid, except to be made manifest; nor is anything secret, except to come to light. 23 If any man has ears to hear, let him hear." 24 And he said to them, "Take heed what you hear; the measure you give will be the measure you get, and still more will be given you.

Comment

The parable begins with a question, "Who lights a lamp and puts it under their bed, why not put it on a stand?" It continues with saying those who have light (faith) will gain more, while those who have little or no faith will lose what they did have. These persons will become like the living dead.

25 For to him who has will more be given; and from him who has not, even what he has will be taken away."

Luke 8:16-18
16 "No one after lighting a lamp covers it with a vessel, or puts it under a bed, but puts it on a stand, that those who enter may see the light. 17 For nothing is hid that shall not be made manifest, nor anything secret that shall not be known and come to light. 18 Take heed then how you hear; for to him who has will more be given, and from him who has not, even what he thinks that he has will be taken away."

Luke 11:33-36
33 "No one after lighting a lamp puts it in a cellar or under a bushel, but on a stand, that those who enter may see the light. 34 Your eye is the lamp of your body; when your eye is sound, your whole body is full of light; but when it is not sound, your body is full of darkness. 35 Therefore be careful lest the light in you be darkness. 36 If then your whole body is full of light, having no part dark, it will be wholly bright, as when a lamp with its rays gives you light."

Mark adds those entering a house will see the light when it is placed on a stand. In the same manner, when you stand in the company of the faithful you are enabled to grow in your own hope and faith.

When the parable says watch what you hear, it means pay close attention to Jesus' teaching. The admonition of how we hear means to hear incorrectly will bring sorrow, while hearing correctly will bring joy and peace.

Only Mark makes the point that you will get back good for good and you will receive even more than you have given.

The Kingdom of God

"The Kingdom of God" is a small term with an enormous meaning. In Jesus' day, every nation, large or small, powerful or weak, had a king. The king made the rules! Subjects obeyed the rules, or suffered the consequences. The same concept governs the "Kingdom of God." God makes the rules as do earthly kings; however, there is a difference. Earthly kings rule in the anticipation of their own comfort, they levy taxes, create inequality, and systems of haves and have-nots. God's goal is for all to experience His love that brings peace and reunion with Him.

Kingdom of God is like a man planting seed	*Kingdom of God is like a man planting seed*
Mark 4:26-29 26 And he said, "The kingdom of God is as if a man should scatter seed upon the ground, 27 and should sleep and rise night and day, and the seed should sprout and grow, he knows not how. 28 The earth produces of itself, first the blade, then the ear, then the full grain in the ear. 29 But when the grain is ripe, at once he puts in the sickle, because the harvest has come."	**Mark 4:26-29** **Comment** This is an independent statement found only in Mark. It is likely everyone listening to Jesus understood the image of the farmer sowing his field. Farmers knew nothing about the science of modern agriculture. They simply knew if the farmer did his work correctly and in a timely fashion with the right amount of rain he would harvest a crop in the fall.

Chapter 9

SEA OF GALILEE

Storm on the sea	*Storm on the sea*
Mark 4:35-41; Matthew 8:23-27; Luke 8:22-25	**Mark 4:35-41; Matthew 8:23-27; Luke 8:22-25**
Mark 4:35-41	**Comment**
35 On that day, when evening had come, he said to them, "Let us go across to the other side." 36 And leaving the crowd, they took him with them in the boat, just as he was. And other boats were with him. 37 And a great storm of wind arose, and the waves beat into the boat, so that the boat was already filling. 38 But he was in the stern, asleep on the cushion; and they woke	In this case, the "other side" means the opposite shore from Tiberius. The boats were in route from the north west area of the Sea of Galilee to a destination near the middle of the south east shoreline. While making the voyage, a great storm arose on the lake. Matthew, Mark, and Luke all give a description of the storm.

him and said to him, "Teacher, do you not care if we perish?" 39 And he awoke and rebuked the wind, and said to the sea, "Peace! Be still!" And the wind ceased, and there was a great calm. 40 He said to them, "Why are you afraid? Have you no faith?" 41 And they were filled with awe, and said to one another, "Who then is this, that even wind and sea obey him?"

Matthew 8:23-27
23 And when he got into the boat, his disciples followed him. 24 And behold, there arose a great storm on the sea, so that the boat was being swamped by the waves; but he was asleep. 25 And they went and woke him, saying, "Save, Lord; we are perishing." 26 And he said to them, "Why are you afraid, O men of little faith?" Then he rose and rebuked the winds and the sea; and there was a great calm. 27 And the men marveled, saying, "What sort of man is this, that even winds and sea obey him?"

Luke 8:22-25
22 One day he got into a boat with his disciples, and he said to them, "Let us go across to the other side of the lake." So they set out, 23 and as they sailed he

Jesus calmed the storm and those caught in the storm. Each of the writers addressed Jesus by a different title: teacher, Lord, and master.

fell asleep. And a storm of wind came down on the lake, and they were filling with water, and were in danger. 24 And they went and woke him, saying, "Master, Master, we are perishing!" And he awoke and rebuked the wind and the raging waves; and they ceased, and there was a calm. 25 He said to them, "Where is your faith?" And they were afraid, and they marveled, saying to one another, "Who then is this, that he commands even wind and water, and they obey him?"

Legion

**Mark 5:1-10;
Matthew 8:28-29;
Luke 8:26-31**

Legion

**Mark 5:1-10;
Matthew 8:28-29;
Luke 8:26-31**

Mark 5:1-10
1 They came to the other side of the sea, to the country of the Ger'asenes. 2 And when he had come out of the boat, there met him out of the tombs a man with an unclean spirit, 3 who lived among the tombs; and no one could bind him any more, even with a chain; 4 for he had often been bound with fetters and chains, but the chains he wrenched apart, and the fetters he broke in pieces; and no one

Comment

Mark leads us through the story in a compelling manner, introducing us to a man that lived among the tombs. The tombs were in reality caves used as burial places in ancient Israel. A person who would live among the tombs would obviously have some sort of mental problem.

Among Legion's many problems was his unexplainable out of

had the strength to subdue him. 5 Night and day among the tombs and on the mountains he was always crying out, and bruising himself with stones. 6 And when he saw Jesus from afar, he ran and worshiped him; 7 and crying out with a loud voice, he said, "What have you to do with me, Jesus, Son of the Most High God? I adjure you by God, do not torment me." 8 For he had said to him, "Come out of the man, you unclean spirit!" 9 And Jesus asked him, "What is your name?" He replied, "My name is Legion; for we are many." 10 And he begged him eagerly not to send them out of the country.

Matthew 8:28-29
28 And when he came to the other side, to the country of the Gadarenes, two demoniacs met him, coming out of the tombs, so fierce that no one could pass that way. 29 And behold, they cried out, "What have you to do with us, O Son of God? Have you come here to torment us before the time?"

Luke 8:26-31
26 Then they arrived at the country of the Ger'asenes, which is opposite Galilee. 27 And as he stepped out on land, there met

control enormous strength. The townspeople had tried ropes to constrain him, and they failed, they tried to bind his hands and feet with fetters and to chain him. With apparent ease he simply broke his bonds and set himself free. One can easily imagine the frightening experience of coming too close to this man.

When Jesus came ashore, Legion ran toward him. Imagine how the disciples felt seeing this fearsome naked man charging them? The hair on the back of their necks must have stood straight up.

Matthew abbreviated the story with one outstanding difference. Rather than one man, Matthew said there were two men who were possessed and who lived among the tombs and had the same conversation with Jesus as did Legion.

him a man from the city who had demons; for a long time he had worn no clothes, and he lived not in a house but among the tombs. 28 When he saw Jesus, he cried out and fell down before him, and said with a loud voice, "What have you to do with me, Jesus, Son of the Most High God? I beseech you, do not torment me." 29 For he had commanded the unclean spirit to come out of the man. (For many a time it had seized him; he was kept under guard, and bound with chains and fetters, but he broke the bonds and was driven by the demon into the desert.) 30 Jesus then asked him, "What is your name?" And he said, "Legion"; for many demons had entered him. 31 And they begged him not to command them to depart into the abyss.

<u>Healing the "Unclean"</u>

The majority of healings Jesus performed were for people who had been declared unclean. The Law observing Jews tried to avoid dealing with those called unclean. The "unclean" included, lepers, prostitutes, cripples, those who were uncircumcised, and those possessed. Jesus cast out the unclean demons of Legion, allowing them to enter the forbidden "swine!" Jesus believed no person made in God's image should be treated as unclean.

<u>*Swine*</u>	<u>*Swine*</u>
Mark 5:11-13; Matthew 8:30-32; Luke 8:32-33	Mark 5:11-13; Matthew 8:30-32; Luke 8:32-33

Mark 5:11-13

11 Now a great herd of swine was feeding there on the hillside; 12 and they begged him, "Send us to the swine, let us enter them." 13 So he gave them leave. And the unclean spirits came out, and entered the swine; and the herd, numbering about two thousand, rushed down the steep bank into the sea, and were drowned in the sea.

Matthew 8:30-32

30 Now a herd of many swine was feeding at some distance from them. 31 And the demons begged him, "If you cast us out, send us away into the herd of swine." 32 And he said to them, "Go." So they came out and went into the swine; and behold, the whole herd rushed down the steep bank into the sea, and perished in the waters.

Luke 8:32-33

32 Now a large herd of swine was feeding there on the hillside; and they begged him to let them

Comment

There was a herd of swine, grazing on the hillside, which were unclean animals to the Israelites. Jews would have nothing to do with swine (hogs),* and coming in contact with one would cause them to become religiously unclean.

* The reference to swine comes from Leviticus 11:7
7 And the swine, because it parts the hoof and is cloven-footed but does not chew the cud, is unclean to you.

When the demons were told to leave Legion they begged Jesus not to drive them out of the region, but to allow them to enter the swine. Jesus granted their request. When the demons entered the swine the herd began to stampede.

The first question most people have concerning the swine is something like this, "Since the Jews did not eat pork why

enter these. So he gave them leave. 33 Then the demons came out of the man and entered the swine, and the herd rushed down the steep bank into the lake and were drowned.	would there be a herd of them present?" The answer is simple; the swine were being raised to sell to the Romans of the region who had a taste for pork.

Preacher Talk

It is common practice for many preachers and teachers to say the swine ran off a cliff and *crashed into the Sea of Galilee*. However, that position is without actual support. There are no such cliffs immediately available for such an event to take place anywhere on the coastline of the Sea of Galilee. The site believed to be the location of this event is where the mountain range rises up from the shoreline to its height. It was down this slope that the herd thundered toward their watery grave. In the panic of the stampede only those leading the rush could see the emerald green water awaiting them. The leading animals tried to stop but the momentum of the herd forced all of them into the deep water. One can imagine the sight of 2,000 drowned swine floating on the surface and drifting toward the outlet of the Jordan River.

Herdsmen	*Herdsmen*
Mark 5:14-15; **Matthew 8:33;** **Luke 8:34-36**	**Mark 5:14-15;** **Matthew 8:33;** **Luke 8:34-36**
Mark 5:14-15 14 The herdsmen fled, and told it in the city and in the country. And people came to see what it was that had happened. 15 And they came to Jesus, and saw the	*Comment* The herdsmen, after running away, returned with the town's people who were shocked to see Legion clothed, seated, and

demoniac sitting there, clothed and in his right mind, the man who had had the legion; and they were afraid.

Matthew 8:33
33 The herdsmen fled, and going into the city they told everything, and what had happened to the demoniacs.

Luke 8:34-36
34 When the herdsmen saw what had happened, they fled, and told it in the city and in the country. 35 Then people went out to see what had happened, and they came to Jesus, and found the man from whom the demons had gone, sitting at the feet of Jesus, clothed and in his right mind; and they were afraid. 36 And those who had seen it told them how he who had been possessed with demons was healed.

<u>Please Leave Now</u>

Mark 5:16-17;
Matthew 8:34;
Luke 8:37

Mark 5:16-17
16 And those who had seen it told what had happened to the demoniac and to the swine. 17 And they began to beg

engaged in civil conversation. The sight of the new Legion and the major loss of the herd of swine were too much and filled them with fear.

<u>Please Leave Now</u>

Mark 5:16-17;
Matthew 8:34;
Luke 8:37

Comment

They asked the miracle worker to leave before he brought some greater calamity upon them.

Jesus to depart from their neighborhood.

Matthew 8:34
34 And behold, all the city came out to meet Jesus; and when they saw him, they begged him to leave their neighborhood.

Luke 8:37
37 Then all the people of the surrounding country of the Ger'asenes asked him to depart from them; for they were seized with great fear; so he got into the boat and returned.

May I Please Go With You?

**Mark 5:18-20;
Luke 8:38-39**

Mark 5:18-20
18 And as he was getting into the boat, the man who had been possessed with demons begged him that he might be with him. 19 But he refused, and said to him, "Go home to your friends, and tell them how much the Lord has done for you, and how he has had mercy on you." 20 And he went away and began to proclaim in the Decap'olis how much Jesus had done for him; and all men marveled.

May I Please Go With You?

**Mark 5:18-20;
Luke 8:38-39**

Comment

Legion asked Jesus to take him with them. Jesus told Legion to go back to his town and tell everyone what the Lord had done for him.

Mark and Luke give us a slightly different version of the healing. Luke's version however, is almost identical to Mark. The most outstanding difference is in verse twenty-

Luke 8:38-39 38 The man from whom the demons had gone begged that he might be with him; but he sent him away, saying, 39 "Return to your home, and declare how much God has done for you." And he went away, proclaiming throughout the whole city how much Jesus had done for him.	seven; Luke says that Legion "wore no clothing."

Jesus commissioned His first Gentile evangelist

This is such a subtle but powerful ending to the story that most readers miss its full impact. Legion is a Gentile, living in a Gentile portion of the region around the Sea of Galilee. When Jesus told Legion to go home and witness to what has happened, Jesus in reality commissioned his first Gentile evangelist. We will later learn that Legion was a very effective witness/evangelist. This is borne out when Jesus returned to the region and was warmly received.

Jairus at Capernaum **Mark 5:21-24;** **Matthew 9:18-19;** **Luke 8:40-42**	*Jairus at Capernaum* **Mark 5:21-24;** **Matthew 9:18-19;** **Luke 8:40-42**
Mark 5:21-24 21 And when Jesus had crossed again in the boat to the other side, a great crowd gathered about him; and he was beside the sea. 22 Then came one of the rulers of the synagogue, Ja'irus by name; and seeing him, he fell	**Comment** Again we encounter the clause "going to the other side." In this case there is no doubt they were coming from the Decapolis to Galilee. We can say this with certainty because there were no

at his feet, 23 and besought him, saying, "My little daughter is at the point of death. Come and lay your hands on her, so that she may be made well, and live." 24 And he went with him. And a great crowd followed him and thronged about him.

Matthew 9:18-19
18 While he was thus speaking to them, behold, a ruler came in and knelt before him, saying, "My daughter has just died; but come and lay your hand on her, and she will live." 19 And Jesus rose and followed him, with his disciples.

Luke 8:40-42
40 Now when Jesus returned, the crowd welcomed him, for they were all waiting for him. 41 And there came a man named Ja'irus, who was a ruler of the synagogue; and falling at Jesus' feet he besought him to come to his house, 42 for he had an only daughter, about twelve years of age, and she was dying. As he went, the people pressed round him.

<u>Woman with flow of blood</u>

Mark 5:25-34;
Matthew 9:20-22;
Luke 8:43-48

Mark 5:25-34

synagogues in the Decapolis.

There are slight variations between the accounts of the three Evangelists. Mark and Luke tell us that the girl is at the point of death. She is his only daughter and about twelve years old. Matthew says that the girl has already died.

<u>Woman with flow of blood</u>

Mark 5:25-34;
Matthew 9:20-22;
Luke 8:43-48

Comment

25 And there was a woman who had had a flow of blood for twelve years, 26 and who had suffered much under many physicians, and had spent all that she had, and was no better but rather grew worse. 27 She had heard the reports about Jesus, and came up behind him in the crowd and touched his garment. 28 For she said, "If I touch even his garments, I shall be made well." 29 And immediately the hemorrhage ceased; and she felt in her body that she was healed of her disease. 30 And Jesus, perceiving in himself that power had gone forth from him, immediately turned about in the crowd, and said, "Who touched my garments?" 31 And his disciples said to him, "You see the crowd pressing around you, and yet you say, 'Who touched me?'" 32 And he looked around to see who had done it. 33 But the woman, knowing what had been done to her, came in fear and trembling and fell down before him, and told him the whole truth. 34 And he said to her, "Daughter, your faith has made you well; go in peace, and be healed of your disease."

Matthew 9:20-22
20 And behold, a woman who had suffered from a hemorrhage

Matthew gives us an abbreviated version of the story.

A menstruating woman was unclean and had to be purified before she could go into the temple. Neither could she deal with others, prepare their food, or wash their clothes without contaminating them. This woman had a continuous flow of blood, making her perpetually unclean and an outcast.

25 "If a woman has a discharge of blood for many days, not at the time of her impurity, or if she has a discharge beyond the time of her impurity, all the days of the discharge she shall continue in uncleanness; as in the days of her impurity, she shall be unclean. 26 Every bed on which she lies, all the days of her discharge, shall be to her as the bed of her impurity; and everything on which she sits shall be unclean, as in the uncleanness of her impurity. 27 And whoever touches these things shall be unclean, and shall wash his clothes, and bathe himself in water, and be unclean until the evening. Leviticus 15:25-27

for twelve years came up behind him and touched the fringe of his garment; 21 for she said to herself, "If I only touch his garment, I shall be made well." 22 Jesus turned, and seeing her he said, "Take heart, daughter; your faith has made you well." And instantly the woman was made well.

Luke 8:43-48
43 And a woman who had had a flow of blood for twelve years and could not be healed by any one, 44 came up behind him, and touched the fringe of his garment; and immediately her flow of blood ceased. 45 And Jesus said, "Who was it that touched me?" When all denied it, Peter said, "Master, the multitudes surround you and press upon you!" 46 But Jesus said, "Some one touched me; for I perceive that power has gone forth from me." 47 And when the woman saw that she was not hidden, she came trembling, and falling down before him declared in the presence of all the people why she had touched him, and how she had been immediately healed. 48 And he said to her, "Daughter, your faith has made you well; go in peace."

This woman was so desperate to be cured she defied the ban on contact with others. She made her way through the crowd in order to reach Jesus. Once close enough she reached out and touched the hem of his garment. Jesus instantly responded, "Who touched me?" Elated as she was at being healed, she was suddenly afraid of the price she may have to pay for breaking the Levitical law.

Jairus, your daughter is dead

**Mark 5:35-43;
Matthew 9:23-26;
Luke 8:49-56**

Mark 5:35-43

35 While he was still speaking, there came from the ruler's house some who said, "Your daughter is dead. Why trouble the Teacher any further?" 36 But ignoring what they said, Jesus said to the ruler of the synagogue, "Do not fear, only believe." 37 And he allowed no one to follow him except Peter and James and John the brother of James. 38 When they came to the house of the ruler of the synagogue, he saw a tumult, and people weeping and wailing loudly. 39 And when he had entered, he said to them, "Why do you make a tumult and weep? The child is not dead but sleeping." 40 And they laughed at him. But he put them all outside, and took the child's father and mother and those who were with him, and went in where the child was. 41 Taking her by the hand he said to her, "Tal'itha cu'mi"; which means, "Little girl, I say to you, arise." 42 And immediately the girl got up and walked (she was twelve years of age), and they were immediately overcome with amazement. 43 And he

Jairus, your daughter is dead

**Mark 5:35-43;
Matthew 9:23-26;
Luke 8:49-56**

Comment

The three accounts of this story are in close harmony.

The servant told the father his child was dead and not to bother the teacher any longer. Jesus ignored the comment of the servant, and told the father to "believe," Luke adds "and the child will be well."

The mourners had already arrived and were doing their job, crying, and wailing, making a great show of sadness. When Jesus told them the child was asleep, the mourners knew better, they recognized death.

Entering the house Jesus allowed only the father, mother, Peter, James, and John to accompany him. Jesus took the child by the hand and told her to arise, which she did. This was the same word Jesus said to the man in Nain, "arise."

This is the second time Jesus raised someone from the dead.

strictly charged them that no one should know this, and told them to give her something to eat.

Matthew 9:23-26
23 And when Jesus came to the ruler's house, and saw the flute players, and the crowd making a tumult, 24 he said, "Depart; for the girl is not dead but sleeping." And they laughed at him. 25 But when the crowd had been put outside, he went in and took her by the hand, and the girl arose. 26 And the report of this went through all that district.

Luke 8:49-56
49 While he was still speaking, a man from the ruler's house came and said, "Your daughter is dead; do not trouble the Teacher any more." 50 But Jesus on hearing this answered him, "Do not fear; only believe, and she shall be well." 51 And when he came to the house, he permitted no one to enter with him, except Peter and John and James, and the father and mother of the child. 52 And all were weeping and bewailing her; but he said, "Do not weep; for she is not dead but sleeping." 53 And they laughed at him, knowing that she was dead. 54 But taking her by the hand he called, saying, "Child, arise." 55 And her spirit returned, and she

got up at once; and he directed that something should be given her to eat. 56 And her parents were amazed; but he charged them to tell no one what had happened.

Parable of the Sower

**Mark 4:1-9;
Matthew 13:1-9;
Luke 8:4-8**

Mark 4:1-9
1 Again he began to teach beside the sea. And a very large crowd gathered about him, so that he got into a boat and sat in it on the sea; and the whole crowd was beside the sea on the land. 2 And he taught them many things in parables, and in his teaching he said to them: 3 "Listen! A sower went out to sow. 4 And as he sowed, some seed fell along the path, and the birds came and devoured it. 5 Other seed fell on rocky ground, where it had not much soil, and immediately it sprang up, since it had no depth of soil; 6 and when the sun rose it was scorched, and since it had no root it withered away. 7 Other seed fell among thorns and the thorns grew up and choked it, and it yielded no grain. 8 And other seeds fell into good soil

Parable of the Sower

**Mark 4:1-9;
Matthew 13:1-9;
Luke 8:4-8**

Comment

In verse one, Mark uses one of his favorite words, "again." He often begins a new thought in this manner. Mark continues by telling us the location is on the sea shore. Clearly he wants us to understand Jesus is on the land not in a boat.

Jesus used parables as a principle means of teaching, the "Sower" is but one of these stories. The parable of the "Sower" is one of the few times when Mark uses more words to tell the story than either Matthew or Luke.

All three gospel writers emphasize seeds landing on four different types of ground.

and brought forth grain, growing up and increasing and yielding thirtyfold and sixtyfold and a hundredfold." 9 And he said, "He who has ears to hear, let him hear."

Matthew 13:1-9
1 That same day Jesus went out of the house and sat beside the sea. 2 And great crowds gathered about him, so that he got into a boat and sat there; and the whole crowd stood on the beach. 3 And he told them many things in parables, saying: "A sower went out to sow. 4 And as he sowed, some seeds fell along the path, and the birds came and devoured them. 5 Other seeds fell on rocky ground, where they had not much soil, and immediately they sprang up, since they had no depth of soil, 6 but when the sun rose they were scorched; and since they had no root they withered away. 7 Other seeds fell upon thorns, and the thorns grew up and choked them. 8 Other seeds fell on good soil and brought forth grain, some a hundredfold, some sixty, some thirty. 9 He who has ears, let him hear."

Luke 8:4-8
4 And when a great crowd came together and people from town after town came to him, he said

1. Seeds land along the path.
2. Seeds land on rocky ground.
3. Seeds land among the thorns.
4. Seeds land on the good ground.

in a parable: 5 "A sower went out to sow his seed; and as he sowed, some fell along the path, and was trodden under foot, and the birds of the air devoured it. 6 And some fell on the rock; and as it grew up, it withered away, because it had no moisture. 7 And some fell among thorns; and the thorns grew with it and choked it. 8 And some fell into good soil and grew, and yielded a hundredfold." As he said this, he called out, "He who has ears to hear, let him hear."

Explanation of The Sower

**Mark 4:10-20;
Matthew 13:10-23;
Luke 8:9-15**

Mark 4:10-20
10 And when he was alone, those who were about him with the twelve asked him concerning the parables. 11 And he said to them, "To you has been given the secret of the kingdom of God, but for those outside everything is in parables; 12 so that they may indeed see but not perceive, and may indeed hear but not understand; lest they should turn again, and be forgiven." 13 And he said to them, "Do you not understand this parable? How

Explanation of The Sower

**Mark 4:10-20;
Matthew 13:10-23;
Luke 8:9-15**

Comment

This is one of the rare times when Jesus explains his parable. We are also given an opportunity to experience the bewilderment of the Inner-Circle as they struggled to understand. If the Inner-Circle did not understand, how baffled were the other followers?

Why did Jesus explain this parable? The Inner-Circle asked

then will you understand all the parables? 14 The sower sows the word. 15 And these are the ones along the path, where the word is sown; when they hear, Satan immediately comes and takes away the word which is sown in them. 16 And these in like manner are the ones sown upon rocky ground, who, when they hear the word, immediately receive it with joy; 17 and they have no root in themselves, but endure for a while; then, when tribulation or persecution arises on account of the word, immediately they fall away. 18 And others are the ones sown among thorns; they are those who hear the word, 19 but the cares of the world, and the delight in riches, and the desire for other things, enter in and choke the word, and it proves unfruitful. 20 But those that were sown upon the good soil are the ones who hear the word and accept it and bear fruit, thirtyfold and sixtyfold and a hundredfold."

Matthew 13:10-23
10 Then the disciples came and said to him, "Why do you speak to them in parables?" 11 And he answered them, "To you it has been given to know the secrets of the kingdom of heaven, but to them it has not been given. 12 For the explanation.

Mark implies in verse twelve it was not intended that the everyday person would understand. Their understanding would come when they accepted the Lordship of Jesus.

Matthew emphasized Jesus was the fulfillment of the Old Testament prophecies (Isa. 6:9-16).

Matthew makes it very clear the Inner-Circle was given the high privilege of understanding the parable. Jesus explained he was giving them the secrets of the kingdom of God.* Everyday followers would not share in this special understanding. Neither had the prophets or the righteous men who lived in ages past have the privilege of hearing, seeing, and understanding afforded the Inner-Circle. Further, those who had little knowledge would lose even what knowledge they possessed. Verse thirteen seems to be a blatant put down to the everyday people. This is without a doubt one of the hard statements of Jesus.

Matthew omits the first seed which fell upon the path.

to him who has will more be given, and he will have abundance; but from him who has not, even what he has will be taken away. 13 This is why I speak to them in parables, because seeing they do not see, and hearing they do not hear, nor do they understand. 14 With them indeed is fulfilled the prophecy of Isaiah which says: 'You shall indeed hear but never understand, and you shall indeed see but never perceive. 15 For this people's heart has grown dull, and their ears are heavy of hearing, and their eyes they have closed, lest they should perceive with their eyes, and hear with their ears, and understand with their heart, and turn for me to heal them.' 16 But blessed are your eyes, for they see, and your ears, for they hear. 17 Truly, I say to you, many prophets and righteous men longed to see what you see, and did not see it, and to hear what you hear, and did not hear it.

18 "Hear then the parable of the sower. 19 When any one hears the word of the kingdom and does not understand it, the evil one comes and snatches away what is sown in his heart; this is what was sown along the path. 20 As for what was sown on rocky ground, this is he who hears the word and

Luke supports the concept of exclusiveness for those who understand the meaning of the parable.

According to Jesus the "Sower" can be the preacher or teacher of every age.

*The Kingdom of God is not a reference to a place but rather to the relationship with God.

immediately receives it with joy; 21 yet he has no root in himself, but endures for a while, and when tribulation or persecution arises on account of the word, immediately he falls away. 22 As for what was sown among thorns, this is he who hears the word, but the cares of the world and the delight in riches choke the word, and it proves unfruitful. 23 As for what was sown on good soil, this is he who hears the word and understands it; he indeed bears fruit, and yields, in one case a hundredfold, in another sixty, and in another thirty."

Luke 8:9-15
9 And when his disciples asked him what this parable meant, 10 he said, "To you it has been given to know the secrets of the kingdom of God; but for others they are in parables, so that seeing they may not see, and hearing they may not understand. 11 Now the parable is this: The seed is the word of God. 12 The ones along the path are those who have heard; then the devil comes and takes away the word from their hearts, that they may not believe and be saved. 13 And the ones on the rock are those who, when they hear the word, receive it with joy; but these have no root, they believe for a

while and in time of temptation fall away. 14 And as for what fell among the thorns, they are those who hear, but as they go on their way they are choked by the cares and riches and pleasures of life, and their fruit does not mature. 15 And as for that in the good soil, they are those who, hearing the word, hold it fast in an honest and good heart, and bring forth fruit with patience.

Parable of the Good Seed and the Weeds

And

Interpretation of the Parable

**Matthew 13:24-30;
Matthew 13:36-43**

Matthew 13:24-30
24 Another parable he put before them, saying, "The kingdom of heaven may be compared to a man who sowed good seed in his field; 25 but while men were sleeping, his enemy came and sowed weeds among the wheat, and went away. 26 So when the plants came up and bore grain, then the weeds appeared also. 27 And the servants of the householder came and said to him, 'Sir, did you not sow good

Parable of the Good Seed and the Weeds

And

Interpretation of the Parable

**Matthew 13:24-30;
Matthew 13:36-43**

Comment

This is an independent parable found only in Matthew.

Parables present multiple ways of interpretation. The introduction of this parable established the characters. The "Kingdom of Heaven" (The creative work of God, and God said, "It is very good,") is compared to a man who

seed in your field? How then has it weeds?' 28 He said to them, 'An enemy has done this.' The servants said to him, 'Then do you want us to go and gather them?' 29 But he said, 'No; lest in gathering the weeds you root up the wheat along with them. 30 Let both grow together until the harvest; and at harvest time I will tell the reapers, Gather the weeds first and bind them in bundles to be burned, but gather the wheat into my barn.'"

Interpretation of the Parable

Matthew 13:36-43
36 Then he left the crowds and went into the house. And his disciples came to him, saying, "Explain to us the parable of the weeds of the field." 37 He answered, "He who sows the good seed is the Son of man; 38 the field is the world, and the good seed means the sons of the kingdom; the weeds are the sons of the evil one, 39 and the enemy who sowed them is the devil; the harvest is the close of the age, and the reapers are angels. 40 Just as the weeds are gathered and burned with fire, so will it be at the close of the age. 41 The Son of man will send his angels, and they will gather out of his kingdom all causes of sin and

prepared his field and planted good seed. The farmer is the "Son of Man."

Comparisons used in the parable and its interpretation.

Man who sowed—Son of Man

good seed—sons of the kingdom

field—World

enemy—devil

weeds—sons of the evil one

harvest—close of the age

reapers—angels, who will gather

gathered weed—burned in furnace of fire

gather the wheat—the righteous will shine like the sun in the Kingdom of the Father

This parable addresses the issue of evil in the world. Where did this evil come from? When did it come? Can anything be done to overcome it?

Jesus laid out the scenario alluding to when the earth

all evildoers, 42 and throw them into the furnace of fire; there men will weep and gnash their teeth. 43 Then the righteous will shine like the sun in the kingdom of their Father. He who has ears, let him hear.	was not under the attack of evil. The man who sowed is a reference to God in the creation of everything, including man. When God completed His creation He looked at it and said it is good. The enemy is the source of evil that entered the Garden of Eden in the form of a serpent. Through the means of lies and twisting truth he convinced Eve that God did not mean she could not take just a taste of the forbidden fruit. What harm could a little taste do? So God allowed the fallen humanity to live side by side with His faithful children. The reapers will gather the unfaithful and destroy them in the place of fire. The faithful will be set aside in the place of safe refuge.

A popular book series

A popular book series talks about the "repentant" suddenly vanishing from earth while the "unrepentant" look on in confused bewilderment asking, "Where did they go?" In this and other parables Jesus said the "unrepentant" are gathered up first and sent to the eternal flames while the "repentant" are ushered into the presence of God.

In my opinion, the left behind theology is a contradiction of this parable of Jesus. The golden rule of theological study always gives first precedence to Jesus' words!

Mustard seed

**Mark 4:30-32;
Matthew 13:31-32;
Luke 13:18-19**

Mark 4:30-32
30 And he said, "With what can we compare the kingdom of God, or what parable shall we use for it? 31 It is like a grain of mustard seed, which, when sown upon the ground, is the smallest of all the seeds on earth; 32 yet when it is sown it grows up and becomes the greatest of all shrubs, and puts forth large branches, so that the birds of the air can make nests in its shade."

Matthew 13:31-32
31 Another parable he put before them, saying, "The kingdom of heaven is like a grain of mustard seed which a man took and sowed in his field; 32 it is the smallest of all seeds, but when it has grown it is the greatest of shrubs and becomes a tree, so that the birds of the air come and make nests in its branches."

Luke 13:18-19
18 He said therefore, "What is the kingdom of God like? And to what shall I compare it? 19 It

Mustard seed

**Mark 4:30-32;
Matthew 13:31-32;
Luke 13:18-19**

Comments

A mustard seed isn't the smallest of seeds. It is about the size of a flake of ground pepper, but it is easily overlooked.

Jesus' parable points to the enormous potential in spite of size. The mustard seed's greatness is found in the shelter it provides that nurtures life. In this parable, shelter is another word for hospitality and hospitality comes from the Old Testament as a duty.

Mark and Luke favor the term "Kingdom of God," while Matthew prefers the "Kingdom of Heaven." Matthew speaks of the man sowing seed in his field, Luke calls it his garden; Mark does not mention it.

Mark and Matthew both say the mustard seed is the smallest of all seeds, while Luke does not mention it. Mark and Matthew tell us it grows to the largest of

is like a grain of mustard seed which a man took and sowed in his garden; and it grew and became a tree, and the birds of the air made nests in its branches."

all shrubs; Luke says it was a tree.

Kingdom of Heaven is like ... leaven

Matthew 13:33;
Luke 13:20-21

Matthew 13:33
33 He told them another parable. "The kingdom of heaven is like leaven which a woman took and hid in three measures of flour, till it was all leavened."

Luke 13:20-21
20 And again he said, "To what shall I compare the kingdom of God? 21 It is like leaven which a woman took and hid in three measures of flour, till it was all leavened."

Kingdom of Heaven is like ... leaven

Matthew 13:33;
Luke 13:20-21

Comment

Every successful baker knows the powerful effect leaven has upon flour. Equal is the affect of the person who embraces the Kingdom of Heaven.

The kingdom of heaven is like treasure hidden in a field

Matthew 13:44
44 "The kingdom of heaven is like treasure hidden in a field, which a man found and covered up; then in his joy he goes and

The kingdom of heaven is like treasure hidden in a field

Matthew 13:44

Comment

sells all that he has and buys that field.	The usual handling of this parable raises more questions than answers. Often the preacher or teacher makes several major presumptions that destroy the true presentation. The misconceptions are like this: the field belonged to someone else. Since the man was working someone else's field, what could he have had valuable enough to buy the field? Look more closely at the wording of the parable. Was the man working the field? Could he have been taking a short cut to somewhere else? The parable does not say he was looking for a treasure, he just found it. As odd as this may sound, the fact of severe earthquakes striking the land of Israel is not all that uncommon and they often uncover what has been hidden. So this man, according to the parable, could easily have had sufficient resources to purchase the field. One truth Jesus was making about the Kingdom of God is that it is not for sale. You cannot buy it. But if the kingdom of God

	were for sale, it would be worth everything you could give in order to buy it!
The kingdom of heaven is like a merchant in search of fine pearls	***The kingdom of heaven is like a merchant in search of fine pearls***
Matthew 13:45-46 45 "Again, the kingdom of heaven is like a merchant in search of fine pearls, 46 who, on finding one pearl of great value, went and sold all that he had and bought it.	**Matthew 13:45-46** **Comment** In this parable we have a "Seeker." He is engaged in the pursuit of the most perfect pearl he can imagine. At last he finds it and it is worth everything he owns. Without hesitation he sells everything and acquires the gem. The Kingdom is not for sale but it requires total commitment for it to become part of one's life.
The kingdom of heaven is like a net	***The kingdom of heaven is like a net***
Matthew 13:47-50 47 "Again, the kingdom of heaven is like a net which was thrown into the sea and gathered fish of every kind; 48 when it was full, men drew it ashore and sat down and sorted the good into vessels but threw away the	**Matthew 13:47-50** **Comment** This parable is the twin of the parable of the wheat and weeds.

bad. ⁴⁹ So it will be at the close of the age. The angels will come out and separate the evil from the righteous, ⁵⁰ and throw them into the furnace of fire; there men will weep and gnash their teeth.

Jesus spoke only in Parables to them

**Mark 4:33-34;
Matthew 13:34-35**

Mark 4:33-34
³³ With many such parables he spoke the word to them, as they were able to hear it; ³⁴ he did not speak to them without a parable, but privately to his own disciples he explained everything.

Matthew 13:34-35
³⁴ All this Jesus said to the crowds in parables; indeed he said nothing to them without a parable. ³⁵ This was to fulfil what was spoken by the prophet: "I will open my mouth in parables, I will utter what has been hidden since the foundation of the world."

Have you understood all this?

Matthew 13:51-52
⁵¹ "Have you understood all

Jesus spoke only in Parables to them

**Mark 4:33-34;
Matthew 13:34-35**

Comment

¹⁰ I spoke to the prophets; it was I who multiplied visions, and through the prophets gave parables. Hosea 12:10

⁴⁹ Then said I, Ah Lord GOD! they say of me, Doth he not speak parables? Ezekiel 20:49 (King James Version)

Parables were a favorite vehicle of Jesus to convey his message. We must not forget that he also used discourse on many occasions.

Have you understood all this?

Matthew 13:51-52

this?" They said to him, "Yes." 52 And he said to them, "Therefore every scribe who has been trained for the kingdom of heaven is like a householder who brings out of his treasure what is new and what is old."

Comment

This is one of the few complimentary statements Jesus utters regarding the scribes.

Crisis at Nazareth

**Mark 6:1-6;
Matthew 13:53-58;
Luke 4:16-30**

Crisis at Nazareth

**Mark 6:1-6;
Matthew 13:53-58;
Luke 4:16-30**

Mark 6:1-6

1 He went away from there and came to his own country; and his disciples followed him. 2 And on the sabbath he began to teach in the synagogue; and many who heard him were astonished, saying, "Where did this man get all this? What is the wisdom given to him? What mighty works are wrought by his hands! 3 Is not this the carpenter, the son of Mary and brother of James and Joses and Judas and Simon, and are not his sisters here with us?" And they took offense at him. 4 And Jesus said to them, "A prophet is not without honor, except in his own country, and among his own kin, and in his own house." 5 And he could do no mighty work there, except

Comment

Mark and Matthew give almost exactly the same account of Jesus preaching in his hometown of Nazareth. Luke's version includes everything found in Matthew and Mark, but adds many additional facts to the event.

Mark and Matthew omit the near lethal confrontation that Luke describes.

Nazareth was Jesus' hometown, and as was his custom, he went to the synagogue to worship on the Sabbath day. Once more we see the standup/sit down method of teaching by a Rabbi.

that he laid his hands upon a few sick people and healed them. 6 And he marveled because of their unbelief. And he went about among the villages teaching.

Matthew 13:53-58
53 And when Jesus had finished these parables, he went away from there, 54 and coming to his own country he taught them in their synagogue, so that they were astonished, and said, "Where did this man get this wisdom and these mighty works? 55 Is not this the carpenter's son? Is not his mother called Mary? And are not his brothers James and Joseph and Simon and Judas? 56 And are not all his sisters with us? Where then did this man get all this?" 57 And they took offense at him. But Jesus said to them, "A prophet is not without honor except in his own country and in his own house." 58 And he did not do many mighty works there, because of their unbelief.

Luke 4:16-30
16 And he came to Nazareth, where he had been brought up; and he went to the synagogue, as his custom was, on the sabbath day. And he stood up to read; 17 and there was given to him the book of the prophet Isaiah. He

Jesus spoke powerfully quoting from Isaiah 61:1-3. This was Jesus' manifesto.

1 The Spirit of the Lord GOD is upon me, because the LORD has anointed me to bring good tidings to the afflicted; he has sent me to bind up the brokenhearted, to proclaim liberty to the captives, and the opening of the prison to those who are bound; 2 to proclaim the year of the Lord's favor, and the day of vengeance of our God; to comfort all who mourn; 3 to grant to those who mourn in Zion—to give them a garland instead of ashes, the oil of gladness instead of mourning, the mantle of praise instead of a faint spirit; that they may be called oaks of righteousness, the planting of the LORD, that he may be glorified. Isaiah 61:1-3

All eyes were now fixed upon this hometown hero.

His astounding claim was that Scripture had been fulfilled by their hearing. This was Jesus' formal announcement of his entry into ministry, the Messiah had arrived!

On first hearing, everyone was excited and pleased. Here was

opened the book and found the place where it was written, ¹⁸ "The Spirit of the Lord is upon me, because he has anointed me to preach good news to the poor. He has sent me to proclaim release to the captives and recovering of sight to the blind, to set at liberty those who are oppressed, ¹⁹ to proclaim the acceptable year of the Lord."

²⁰ And he closed the book, and gave it back to the attendant, and sat down; and the eyes of all in the synagogue were fixed on him. ²¹ And he began to say to them, "Today this scripture has been fulfilled in your hearing." ²² And all spoke well of him, and wondered at the gracious words which proceeded out of his mouth; and they said, "Is not this Joseph's son?" ²³ And he said to them, "Doubtless you will quote to me this proverb, 'Physician, heal yourself; what we have heard you did at Caper'na-um, do here also in your own country.'" ²⁴ And he said, "Truly, I say to you, no prophet is acceptable in his own country. ²⁵ But in truth, I tell you, there were many widows in Israel in the days of Eli'jah, when the heaven was shut up three years and six months, when there came a great famine over

a hometown son who had made good.

The proverb about the physician is not found in our Old Testament Scripture.

Jesus knew exactly where the remainder of this conversation was headed.

Jesus referred to the greatest of all the prophets, Elijah, to establish the grounds for what he was about to say. He knew his words would be very unpopular with his audience. He proceeded to tell them that God is not just the God of Israel He is God of all humanity.

The people were angry enough now to put him to death. They took him to the crest of the hill upon which the city was built and prepared to throw him down. But Jesus walked through them and away from them.

all the land; 26 and Eli'jah was sent to none of them but only to Zar'ephath, in the land of Sidon, to a woman who was a widow. 27 And there were many lepers in Israel in the time of the prophet Eli'sha; and none of them was cleansed, but only Na'aman the Syrian." 28 When they heard this, all in the synagogue were filled with wrath. 29 And they rose up and put him out of the city, and led him to the brow of the hill on which their city was built, that they might throw him down headlong. 30 But passing through the midst of them he went away.

Jesus sends out the Disciples 2 x 2

**Mark 6:7;
Matthew 10:1-4;
Luke 9:1**

Mark 6:7
7 And he called to him the twelve, and began to send them out two by two, and gave them authority over the unclean spirits.

Matthew 10:1-4
1 And he called to him his twelve disciples and gave them authority over unclean spirits, to

Jesus sends out the Disciples 2 x 2

**Mark 6:7;
Matthew 10:1-4;
Luke 9:1**

Comment

All three sources open by telling us that Jesus called the Inner-Circle together. Only Mark tells us that Jesus sent them out two by two. Only Matthew gives us the full list of the names of the twelve. All three writers tell us that Jesus gave the disciples

cast them out, and to heal every disease and every infirmity. 2 The names of the twelve apostles are these: first, Simon, who is called Peter, and Andrew his brother; James the son of Zeb'edee, and John his brother; 3 Philip and Bartholomew; Thomas and Matthew the tax collector; James the son of Alphaeus, and Thaddaeus; 4 Simon the Cananaean, and Judas Iscariot, who betrayed him.

Luke 9:1
1 And he called the twelve together and gave them power and authority over all demons and to cure diseases,

authority over unclean spirits.

<u>*Marching orders*</u>

**Mark 6:8-9;
Matthew 10:5-13;
Luke 9:2-4**

<u>*Marching orders*</u>

**Mark 6:8-9;
Matthew 10:5-13;
Luke 9:2-4**

Mark 6:8-9
8 He charged them to take nothing for their journey except a staff; no bread, no bag, no money in their belts; 9 but to wear sandals and not put on two tunics.

Matthew 10:5-13
5 These twelve Jesus sent out, charging them, "Go nowhere

Comment

Jesus told them to take nothing with them, no money, no bread, no bag, how to dress, where to stay, and how to conduct themselves. They were not to go anywhere among the Gentiles. Neither were they to go to the Samaritans. They were to go

among the Gentiles, and enter no town of the Samaritans, 6 but go rather to the lost sheep of the house of Israel. 7 And preach as you go, saying, 'The kingdom of heaven is at hand.' 8 Heal the sick, raise the dead, cleanse lepers, cast out demons. You received without paying, give without pay. 9 Take no gold, nor silver, nor copper in your belts, 10 no bag for your journey, nor two tunics, nor sandals, nor a staff; for the laborer deserves his food. 11 And whatever town or village you enter, find out who is worthy in it, and stay with him until you depart. 12 As you enter the house, salute it. 13 And if the house is worthy, let your peace come upon it;

Luke 9:2-4
2 and he sent them out to preach the kingdom of God and to heal. 3 And he said to them, "Take nothing for your journey, no staff, nor bag, nor bread, nor money; and do not have two tunics. 4 And whatever house you enter, stay there, and from there depart.

<u>*Warning of the dangers*</u>

Matthew 10:16-23
16 "Behold, I send you out as sheep in the midst of wolves; so

only to the lost sheep of Israel. They were to preach a message that the kingdom of God was at hand. They were to heal the sick, cleanse the leper, and raise the dead. Wherever they found a receptive community they were to stay with them.

<u>*Warning of the dangers*</u>

Matthew 10:16-23

Comment

be wise as serpents and innocent as doves. 17 Beware of men; for they will deliver you up to councils, and flog you in their synagogues, 18 and you will be dragged before governors and kings for my sake, to bear testimony before them and the Gentiles. 19 When they deliver you up, do not be anxious how you are to speak or what you are to say; for what you are to say will be given to you in that hour; 20 for it is not you who speak, but the Spirit of your Father speaking through you. 21 Brother will deliver up brother to death, and the father his child, and children will rise against parents and have them put to death; 22 and you will be hated by all for my name's sake. But he who endures to the end will be saved. 23 When they persecute you in one town, flee to the next; for truly, I say to you, you will not have gone through all the towns of Israel, before the Son of man comes.	This is an individual statement of Matthew. Jesus warned them that he was sending them out as innocence among the shrewd. Then Jesus warned them of what it would be like in the future when they would be hauled before the authorities to give account of their statements. He told them not to be worried about what they would say because the Spirit of God would lead them. Families would be torn apart, some loving and some hating the Savior. Those who persevered would be saved in the end.
What they are to do if they are rejected **Mark 6:10-11;** **Matthew 10:13b-15;** **Luke 9:5-6**	**_What they are to do if they are rejected_** **Mark 6:10-11;** **Matthew 10:13b-15;** **Luke 9:5-6**

Mark 6:10-11 10 And he said to them, "Where you enter a house, stay there until you leave the place. 11 And if any place will not receive you and they refuse to hear you, when you leave, shake off the dust that is on your feet for a testimony against them." **Matthew 10:13b-15** 13 but if it is not worthy, let your peace return to you. 14 And if any one will not receive you or listen to your words, shake off the dust from your feet as you leave that house or town. 15 Truly, I say to you, it shall be more tolerable on the day of judgment for the land of Sodom and Gomor'rah than for that town. **Luke 9:5-6** 5 And wherever they do not receive you, when you leave that town shake off the dust from your feet as a testimony against them." 6 And they departed and went through the villages, preaching the gospel and healing everywhere.	**Comment** Jesus told them when they were invited into a home to stay there. Do not look for a better place to stay and move about. If you are refused a place to stay as you leave the town, shake the dust off of your feet. For those who refuse you hospitality, it will be more intolerable than it was for Sodom and Gomorrah.

A disciple is not above his teacher

Always remember the word disciple means student. Jesus said the servant is not above his master, it is important to note that this passage was written in a period of history when the society was made up of slaves and masters. For a slave to ever be like his master would be a major accomplishment.

A disciple is not above his teacher Matthew 10:24-25; Luke 6:40	*A disciple is not above his teacher* Matthew 10:24-25; Luke 6:40
Matthew 10:24-25 24 "A disciple is not above his teacher, nor a servant above his master; 25 it is enough for the disciple to be like his teacher, and the servant like his master. If they have called the master of the house Be-el'zebul, how much more will they malign those of his household. **Luke 6:40** 40 A disciple is not above his teacher, but every one when he is fully taught will be like his teacher.	**Comment** In the beginning of the student-teacher relationship, the teacher has more knowledge than the student. In some cases, the student one day becomes as knowledgeable as his or her teacher. In some cases, the student's knowledge may come to exceed that of his teacher.
Fear God Matthew 10:26-27; Luke 12:2-3	*Fear God* Matthew 10:26-27; Luke 12:2-3

Matthew 10:26-27	Comment
26 "So have no fear of them; for nothing is covered that will not be revealed, or hidden that will not be known. 27 What I tell you in the dark, utter in the light; and what you hear whispered, proclaim upon the housetops. **Luke 12:2-3** 2 Nothing is covered up that will not be revealed, or hidden that will not be known. 3 Therefore whatever you have said in the dark shall be heard in the light, and what you have whispered in private rooms shall be proclaimed upon the housetops.	Jesus told them whatever you do, whatever you try to cover up, whatever you try to keep secret, all will become known.
Do not fear those who kill the body **Matthew 10:28a;** **Luke 12:4**	***Do not fear those who kill the body*** **Matthew 10:28a;** **Luke 12:4**
Matthew 10:28a 28 And do not fear those who kill the body but cannot kill the soul; **Luke 12:4** 4 "I tell you, my friends, do not fear those who kill the body, and after that have no more that they can do.	**Comment** Life is important, but the one to really fear is the one who can take your life and also put you in hell.

Fear him who can destroy both soul and body in hell

Matthew 10:28b-31;
Luke 12:5-7

Matthew 10:28b-31
28 rather fear him who can destroy both soul and body in hell. 29 Are not two sparrows sold for a penny? And not one of them will fall to the ground without your Father's will. 30 But even the hairs of your head are all numbered. 31 Fear not, therefore; you are of more value than many sparrows.

Luke 12:5-7
5 But I will warn you whom to fear: fear him who, after he has killed, has power to cast into hell; yes, I tell you, fear him! 6 Are not five sparrows sold for two pennies? And not one of them is forgotten before God. 7 Why, even the hairs of your head are all numbered. Fear not; you are of more value than many sparrows.

Fear him who can destroy both soul and body in hell

Matthew 10:28b-31;
Luke 12:5-7

Comment

Here Jesus was speaking of the condition of the Spirit. When one dies, and his relationship with God is in tatters his eternal dwelling place would be in the fires of hell. How would God know if such relationship did not exist? If He was concerned about even a sparrow falling to the earth dead, certainly He was concerned about His relationship with the human. If He were not concerned why would He bother to know how many hairs were on one's head?

To acknowledge or deny

Matthew 10:32-33;
Luke 12:8-9

To acknowledge or deny

Matthew 10:32-33;
Luke 12:8-9

Matthew 10:32-33	Comment
32 So every one who acknowledges me before men, I also will acknowledge before my Father who is in heaven; 33 but whoever denies me before men, I also will deny before my Father who is in heaven. **Luke 12:8-9** 8 "And I tell you, every one who acknowledges me before men, the Son of man also will acknowledge before the angels of God; 9 but he who denies me before men will be denied before the angels of God.	There is a positive result from acknowledging Jesus as Lord. This positive is, Jesus promised to acknowledge them to God. Those who deny Jesus, he in turn will deny them before God.

I have not come to bring peace   *I have not come to bring peace*

Matthew 10:34-36;   **Matthew 10:34-36;**
Luke 12:49-53   **Luke 12:49-53**

Matthew 10:34-36	**Comment**
34 "Do not think that I have come to bring peace on earth; I have not come to bring peace, but a sword. 35 For I have come to set a man against his father, and a daughter against her mother, and a daughter-in-law against her mother-in-law; 36 and a man's foes will be those of his own household.	These are very disturbing statements by Jesus. We are deeply impressed with the angel's message at the announcement of Jesus' birth of peace on earth. Now Jesus tells us that he has come to bring discord and discomfort. How is this to be so? It is based upon the fact that those who followed

Luke 12:49-53 ⁴⁹ "I came to cast fire upon the earth; and would that it were already kindled! ⁵⁰ I have a baptism to be baptized with; and how I am constrained until it is accomplished! ⁵¹ Do you think that I have come to give peace on earth? No, I tell you, but rather division; ⁵² for henceforth in one house there will be five divided, three against two and two against three; ⁵³ they will be divided, father against son and son against father, mother against daughter and daughter against her mother, mother-in-law against her daughter-in-law and daughter-in-law against her mother-in-law."	Jesus would not be in favor with those who rejected him. Belief in Jesus would result in fragmentation of many families and friendships.
The Cost of Discipleship **Matthew 10:37-39;** **Luke 14:25-33**	*The Cost of Discipleship* **Matthew 10:37-39;** **Luke 14:25-33**
Matthew 10:37-39 ³⁷ He who loves father or mother more than me is not worthy of me; and he who loves son or daughter more than me is not worthy of me; ³⁸ and he who does not take his cross and follow me is not worthy of me. ³⁹ He who finds his life will lose it, and he who loses his life for my sake will find it.	**Comment** Why would Jesus have made such a statement as this? Simply put, it is to advise the would-be follower of the high cost involved. It is the cost of everything that one loved and cared for becoming secondary to their commitment to Jesus. Only the "called" can make this

Luke 14:25-33

25 Now great multitudes accompanied him; and he turned and said to them, 26 "If any one comes to me and does not hate his own father and mother and wife and children and brothers and sisters, yes, and even his own life, he cannot be my disciple. 27 Whoever does not bear his own cross and come after me, cannot be my disciple. 28 For which of you, desiring to build a tower, does not first sit down and count the cost, whether he has enough to complete it? 29 Otherwise, when he has laid a foundation, and is not able to finish, all who see it begin to mock him, 30 saying, 'This man began to build, and was not able to finish.' 31 Or what king, going to encounter another king in war, will not sit down first and take counsel whether he is able with ten thousand to meet him who comes against him with twenty thousand? 32 And if not, while the other is yet a great way off, he sends an embassy and asks terms of peace. 33 So therefore, whoever of you does not renounce all that he has cannot be my disciple.

deep pervasive commitment. It is truly a burden, as represented by the cross of Christ. It is indeed the losing of one's life as we generally think of it in finding a life of deeper dedication.

To emphasize his point Jesus told the story of a man who wanted to build a tower. There is a cost associated with building the tower, and one who does not plan for it will be embarrassed at his inability to complete his undertaking.

To further emphasize its meaning, Jesus told a second story of a king going to war. The king of the story underestimated the cost. In this case the king understands his shortcoming and sues for peace.

Jesus said you must count the cost before you become my disciple.

Chapter 10

JERUSALEM AS SEEN FROM THE MOUNT OF OLIVES

Inner-Circle on mission *Jesus goes to Jerusalem*	*Inner-Circle on mission* *Jesus goes to Jerusalem*
Matthew 11:1 1 And when Jesus had finished instructing his twelve disciples, he went on from there to teach and preach in their cities.	**Matthew 11:1** **Comment** Jesus had just dispatched the Inner-Circle on their first authorized missionary journey.
John, in prison, hears of Jesus	*John, in prison, hears of Jesus*
Matthew 11:2-6; **Luke 7:18-23**	**Matthew 11:2-6;** **Luke 7:18-23**

Matthew 11:2-6	**Comment**
2 Now when John heard in prison about the deeds of the Christ, he sent word by his disciples 3 and said to him, "Are you he who is to come, or shall we look for another?" 4 And Jesus answered them, "Go and tell John what you hear and see: 5 the blind receive their sight and the lame walk, lepers are cleansed and the deaf hear, and the dead are raised up, and the poor have good news preached to them. 6 And blessed is he who takes no offense at me."	The arrest of John the Baptist is found in chapter 6. This present section marks another point on the Gospel Timeline, John is in prison.
Luke 7:18-23	While in prison, John the Baptist heard reports concerning Jesus. Matthew used the title "Christ" which is another way to define Jesus as the Messiah. The title "Christ" is used by the four Evangelists:
18 The disciples of John told him of all these things. 19 And John, calling to him two of his disciples, sent them to the Lord, saying, "Are you he who is to come, or shall we look for another?" 20 And when the men had come to him, they said, "John the Baptist has sent us to you, saying, 'Are you he who is to come, or shall we look for another?'" 21 In that hour he cured many of diseases and plagues and evil spirits, and on many that were blind he bestowed sight. 22 And he answered them, "Go and tell John what you have seen and heard: the blind receive their sight, the lame walk, lepers are cleansed, and the deaf hear, the	Mark 8 Matthew 17 Luke 12 John 19 total 56 Luke, while not saying he was in prison, says John the Baptist called two of his disciples and sent them to the "Lord." This is another title for The Messiah. Matthew and Luke refer to Jesus by titles to establish his authority and divinity. Luke agrees the emissaries from John asked the same question, "Are you the one?" The scribes and Pharisees had much earlier posed this same question to John the Baptist.

dead are raised up, the poor have good news preached to them. 23 And blessed is he who takes no offense at me."

He answered unequivocally no. If Jesus had said no, they were prepared to wait and pray for the advent of the Christ. Isaiah had promised the Messiah would heal, restore sight to the bind, and preach to the poor. All these things Jesus demonstrated while the messengers were in his presence. Then Jesus told them to go and tell John all they had witnessed with their own eyes.

Jesus praises John

**Matthew 11:7-15;
Luke 7:24-30**

Matthew 11:7-15
7 As they went away, Jesus began to speak to the crowds concerning John: "What did you go out into the wilderness to behold? A reed shaken by the wind? 8 Why then did you go out? To see a man clothed in soft raiment? Behold, those who wear soft raiment are in kings' houses. 9 Why then did you go out? To see a prophet? Yes, I tell you, and more than a prophet. 10 This is he of whom it is written, 'Behold, I send my messenger before thy face, who shall prepare thy way before thee.' 11 Truly, I say to you, among those born of women there has

Jesus praises John

**Matthew 11:7-15;
Luke 7:24-30**

Comment

All eyes were upon the disciples of John as they disappeared down the road. Jesus faced the crowd and began to speak about The Baptist. He asked them, "What did you go out in the wilderness to see? Certainly not a fragile reed easily swayed by the wind! Was it John's beautiful garments?" He concluded saying, "You went out to see a prophet! I tell you he was more than a prophet!"

Matthew and Luke are virtually word for word to this point in

risen no one greater than John the Baptist; yet he who is least in the kingdom of heaven is greater than he. 12 From the days of John the Baptist until now the kingdom of heaven has suffered violence, and men of violence take it by force. 13 For all the prophets and the law prophesied until John; 14 and if you are willing to accept it, he is Eli'jah who is to come. 15 He who has ears to hear, let him hear.

Luke 7:24-30
24 When the messengers of John had gone, he began to speak to the crowds concerning John: "What did you go out into the wilderness to behold? A reed shaken by the wind? 25 What then did you go out to see? A man clothed in soft clothing? Behold, those who are gorgeously appareled and live in luxury are in kings' courts. 26 What then did you go out to see? A prophet? Yes, I tell you, and more than a prophet. 27 This is he of whom it is written, 'Behold, I send my messenger before thy face, who shall prepare thy way before thee.' 28 I tell you, among those born of women none is greater than John; yet he who is least in the kingdom of God is greater than he." 29 (When they heard

their accounts; however, each adds independent material to the story.

Matthew said from the beginning the kingdom of heaven had suffered violence as men tried to take the kingdom by force. All of the prophets and the Law spoke of John up until that moment. Jesus warned them he was about to say something that might be hard for some of them to accept, Elijah had come in the person of John the Baptist! "Let him who has ears to hear, let him hear," is another way of saying I have spoken the truth do you have the trust to believe me?

Luke added, when the people and the tax collectors heard all Jesus said they believed in God.

According to Luke, the people who had been baptized by John, and accepted John as a prophet from God were listening to Jesus. At the same time the Pharisees and lawyers rejected Jesus' words because they had not been baptized by John and neither did they accept him as a prophet.

Mark is silent on this part of the subject.

this all the people and the tax collectors justified God, having been baptized with the baptism of John; 30 but the Pharisees and the lawyers rejected the purpose of God for themselves, not having been baptized by him.)

You don't really like John or Me

**Matthew 11:16-19;
Luke 7:31-35**

Matthew 11:16-19
16 "But to what shall I compare this generation? It is like children sitting in the market places and calling to their playmates, 17 'We piped to you, and you did not dance; we wailed, and you did not mourn.' 18 For John came neither eating nor drinking, and they say, 'He has a demon'; 19 the Son of man came eating and drinking, and they say, 'Behold, a glutton and a drunkard, a friend of tax collectors and sinners!' Yet wisdom is justified by her deeds."

Luke 7:31-35
31 "To what then shall I compare the men of this generation, and what are they like? 32 They are like children sitting in the market

You don't really like John or Me

**Matthew 11:16-19;
Luke 7:31-35**

Comment

The ambivalent attitude of the people bewildered Jesus. This is the only time Jesus refers to children in a negative manner, referencing to how this generation acted. Jesus said he and John had "piped (to play a flute or pipe) for you." They gave them a song for the heart and it was heard only by those who believed. Unfortunately the others heard nothing that moved them.

Jesus and John "wailed," (to mourn or lament). The people saw their sorrow and anguish but still were not moved to repentance. Because they were different, the multitude

place and calling to one another, 'We piped to you, and you did not dance; we wailed, and you did not weep.' 33 For John the Baptist has come eating no bread and drinking no wine; and you say, 'He has a demon.' 34 The Son of man has come eating and drinking; and you say, 'Behold, a glutton and a drunkard, a friend of tax collectors and sinners!' 35 Yet wisdom is justified by all her children."

dismissed them saying John had a demon, and Jesus was a glutton and a drunkard. Time indeed has revealed who was right, Jesus and John!

Luke has only one change from Matthew's account, he refers to this present generation as "men" while Matthew calls them "children."

Beware of all covetousness

Luke 12:13-21;
Luke 6:24

Beware of all covetousness

Luke 12:13-21;
Luke 6:24

Luke 12:13-21

13 One of the multitude said to him, "Teacher, bid my brother divide the inheritance with me." 14 But he said to him, "Man, who made me a judge or divider over you?" 15 And he said to them, "Take heed, and beware of all covetousness; for a man's life does not consist in the abundance of his possessions." 16 And he told them a parable, saying, "The land of a rich man brought forth plentifully; 17 and he thought to himself, 'What shall I do, for I have nowhere to store my crops?' 18 And he said, 'I will do this:

Comment

This is an independent statement of Luke.

An unnamed man brings his unresolved dispute to Jesus expecting him to render a judgment favorable to him. This was historically one of the roles of the judges of ancient Israel. Jesus rejected such a role for himself. Jesus spoke to the heart of the dispute—covetousness (greedy desire to have more, avarice). Perhaps Jesus' comment was an indictment on both the brothers.

I will pull down my barns, and build larger ones; and there I will store all my grain and my goods. ^{19} And I will say to my soul, Soul, you have ample goods laid up for many years; take your ease, eat, drink, be merry.' ^{20} But God said to him, 'Fool! This night your soul is required of you; and the things you have prepared, whose will they be?' ^{21} So is he who lays up treasure for himself, and is not rich toward God."

Luke 6:24
^{24} "But woe to you that are rich, for you have received your consolation.

Then Jesus told the parable of a greedy farmer, who had everything he had ever dreamed of given to him. So what did he decide to do? He decided to go to radical lengths to secure his wealth for himself only! God was not pleased with such a greedy and selfish decision. Pronouncing the death sentence on the farmer God asked, "Now who will enjoy your wealth?"

No fault is found with the bounty one may receive as the result of his hard work and good management. Condemnation comes because of the selfishness inherent in the idea of keeping all the reward as one's own personal treasure. God views his gifts to humanity as a stewardship and a trust.

Jesus spoke sternly against hoarding. In times of shortages only the rich can afford to be over stocked.

Good tree/Bad tree

**Matthew 12:33-37;
Luke 6:43-45**

Matthew 12:33-37
^{33} "Either make the tree good, and its fruit good; or make the

Good tree/Bad tree

**Matthew 12:33-37;
Luke 6:43-45**

Comment

Continuing to address the

tree bad, and its fruit bad; for the tree is known by its fruit. 34 You brood of vipers! how can you speak good, when you are evil? For out of the abundance of the heart the mouth speaks. 35 The good man out of his good treasure brings forth good, and the evil man out of his evil treasure brings forth evil. 36 I tell you, on the day of judgment men will render account for every careless word they utter; 37 for by your words you will be justified, and by your words you will be condemned."

Luke 6:43-45
43 "For no good tree bears bad fruit, nor again does a bad tree bear good fruit; 44 for each tree is known by its own fruit. For figs are not gathered from thorns, nor are grapes picked from a bramble bush. 45 The good man out of the good treasure of his heart produces good, and the evil man out of his evil treasure produces evil; for out of the abundance of the heart his mouth speaks.

gathering Jesus said the obvious, a good tree bears good fruit, and a bad tree bears bad fruit. The tree, like a man, is known by the fruits of their life.

Looking once more at the Pharisees and the lawyers, Jesus borrows an epitaph from John's vocabulary saying, "You brood of vipers!" Jesus marveled that they could talk so well while living so misguidedly.

The true person is revealed by the likeness or disparity between his life and his words. Jesus enforced his point saying figs are not gathered from thorn bushes and neither are grapes found on bramble bushes.

Jesus warned when judgment day comes all will give account of every word, careless, or thought out, that they have uttered.

Jesus divided the good and the bad in the following groupings:

As good fruit he singles out:
- John the Baptist

- Believers, people in general

- Tax collectors in specific

	As Evil or bad fruit people: • Herod • Pharisees • Lawyers/Scribes
When an Unclean Spirit returns **Matthew 12:43-45;** **Luke 11:24-26** **Matthew 12:43-45** 43 "When the unclean spirit has gone out of a man, he passes through waterless places seeking rest, but he finds none. 44 Then he says, 'I will return to my house from which I came.' And when he comes he finds it empty, swept, and put in order. 45 Then he goes and brings with him seven other spirits more evil than himself, and they enter and dwell there; and the last state of that man becomes worse than the first. So shall it be also with this evil generation." **Luke 11:24-26** 24 "When the unclean spirit has gone out of a man, he passes through waterless places seeking rest; and finding none he says, 'I will return to my house from which I came.' 25 And when he comes he finds it swept and put	***When an Unclean Spirit returns*** **Matthew 12:43-45;** **Luke 11:24-26** **Comment** N.T. Wright, Anglican Bishop and biblical scholar, believes this parable also refers to the Temple. The House referred to was the Temple, cleaned and put into order by the Maccabees. Later, reformers came only to find that the Temple had reverted to even worse abuses with the passage of years. When one returns to their old bad ways of living the new is often far worse than the first.

in order. 26 Then he goes and brings seven other spirits more evil than himself, and they enter and dwell there; and the last state of that man becomes worse than the first."

Blessed is the womb that bore you

Luke 11:27-28
27 As he said this, a woman in the crowd raised her voice and said to him, "Blessed is the womb that bore you, and the breasts that you sucked!" 28 But he said, "Blessed rather are those who hear the word of God and keep it!"

Blessed is the womb that bore you

Luke 11:27-28

Comment

This is an independent statement of Luke.

The unnamed woman shouts praise for Jesus' mother. Jesus' words once again sound sharp. If only we could hear the tone of his voice we would have a better understanding of how to interpret this comment.

Feast of the Jews

John 5:1-5
1 After this there was a feast of the Jews, and Jesus went up to Jerusalem. 2 Now there is in Jerusalem by the Sheep Gate a pool, in Hebrew called Bethesda which has five porticoes. 3 In these lay a multitude of invalids,

Feast of the Jews

John 5:1-5

Comment

This is the second visit Jesus made to Jerusalem following His baptism.

blind, lame, paralyzed. 5 One man was there, who had been ill for thirty-eight years.

Covered colonnades surrounded the Bethesda Pools whose waters were divided into northern and southern pools. Water was conveyed from the pools for use at the nearby Temple court. Near the pools were smaller basins containing water, to which healing abilities were attributed. As Jesus entered, he found many waiting to be healed. Although it was the Sabbath, Jesus healed a man who had been ill for thirty-eight years.

Do you want to be healed?

John 5:6-9a

6 When Jesus saw him and knew that he had been lying there a long time, he said to him, "Do you want to be healed?" 7 The sick man answered him, "Sir, I have no man to put me into the pool when the water is troubled, and while I am going another steps down before me." 8 Jesus said to him, "Rise, take up your pallet, and walk." 9 And at once the man was healed, and he took up his pallet and walked.

Do you want to be healed?

John 5:6-9a

Comment

Jesus never invaded another person's privacy. When the man gave him an evasive answer Jesus accepted his response as a yes, and then told him to rise up and walk.

### *On a Sabbath day*	### *On a Sabbath day*
John 5:9b Now that day was the sabbath.	**John 5:9b** **Comment** Remember, you do not do any work on the Sabbath! More trouble is brewing. Jesus took his usual radical position caring more for people than for tradition. Exodus 35:2 clearly states that one should be put to death for works performed on the Sabbath day. *2 Six days shall work be done, but on the seventh day you shall have a holy sabbath of solemn rest to the LORD; whoever does any work on it shall be put to death; 3 you shall kindle no fire in all your habitations on the sabbath day." Exodus 35:2-3*
### *Can't carry your pallet on the Sabbath*	### *Can't carry your pallet on the Sabbath*
John 5:10-14 10 So the Jews said to the man who was cured, "It is the sabbath, it is not lawful for you to carry your pallet." 11 But he answered them, "The man who healed me	**John 5:10-14** **Comment** Neither the man nor the Jews knew who had healed him. Jesus

said to me, 'Take up your pallet, and walk.'" 12 They asked him, "Who is the man who said to you, 'Take up your pallet, and walk'?" 13 Now the man who had been healed did not know who it was, for Jesus had withdrawn, as there was a crowd in the place. 14 Afterward, Jesus found him in the temple, and said to him, "See, you are well! Sin no more, that nothing worse befall you."

implies the man's thirty-eight years of suffering were caused by his sinning. Jesus does not mince words, do not sin again!

Why the Jews persecuted Jesus

John 5:15-18

15 The man went away and told the Jews that it was Jesus who had healed him. 16 And this was why the Jews persecuted Jesus, because he did this on the sabbath. 17 But Jesus answered them, "My Father is working still, and I am working." 18 This was why the Jews sought all the more to kill him, because he not only broke the sabbath but also called God his Father, making himself equal with God.

Why the Jews persecuted Jesus

John 5:15-18

Comment

In verse sixteen, John tells us why the Jews persecuted Jesus. It was not that he healed the man, but because he did it on the Sabbath. Healing the man was bad enough but when Jesus said His Father works on the Sabbath, and so does he, their anger boiled over and they wanted to kill him, because he had made himself equal with God, which was blasphemy to them.

The Son can do nothing of his own accord

The Son can do nothing of his own accord

John 5:19-24 19 Jesus said to them, "Truly, truly, I say to you, the Son can do nothing of his own accord, but only what he sees the Father doing; for whatever he does, that the Son does likewise. 20 For the Father loves the Son, and shows him all that he himself is doing; and greater works than these will he show him, that you may marvel. 21 For as the Father raises the dead and gives them life, so also the Son gives life to whom he will. 22 The Father judges no one, but has given all judgment to the Son, 23 that all may honor the Son, even as they honor the Father. He who does not honor the Son does not honor the Father who sent him. 24 Truly, truly, I say to you, he who hears my word and believes him who sent me, has eternal life; he does not come into judgment, but has passed from death to life.	**John 5:19-24** **Comment** Simply stated, Jesus said he takes directions from God and only God. If God sees fit to do good things on the Sabbath then so will Jesus. God has authorized him to render judgment. Eternal life is offered to those who believe in Jesus as the son of God.
<u>*The dead will hear*</u> **John 5:25-29** 25 "Truly, truly, I say to you, the hour is coming, and now is, when the dead will hear the voice of the Son of God, and those who hear will live. 26 For as the Father has life in himself, so he has	<u>*The dead will hear*</u> **John 5:25-29** **Comment** Here Jesus answered the question of what happens to people who died before he

granted the Son also to have life in himself, 27 and has given him authority to execute judgment, because he is the Son of man. 28 Do not marvel at this; for the hour is coming when all who are in the tombs will hear his voice 29 and come forth, those who have done good, to the resurrection of life, and those who have done evil, to the resurrection of judgment.

came. The "good" go to the resurrection of life. The evil go to the resurrection of judgment.

Jesus can do nothing of His own authority

John 5:30-32
30 "I can do nothing on my own authority; as I hear, I judge; and my judgment is just, because I seek not my own will but the will of him who sent me. 31 If I bear witness to myself, my testimony is not true; 32 there is another who bears witness to me, and I know that the testimony which he bears to me is true.

Jesus can do nothing of His own authority

John 5:30-32

Comment

Again, while in Jerusalem, Jesus declares that he does nothing by his own authority but by the authority of God. God is his witness.

God is Jesus' witness

John 5:33-38
33 You sent to John, and he has borne witness to the truth. 34 Not that the testimony which I receive is from man; but I say this that you may be saved.

God is Jesus' witness

John 5:33-38

Comment

They believed John had power given to him from God. They

35 He was a burning and shining lamp, and you were willing to rejoice for a while in his light. 36 But the testimony which I have is greater than that of John; for the works which the Father has granted me to accomplish, these very works which I am doing, bear me witness that the Father has sent me. 37 And the Father who sent me has himself borne witness to me. His voice you have never heard, his form you have never seen; 38 and you do not have his word abiding in you, for you do not believe him whom he has sent.

Search the Scriptures

John 5:39-47

39 You search the scriptures, because you think that in them you have eternal life; and it is they that bear witness to me; 40 yet you refuse to come to me that you may have life. 41 I do not receive glory from men. 42 But I know that you have not the love of God within you. 43 I have come in my Father's name, and you do not receive me; if another comes in his own name, him you will receive. 44 How can you believe, who receive glory from one another and do not seek did not believe in Jesus because God's word was not in them.

Search the Scriptures

John 5:39-47

Comment

Their eyes are blinded to the full truth revealed in Scripture. Jesus claims God as his Father and the Jews cannot abide this. Jesus must die! Jesus knew how they would respond but did not back down.

the glory that comes from the only God? 45 Do not think that I shall accuse you to the Father; it is Moses who accuses you, on whom you set your hope. 46 If you believed Moses, you would believe me, for he wrote of me. 47 But if you do not believe his writings, how will you believe my words?"

Scribes and Pharisees want a sign

**Matthew 12:38-42;
Luke 11:29-32**

Matthew 12:38-42

38 Then some of the scribes and Pharisees said to him, "Teacher, we wish to see a sign from you." 39 But he answered them, "An evil and adulterous generation seeks for a sign; but no sign shall be given to it except the sign of the prophet Jonah. 40 For as Jonah was three days and three nights in the belly of the whale, so will the Son of man be three days and three nights in the heart of the earth. 41 The men of Nin'eveh will arise at the judgment with this generation and condemn it; for they repented at the preaching of Jonah, and behold, something greater than Jonah is

Scribes and Pharisees want a sign

**Matthew 12:38-42;
Luke 11:29-32**

Comment

Jesus did not work miracles for purposes of entertainment and sternly rebuked those who asked him to do so. His miracles were targeted to teach lessons about the heavenly reign he was announcing.

Jesus' reference to Jonah is found in the book Jonah in the Old Testament. The essence of the story is God called Jonah to go to the great and wicked city of Nineveh and tell them that unless they repented of their sins He was going to destroy them. Jonah did not like the

here. ⁴² The queen of the South will arise at the judgment with this generation and condemn it; for she came from the ends of the earth to hear the wisdom of Solomon, and behold, something greater than Solomon is here.

people of Nineveh so he tried to run away from God and not go to Nineveh. Jonah soon learned that God was universal not territorial. Reluctantly, Jonah finally reached Nineveh and preached, "Forty days and Nineveh will be no more!" The king and all the people repented and God spared the city. Jonah was very angry with God. God pointed out that sinners were important to Him and He did not want anyone to perish.

Luke 11:29-32
²⁹ When the crowds were increasing, he began to say, "This generation is an evil generation; it seeks a sign, but no sign shall be given to it except the sign of Jonah. ³⁰ For as Jonah became a sign to the men of Nin'eveh, so will the Son of man be to this generation. ³¹ The queen of the South will arise at the judgment with the men of this generation and condemn them; for she came from the ends of the earth to hear the wisdom of Solomon, and behold, something greater than Solomon is here. ³² The men of Nin'eveh will arise at the judgment with this generation and condemn it; for they repented at the preaching of Jonah, and behold, something greater than Jonah is here.

Luke 11:29-32

The sign of Jonah in the traditional interpretation is a statement of Jesus' pending resurrection. But what if he was holding up a mirror for the Pharisees to see themselves as God sees them?

The Pharisees would see their own image and the symbolic image of their nation Israel. Notice the similarities:

1) Both the Pharisees and Jonah heard God's call to service.

2) Both the Pharisees and Jonah run from God's call. Both refuse to do God's will and seek to find their own destiny.

	3) Their flight leads to tribulation; Jonah ends up in the belly of a big fish rather than proclaiming God's love. The Pharisees built walls around God's Word rather than opening the Word to everyone. 4) When at last both attempt to fulfill God's will, they do not like the results. In Jonah's case, the people of Nineveh repent of their sins. God is merciful to them and forgives them, while Jonah wants God to destroy them.

Chapter 11

The Disciples return from their mission

Mark 6:12-13

12 So they went out and preached that men should repent. 13 And they cast out many demons, and anointed with oil many that were sick and healed them.

Inner-Circle reports back to Jesus

**Mark 6:30-32;
Matthew 14:13-14;
Luke 9:10**

Mark 6:30-32
30 The apostles returned to Jesus, and told him all that they had done and taught. 31 And he said to them, "Come away by yourselves to a lonely place, and rest a while." For many were coming and going, and they had no leisure even to eat. 32 And they went away in the boat to a lonely place by themselves.

The Disciples return from their mission

Comment

Mark 6:12-13

After receiving their instructions they faithfully carried out their mission. Their success was overwhelming.

Inner-Circle reports back to Jesus

Comment

**Mark 6:30-32;
Matthew 14:13-14;
Luke 9:10**

Trying to get away by boat proved futile, the watchful crowd saw and followed. It helps to understand this by realizing the Sea of Galilee is little more than a very large lake. More than once the crowd followed on foot as the boat moved to a distant destination.

Matthew 14:13-14 13 Now when Jesus heard this, he withdrew from there in a boat to a lonely place apart. But when the crowds heard it, they followed him on foot from the towns. 14 As he went ashore he saw a great throng; and he had compassion on them, and healed their sick **Luke 9:10** 10 On their return the apostles told him what they had done. And he took them and withdrew apart to a city called Beth-sa'ida.	As Jesus stepped ashore he saw the faith and needs of the people. We are told he had compassion on them and healed their sick.

Return of the Inner-Circle

Both Mark and Luke referred to the Inner-Circle as "apostles." The word apostle as used here refers uniquely to the twelve members of the Inner-Circle. In time it included the great teachers and missionaries of the early church. Before the time of Emperor Constantine the definition had grown to include those who established churches and had oversight of them.

We are not told how much time was given to the mission of the Inner-Circle. We do know there is no mention of the Inner-Circle being with Jesus during the early days of John's confinement. To accomplish the healing and exorcism of so many would have been a time consuming mission. When they returned Jesus immediately attempted to take them away to create a break from the endless pressure of the crowd.

Not washing hands

Mark 7:1-8;
Matthew 15:1-3;
Luke 11:37-41

Mark 7:1-8

1 Now when the Pharisees gathered together to him, with some of the scribes, who had come from Jerusalem, 2 they saw that some of his disciples ate with hands defiled, that is, unwashed. 3 (For the Pharisees, and all the Jews, do not eat unless they wash their hands, observing the tradition of the elders; 4 and when they come from the market place, they do not eat unless they purify themselves; and there are many other traditions which they observe, the washing of cups and pots and vessels of bronze.) 5 And the Pharisees and the scribes asked him, "Why do your disciples not live according to the tradition of the elders, but eat with hands defiled?" 6 And he said to them, "Well did Isaiah prophesy of you hypocrites, as it is written,
'This people honors me with their lips,
but their heart is far from me;
7 in vain do they worship me,
teaching as doctrines the precepts of men.'

Not washing hands

Mark 7:1-8;
Matthew 15:1-3;
Luke 11:37-41

Comment

All three evangelists address the same issue of eating with hands that have not been washed. Mark and Matthew reported the Pharisees and scribes accused the disciples of eating with dirty hands. The Pharisees were adamant in their demand for observance of the traditions of the elders. In defense of the disciples, Jesus accused the Pharisees and scribes of being hypocrites. He quoted Isaiah saying "you are people who honor me (God) with your lips but your hearts are far from me. You have left the Commandments in favor of the traditions."

Jesus referred to Isaiah 29:13-14.
13 And the Lord said: "Because this people draw near with their mouth and honor me with their lips, while their hearts are far from me, and their fear of me is a commandment of men learned by rote; 14 therefore, behold, I

8 You leave the commandment of God, and hold fast the tradition of men."

Matthew 15:1-3
1 Then Pharisees and scribes came to Jesus from Jerusalem and said, 2 "Why do your disciples transgress the tradition of the elders? For they do not wash their hands when they eat." 3 He answered them, "And why do you transgress the commandment of God for the sake of your tradition?

Luke 11:37-41
37 While he was speaking, a Pharisee asked him to dine with him; so he went in and sat at table. 38 The Pharisee was astonished to see that he did not first wash before dinner. 39 And the Lord said to him, "Now you Pharisees cleanse the outside of the cup and of the dish, but inside you are full of extortion and wickedness. 40 You fools! Did not he who made the outside make the inside also? 41 But give for alms those things which are within; and behold, everything is clean for you.

will again do marvelous things with this people, wonderful and marvelous; and the wisdom of their wise men shall perish, and the discernment of their discerning men shall be hid."

Luke has a significantly different version of this experience. He said a Pharisee invited Jesus to eat with him. When Jesus began to eat without having washed his hands, the Pharisee was astonished and dismayed. Knowing his thoughts Jesus immediately said to him you spend a great deal of time washing the outside of the cup. But inside, you are filled with extortion and wickedness. Jesus' reference is clearly to God being the potter who made the cup (person). The same one who made the outside made the inside. Then Jesus gave an inspirational interpretation of what this means. If you give your alms from the inside, they will always be clean regardless of how the outside appears.

<u>*Woe to you Pharisees*</u>

Luke 11:42-44

<u>*Woe to you Pharisees*</u>

Luke 11:42-44

⁴² "But woe to you Pharisees! for you tithe mint and rue and every herb, and neglect justice and the love of God; these you ought to have done, without neglecting the others. ⁴³ Woe to you Pharisees! for you love the best seat in the synagogues and salutations in the market places. ⁴⁴ Woe to you! for you are like graves which are not seen, and men walk over them without knowing it."	**Comment** Woe is a way of saying, "You have messed up big time now!" The pitfall of the Pharisees was they were more careful about tithing the mint and rue than about weightier matters. Wild mint grows larger than garden mint and was used as a condiment, and a medicine. The paying of tithes of the seeds was in accordance with the Law. *"You shall tithe all the yield of your seed, which comes forth from the field year by year. Deuteronomy 14:22* *Rue* is a garden herb that the Pharisees were careful to tithe. Jesus admonished the Pharisees, saying you do great in minutia but you fail in the things that really count like love and justice! You should do both. The "best seat" they coveted was the one in front middle where everyone could see them. They loved to be acclaimed in public places. To be like graves that are walked over without notice means they are not as important as they think they are!

Lawyer is offended

Luke 11:45-52

45 One of the lawyers answered him, "Teacher, in saying this you reproach us also." 46 And he said, "Woe to you lawyers also! for you load men with burdens hard to bear, and you yourselves do not touch the burdens with one of your fingers. 47 Woe to you! for you build the tombs of the prophets whom your fathers killed. 48 So you are witnesses and consent to the deeds of your fathers; for they killed them, and you build their tombs. 49 Therefore also the Wisdom of God said, 'I will send them prophets and apostles, some of whom they will kill and persecute,' 50 that the blood of all the prophets, shed from the foundation of the world, may be required of this generation, 51 from the blood of Abel to the blood of Zechari'ah, who perished between the altar and the sanctuary. Yes, I tell you, it shall be required of this generation. 52 Woe to you lawyers! for you have taken away the key of knowledge; you did not enter yourselves, and you hindered those who were entering."

Lawyer is offended

Luke 11:45-52

Comment

The comments Jesus made about their fathers killing the prophets and them building tombs has a deeper meaning. The tombs would be considered as monuments to the slain prophets. The problem lay in the fact that the lawyers did not repudiate the deeds of their fathers as they memorialized the prophets, making it a hypocritical act.

Jesus used *"Zechari'ah, who perished between the altar and the sanctuary,"* as an illustration of the treatment of the prophets by the nations rulers.

20 Then the Spirit of God took possession of Zechari'ah the son of Jehoi'ada the priest; and he stood above the people, and said to them, "Thus says God, 'Why do you transgress the commandments of the LORD, so that you cannot prosper? Because you have forsaken the LORD, he has forsaken you.'"
21 But they conspired against him, and by command of the

	king they stoned him with stones in the court of the house of the LORD. 22 Thus Jo'ash the king did not remember the kindness which Jehoi'ada, Zechari'ah's father, had shown him, but killed his son. 2 Chronicles 24:20-22 Jesus further charged the lawyers of taking away the opportunity for ordinary people to understand the law. The lawyers did not teach the law to others. They kept their learning for their own benefit. Thus hindering people from living within the law.

<u>Jesus had harsh words for the Lawyers</u>

The lawyers were the scribes. Their duties enabled them to become the most knowledgeable people of the Law. They zealously protected the Law from violation. Their zeal resulted in additional laws being written to protect the main Law. This additional body of laws became such a burden on the average person, that there was no way he or she could avoid violating the Law of Moses. Rather than modify their additional laws to make adherence more possible, they simply continued to make the law more complex. Hearing this statement, a friend of mine commented, do you mean like our present day tax code?

Pharisees began to press him hard

Luke 11:53-54

53 As he went away from there, the scribes and the Pharisees began to press him hard, and to provoke him to speak of many things, 54 lying in wait for him, to catch at something he might say.

Pharisees began to press him hard

Luke 11:53-54

Comment

They hounded Jesus like a pack of hyenas after a wounded prey, always circling and constantly attacking from the rear.

Jesus warns the Pharisees

**Mark 7:9-13;
Matthew 15:4-9**

Mark 7:9-13

9 And he said to them, "You have a fine way of rejecting the commandment of God, in order to keep your tradition! 10 For Moses said, 'Honor your father and your mother'; and, 'He who speaks evil of father or mother, let him surely die'; 11 but you say, 'If a man tells his father or his mother, What you would have gained from me is Corban' (that is, given to God)— 12 then you no longer permit him to do anything for his father or mother, 13 thus making void the word of God through your tradition which you hand on. And many such things you do."

Jesus warns the Pharisees

**Mark 7:9-13;
Matthew 15:4-9**

Comment

The word "Corban" is used only twice in the entire Bible. The term meant a gift offered or to be offered to God. The Pharisees interpreted Corban to mean a gift that should have gone for the support of one's parents could be redirected as a gift to God through the temple. This provided two corrupt attributes for the giver. The first was to permit neglect of one's parents. The second permitted this gift to be used to pay one's taxes to the temple.

Jesus cited the fifth

Matthew 15:4-9	commandment, *12 "Honor your father and your mother, that your days may be long in the land which the LORD your God gives you. Exodus 20:12*
4 For God commanded, 'Honor your father and your mother,' and, 'He who speaks evil of father or mother, let him surely die.' 5 But you say, 'If any one tells his father or his mother, What you would have gained from me is given to God, he need not honor his father.' 6 So, for the sake of your tradition, you have made void the word of God. 7 You hypocrites! Well did Isaiah prophesy of you, when he said: 8 'This people honors me with their lips, but their heart is far from me; 9 in vain do they worship me, teaching as doctrines the precepts of men.'"	Next He reminded them of the punishment prescribed in Exodus 21:17, *17 "Whoever curses his father or his mother shall be put to death.* It was a despicable thing to dishonor ones mother or father, *16 "'Cursed be he who dishonors his father or his mother.' And all the people shall say, 'Amen.' Deuteronomy 27:16* Once more Jesus pointed out the Pharisees were more concerned with their traditions, than with the strict adherence to God's word.

Jesus accused the Lawyers of rejecting the Commandments

Accusing the Pharisees of rejecting the Commandments of God would have been the most profound accusation they would have ever imagined. They were caught completely off guard, and could offer no rebuttal. Jesus quickly drove home his point by accusing them of honoring Corban over observing the Fifth Commandment.

Nothing you eat can defile you

Mark 7:14-23;
Matthew 15:10-20;
Luke 6:39

Mark 7:14-23
14 And he called the people to him again, and said to them, "Hear me, all of you, and understand: 15 there is nothing outside a man which by going into him can defile him; but the things which come out of a man are what defile him." 17 And when he had entered the house, and left the people, his disciples asked him about the parable. 18 And he said to them, "Then are you also without understanding? Do you not see that whatever goes into a man from outside cannot defile him, 19 since it enters, not his heart but his stomach, and so passes on?" (Thus he declared all foods clean.) 20 And he said, "What comes out of a man is what defiles a man. 21 For from within, out of the heart of man, come evil thoughts, fornication, theft, murder, adultery, 22 coveting, wickedness, deceit, licentiousness, envy, slander, pride, foolishness. 23 All these evil things come from within, and they defile a man."

Nothing you eat can defile you

Mark 7:14-23;
Matthew 5:10-20;
Luke 6:39

Comment

Jesus spoke concerning the dietary laws of the Jewish people. There was a lengthy list of unclean foods they were prohibited from eating. Jesus proclaimed all food was acceptable for the human body. Foods do not defile the person. The point overlooked by the Pharisees was, it is what comes out of the mouth of the individual that defiles him or her.

Once more, the Inner-Circle requested clarification of what Jesus meant. Verse eighteen implies Jesus' frustration with the slowness of the Inner-Circle to grasp the meaning of his teaching. Jesus told them it is so simple even a child should be able to understand. He went on to express the path of food within the body. Then he catalogs the vileness that comes out of an individual making sure not to attribute these to the food he or she has eaten.

Matthew 15:10-20 10 And he called the people to him and said to them, "Hear and understand: 11 not what goes into the mouth defiles a man, but what comes out of the mouth, this defiles a man." 12 Then the disciples came and said to him, "Do you know that the Pharisees were offended when they heard this saying?" 13 He answered, "Every plant which my heavenly Father has not planted will be rooted up. 14 Let them alone; they are blind guides. And if a blind man leads a blind man, both will fall into a pit." 15 But Peter said to him, "Explain the parable to us." 16 And he said, "Are you also still without understanding? 17 Do you not see that whatever goes into the mouth passes into the stomach, and so passes on? 18 But what comes out of the mouth proceeds from the heart, and this defiles a man. 19 For out of the heart come evil thoughts, murder, adultery, fornication, theft, false witness, slander. 20 These are what defile a man; but to eat with unwashed hands does not defile a man." **Luke 6:39** 39 He also told them a parable: "Can a blind man lead a blind man? Will they not both fall into a pit?	Matthew adds the Pharisees were offended by Jesus' teaching. Jesus then called the Pharisees blind guides, and spoke to the danger inherent in following one who cannot see.

Woe to the world for temptations to sin

**Matthew 18:7-9;
Luke 17:1-4;
Luke 6:26**

Matthew 18:7-9

7 "Woe to the world for temptations to sin! For it is necessary that temptations come, but woe to the man by whom the temptation comes! 8 And if your hand or your foot causes you to sin, cut it off and throw it away; it is better for you to enter life maimed or lame than with two hands or two feet to be thrown into the eternal fire. 9 And if your eye causes you to sin, pluck it out and throw it away; it is better for you to enter life with one eye than with two eyes to be thrown into the hell of fire.

Luke 17:1-4

1 And he said to his disciples, "Temptations to sin are sure to come; but woe to him by whom they come! 2 It would be better for him if a millstone were hung round his neck and he were cast into the sea, than that he should cause one of these little ones to sin. 3 Take heed to yourselves; if your brother sins, rebuke him, and if he repents, forgive him;

Woe to the world for temptations to sin

**Matthew 18:7-9;
Luke 17:1-4;
Luke 6:26**

Comment

Jesus said it was necessary that temptations come, but woe to the one who brings them. Next comes one of the most radical ideas one would ever expect to hear. Jesus said if your hand or your foot causes you to sin then cut it off! Indeed, this concept is abhorrent to us. This was a forceful way of saying even if one is handicapped to receive entry into the kingdom of heaven is more important than being whole here on earth and losing their reward.

⁴ and if he sins against you seven times in the day, and turns to you seven times, and says, 'I repent,' you must forgive him."

Luke 6:26
²⁶ "Woe to you, when all men speak well of you, for so their fathers did to the false prophets.

Chapter 12

THE MOUNT OF OLIVES AS SEEN FROM JERUSALEM

Note: only Matthew gives us the Sermon on the Mount.

The fifth chapter of Matthew opens with what is called the Beatitudes. In the sixth chapter of Luke's Gospel we also find a series of blessings or Beatitudes. I have brought these together because at first glance, they seem to be identical. However, there are significant differences between the two but they convey largely the same themes.

Sermon on the Mount	Sermon on the Mount
Matthew chapters 5, 6, and 7	**Matthew chapters 5, 6, and 7**
Luke: Selected verses from chapters 6, 11, 12, and 18.	**Luke: Selected verses from chapters 6, 11, 12, and 18.**
<u>*Blessed are the poor in spirit*</u>	<u>*Blessed are the poor in spirit*</u>

Matthew 5:1-3; Luke 6:20

Matthew 5:1-3
¹ Seeing the crowds, he went up on the mountain, and when he sat down his disciples came to him. ² And he opened his mouth and taught them, saying: ³ "Blessed are the poor in spirit, for theirs is the kingdom of heaven.

Luke 6:20
²⁰ And he lifted up his eyes on his disciples, and said: "Blessed are you poor, for yours is the kingdom of God.

Matthew 5:1-3; Luke 6:20

Comment

It appears Jesus was teaching the Inner-Circle while the crowd listened in. Jesus spoke of those who felt spiritual emptiness, he affirmed how they felt. He promised their reward would be the kingdom of heaven filling them with joy. Jesus knew living in harmony with God's desire brought blessings regardless of one's outer circumstances.

Even in this mixed crowd the dominant percentage were the poor.

Blessed are those who mourn

Matthew 5:4; Luke 6:25b

Matthew 5:4
⁴ "Blessed are those who mourn, for they shall be comforted.

Luke 6:25b
²⁵ᵇ "Woe to you that laugh now, for you shall mourn and weep.

Blessed are those who mourn

Matthew 5:4; Luke 6:25b

Comment

When speaking of mourning, we generally think in terms of the death of one who has been loved. Mourning includes an emotion that encompasses more than just death. One can mourn the loss of many

	changing of societal norms for the worst. Jesus said those who are sensitive enough to sense change and feel hurt will be comforted. Luke warns those who are insensitive to the hurt of others will someday share their anguish.
Blessed are you that weep **Luke 6:21b** 21b "Blessed are you that weep now, for you shall laugh.	***Blessed are you that weep*** **Luke 6:21b** **Comment** Those who weep shall laugh, meaning they shall recover from the source of their weeping.
Blessed are the meek **Matthew 5:5** 5 "Blessed are the meek, for they shall inherit the earth.	***Blessed are the meek*** **Matthew 5:5** **Comment** To be blessed means to be happy. Strong's Greek Dictionary defines "meek" as: "Mildness of disposition, gentleness of spirit, the disposition of spirit in which we accept God's dealings with us as good, and therefore without disputing or resisting."

	In the Old Testament, the meek were those who relied totally upon God and not upon themselves. The way they dealt with the evil someone inflicted upon a person was to believe God permitted the injuries for the purpose of purifying His elect, and He would deliver His elect in His time (Isa. 41:17; Luke 18:1-8). Gentleness and meekness are the opposite of self-assertiveness and self-interest. They stem from trust in God's goodness and control over the situation. The gentle person is not occupied with self.
<u>**Blessed are those who hunger and thirst for righteousness**</u> **Matthew 5:6;** **Luke 6:21a** **Matthew 5:6** 6 "Blessed are those who hunger and thirst for righteousness, for they shall be satisfied. **Luke 6:21a** 21a "Blessed are you that hunger now, for you shall be satisfied.	<u>**Blessed are those who hunger and thirst for righteousness**</u> **Matthew 5:6;** **Luke 6:21a** **Comment** Among Jesus' audience were those who understood "hunger" to mean their grumbling stomach. All were hungry for their needs to be met, but Jesus clearly informed them he was speaking of the hunger of the heart to be connected to God.

Woe to you that are full now	***Woe to you that are full now***
Luke 6:25a "Woe to you that are full now, for you shall hunger.	**Luke 6:25a** **Comment** Luke begins each of the blessings with a "Woe" you may be full now but the day will come when you will be hungry.
Blessed are the merciful	***Blessed are the merciful***
Matthew 5:7 7 "Blessed are the merciful, for they shall obtain mercy.	**Matthew 5:7** **Comment** Merciful means the remission of a penalty. Mercy is the opposite of self-centeredness. Jesus knew how merciless and cruel the world they lived in could be.
Blessed are the pure in heart	***Blessed are the pure in heart***
Matthew 5:8 8 "Blessed are the pure in heart, for they shall see God.	**Matthew 5:8** **Comment** No one has ever seen God. Even the Old Testament prophet hid in the cleft of the rock as God passed by. To "see" God can only be explained by assumption. While in this

world to see God as a physical experience is impossible, unless God should permit it. To see God now is more likely to mean understanding more fully. In the next world anything is possible.

Blessed are the peacemakers

Matthew 5:9

9 "Blessed are the peacemakers, for they shall be called sons of God.

Blessed are the peacemakers

Matthew 5:9

Comment

Among the most rejected of the world's rejected are the peacemakers. Peacemakers are the very ones every generation desperately needs.

Blessed are those who are persecuted

Matthew 5:10

10 "Blessed are those who are persecuted for righteousness' sake, for theirs is the kingdom of heaven.

Blessed are those who are persecuted

Matthew 5:10

Comment

Being "persecuted," is not what most of us want as part of our resume of life.

However, this persecution is not just for anything, it is for the sake of righteousness.

In part, being righteous means to live with integrity and virtue. Righteousness is the condition acceptable to God. The blessing is for those who withstand the persecution along with those who are poor in spirit. Together they shall receive the kingdom of heaven.

Blessed are you when men revile you

**Matthew 5:11-12;
Luke 6:22-23**

Matthew 5:11-12

11 "Blessed are you when men revile you and persecute you and utter all kinds of evil against you falsely on my account. 12 Rejoice and be glad, for your reward is great in heaven, for so men persecuted the prophets who were before you.

Luke 6:22-23

22 "Blessed are you when men hate you, and when they exclude you and revile you, and cast out your name as evil, on account of the Son of man! 23 Rejoice in that day, and leap for joy, for behold, your reward is great in heaven; for so their fathers did to the prophets.

Blessed are you when men revile you

**Matthew 5:11-12;
Luke 6:22-23**

Comment

The word persecuted is used seventeen times in the four Gospels. It means to make one run or flee, put to flight, drive away, to run swiftly in order to catch a person or thing, to harass, trouble, molest, mistreat, and to suffer.

Jesus reminded them the prophets of old had suffered persecutions. To be a follower of Jesus made one liable to the possibility of persecution.

There is an old cliché that says "sticks and stones may break my bones but words will never hurt me," it should probably read sticks and stones break my bones and words leave lasting wounds.

The word reward appears in the Gospels fourteen times.

Luke refers to Jesus as the Son of Man reiterating the title Jesus used to define himself on many occasions.

You are the salt of the earth

Matthew 5:13;
Luke 14:34-35

Matthew 5:13
13 "You are the salt of the earth; but if salt has lost its taste, how shall its saltness be restored? It is no longer good for anything except to be thrown out and trodden under foot by men.

Luke 14:34-35
34 "Salt is good; but if salt has lost its taste, how shall its saltness be restored? 35 It is fit neither for the land nor for the dunghill; men throw it away. He who has ears to hear, let him hear.

You are the salt of the earth

Matthew 5:13;
Luke 14:34-35

Comment

Salt has been an essential for life predating all written history. In ancient times it was used as legal tender. People bought and sold their goods in return for salt. Roman soldiers were once paid by measures of salt. Salt is a natural preserver of foods, it enhances flavor and brings out distinctive taste in food. Jesus made it plain his followers were to make a major impact for good upon the world.

When Jesus said, "What will you do with salt that has lost its

Jesus and the Gospel Timeline

saltiness," he was saying any one who no longer has zest for the Christian faith, is no longer moved by the knowledge of God's presence, has lost the joy of life. Like salt without flavor the person who rejects God's love and presence is beyond our help.

You are the light of the world

Matthew 5:14-16

14 "You are the light of the world. A city set on a hill cannot be hid. 15 Nor do men light a lamp and put it under a bushel, but on a stand, and it gives light to all in the house. 16 Let your light so shine before men, that they may see your good works and give glory to your Father who is in heaven.

You are the light of the world

Matthew 5:14-16

Comment

When Jesus spoke of "the light of the world," he was pointing out a major condition most of the modern world has little knowledge of. The modern world does not live with endless darkened nights. Light overcoming darkness is a gift. In the world before electricity, light in the dark hours was almost a magical condition. A city set upon a hill casting a glow of light shattered the night and could be seen for miles. Jesus said the obvious, no one lights a candle and puts it under a bushel or under a bed where it would be concealed and its flame would become a danger. A lamp is to be put upon a stand where it will brighten its surroundings.

Jesus said his followers were to let their light shine. His followers were to be reflections of himself and of God's love. The work to be done should be done in an attitude of serving God.

I have not come to abolish the law and the prophets

Mathew 5:17-20

17 "Think not that I have come to abolish the law and the prophets; I have come not to abolish them but to fulfil them. 18 For truly, I say to you, till heaven and earth pass away, not an iota, not a dot, will pass from the law until all is accomplished. 19 Whoever then relaxes one of the least of these commandments and teaches men so, shall be called least in the kingdom of heaven; but he who does them and teaches them shall be called great in the kingdom of heaven. 20 For I tell you, unless your righteousness exceeds that of the scribes and Pharisees, you will never enter the kingdom of heaven.

I have not come to abolish the law and the prophets

Mathew 5:17-20

Comment

Jesus was not talking about just the Ten Commandments he was speaking of the entire body of law contained in the Books of Moses. The religious community thought Jesus was trying to establish a new law based on his interpretation of God. Jesus stated unmistakably he had not come to abolish the law, or to change the teachings of Moses. He had not come to do away with the Ten Commandments. He came to fulfil the Law and the prophets. This was none other than the role of the Messiah!

He announced anyone who relaxed or weakened the teachings of the Law or the Commandments would be called least in the kingdom of heaven. Interestingly he does not say such a person would be thrown out of the kingdom of heaven but they will be called the least in the kingdom of heaven. On the other hand those who teach the Law and the Prophets shall be called great in the kingdom of heaven. He continued saying his followers were to have a righteousness exceeding that exemplified by the scribes and the Pharisees. If their righteousness did not exceed that of the Pharisees they would never enter the kingdom of heaven!

Judging

Matthew 5:21-26

21 "You have heard that it was said to the men of old, 'You shall not kill; and whoever kills shall be liable to judgment.' 22 But I say to you that every one who is angry with his brother shall be liable to judgment; whoever insults his brother shall be liable to the council, and whoever says, 'You fool!' shall be liable to the hell of fire. 23 So if you are offering your gift at the altar, and there remember that your brother has something against you,

Judging

Matthew 5:21-26

Comment

Jesus' audience was a mixture of every level of society. The crowd included Pharisees, scribes, fishermen, tax collectors, Roman soldiers, and perhaps an equal number of women and children. Jesus began this part of his address laying out the progression of the small events that led to major mayhem. It included anger,

24 leave your gift there before the altar and go; first be reconciled to your brother, and then come and offer your gift. 25 Make friends quickly with your accuser, while you are going with him to court, lest your accuser hand you over to the judge, and the judge to the guard, and you be put in prison; 26 truly, I say to you, you will never get out till you have paid the last penny.

insult, and culminated with the urge to kill.

When Jesus announced, "I say to you," it was more than a simple off the cuff comment. He boldly said he had come to write a new chapter in their relationship to God and with other people.

Jesus included another amazing statement, saying if you were at the altar with your gift and you remembered you had something against a brother leave your gift and go find your brother. If possible be reconciled and then return to offer your gift of God. Jesus warned bringing a heart filled with malice and anger negates the gift to God. Reconciliation is worth more than any gift we may choose to bring.

Jesus strongly urged them to settle their grievances and not to resort to the court. This was another way of saying the courts are not your friend. Stay away from them as much as you can.

Judge what is right

Luke 12:57-59
57 "And why do you not judge for

Judge what is right

Luke 12:57-59

yourselves what is right? 58 As you go with your accuser before the magistrate, make an effort to settle with him on the way, lest he drag you to the judge, and the judge hand you over to the officer, and the officer put you in prison. 59 I tell you, you will never get out till you have paid the very last copper."

Comment

In these verses Jesus gives us a glimpse of the reality of life in his day. There were conflicts among people that needed resolution. There were lawsuits that had to be resolved. Jesus says, "Use your own common sense and try to settle the dispute before the other party takes you before the judge." He knew those at the bottom end of the social scale were not going to receive mercy at the hands of the judge. Judicial decrees would often bring greater hardship than settling the dispute out of court.

Adultery

Matthew 5:27-30

27 "You have heard that it was said, 'You shall not commit adultery.' 28 But I say to you that every one who looks at a woman lustfully has already committed adultery with her in his heart. 29 If your right eye causes you to sin, pluck it out and throw it away; it is better that you lose one of your members than that your whole body be thrown into hell. 30 And if your right hand causes you to sin, cut it off and throw

Adultery

Matthew 5:27-30

Comment

Here is another, "I say to you," comment.

Everyone in Jesus' audience had been taught adultery was a violation of one of the Ten Commandments. Jesus expands the scope of the commandment to include lust of the heart.

it away; it is better that you lose one of your members than that your whole body go into hell.	Jesus had no qualms about making radical statements, admonishing one to pluck out their eye and throw it away. His point was it would be better to be without sight than to allow sight to lead one into sin.

When Jesus spoke of the hand he was speaking directly to the thief of every category.

As awful as it sounds to be crippled by the loss of eye or limb, Jesus contended it would be better to have these appendages lost than to be thrown into the fires of hell because of them. |
| ### *Whoever divorces his wife*

Matthew 5:31-32
31 "It was also said, 'Whoever divorces his wife, let him give her a certificate of divorce.' 32 But I say to you that every one who divorces his wife, except on the ground of unchastity, makes her an adulteress; and whoever marries a divorced woman commits adultery. | ### *Whoever divorces his wife*

Matthew 5:31-32

Comment

This "I say to you" statement is specifically on divorce.

The enormity of this institution in our society requires a more lengthy discussion of divorce.

The certificate of divorce, referred to, was given by Moses allowing the husband to divorce or dismiss his wife. |

	1 "When a man takes a wife and marries her, if then she finds no favor in his eyes because he has found some indecency in her, and he writes her a bill of divorce and puts it in her hand and sends her out of his house, and she departs out of his house, Deuteronomy 24:1

There was no concept of Equal Rights

There is no "equal rights" provision in the statement. This is evidence of a male dominant society. In this mindset, a woman is little more than a piece of chattel mortgage. Jesus challenges this understanding, at its very core. Jesus was a champion of "equality of rights." We must remember marriages were arranged during this period of history. Divorce is an ageless malady that has afflicted humanity.

3 And Pharisees came up to him and tested him by asking, "Is it lawful to divorce one's wife for any cause?" 4 He answered, "Have you not read that he who made them from the beginning made them male and female, 5 and said, 'For this reason a man shall leave his father and mother and be joined to his wife, and the two shall become one flesh'? 6 So they are no longer two but one flesh. What therefore God has joined together, let not man put asunder." 7 They said to him, "Why then did Moses command one to give a certificate of divorce, and to put her away?" 8 He said to them, "For your hardness of heart Moses allowed you to divorce your wives, but from the beginning it was not so. 9 And I say to you: whoever divorces his wife, except for unchastity, and marries another, commits adultery." 10 The disciples said to him, "If such is the case of a man with his wife, it is not expedient to marry." 11 But he said to them, "Not all men can receive this saying, but only those to whom it is given. 12 For there are eunuchs who have been so from birth, and there are eunuchs who have been made eunuchs by men, and there are eunuchs who have made themselves eunuchs for the sake of the kingdom of heaven. He who is able to receive this, let him receive it." Matthew 19:3-12 and Mark 10:2-12

Divorce was a hot button issue in Jesus' day. His adversaries attempted to use it to disadvantage him. They believed they had confronted Jesus with a no-win question. No matter what he said it would offend at least half of the people listening to him.

They were a persistent lot, and never gave up trying to ensnare Jesus.

3 The scribes and the Pharisees brought a woman who had been caught in adultery, and placing her in the midst 4 they said to him, "Teacher, this woman has been caught in the act of adultery. 5 Now in the law Moses commanded us to stone such. What do you say about her?" 6 This they said to test him, that they might have some charge to bring against him. Jesus bent down and wrote with his finger on the ground. 7 And as they continued to ask him, he stood up and said to them, "Let him who is without sin among you be the first to throw a stone at her." 8 And once more he bent down and wrote with his finger on the ground. 9 But when they heard it, they went away, one by one, beginning with the eldest, and Jesus was left alone with the woman standing before him. 10 Jesus looked up and said to her, "Woman, where are they? Has no one condemned you?" 11 She said, "No one, Lord." And Jesus said, "Neither do I condemn you; go, and do not sin again." John 8:3-11

This incident may be summed up by saying Jesus made the point that Divorce and Adultery were the two most explosive issues of that day or any other. It left all the participants realizing that Adultery and Divorce were no more condemnable than any other sin of major consequence. God's mercy and forgiveness availed here too.

I came that they may have life, and have it abundantly. John 10:10b

Simple yes or no will do

Matthew 5:33-37

33 "Again you have heard that it was said to the men of old, 'You shall not swear falsely, but shall perform to the Lord what you have sworn.' 34 But I say to you, Do not swear at all, either by heaven, for it is the throne of God, 35 or by the earth, for it is his footstool, or by Jerusalem, for it is the city of the great King. 36 And do not swear by your head, for you cannot make one hair white or black. 37 Let what you say be simply 'Yes' or 'No'; anything more than this comes from evil.

Simple yes or no will do

Matthew 5:33-37

Comment

This is another "I say to you" passage.

Here is another glimpse of Jesus expanding the law, moving from the letter of the law to the deeper spirit of the law.

He began by saying, "You have heard," midway through the statement he said, "I say to you," though he had been impacted by the pharisaic interpretation of the law he now proclaims his own dogma. He admonished his hearers to speak plainly, concisely, not elaborately saying, "let your yes be yes and your no be no."

Jesus' prohibition to swearing an oath was also a statement of treason to the dictators of Rome. The Emperor demanded all subjects to swear allegiance to Rome, saying "Caesar is Lord." When Jesus said do not swear he defied Roman authority. In the early Christian church refusing to say, "Caesar is Lord," caused many

Christians to be put to death. Their allegiance was to Jesus and they affirmed it saying, "Jesus is Lord!"

An eye for an eye

Matthew 5:38-42

Comment

This is another "I say to you" statement.

These verses contained perhaps the most radical and difficult teachings Jesus ever uttered. Again we hear him moving from the old dogma to the new. "You have heard but I say to you." The old dogma called for an eye for an eye, Jesus said do not resist one who is evil. If you're struck on one cheek offer the other also, if you're sued for your overcoat, give him your sweater as well.

A Roman soldier had the legal right to compel anyone to carry his burden for one-mile, Jesus said carry it two miles. Our prime example of this comes when Simon of Cyrene is compelled to carry the cross of Jesus.

An eye for an eye

Matthew 5:38-42

38 "You have heard that it was said, 'An eye for an eye and a tooth for a tooth.' 39 But I say to you, Do not resist one who is evil. But if any one strikes you on the right cheek, turn to him the other also; 40 and if any one would sue you and take your coat, let him have your cloak as well; 41 and if any one forces you to go one mile, go with him two miles. 42 Give to him who begs from you, and do not refuse him who would borrow from you.

Love your enemies

**Matthew 5:43-48;
Luke 6:27-31**

Matthew 5:43-48
43 "You have heard that it was said, 'You shall love your neighbor and hate your enemy.' 44 But I say to you, Love your enemies and pray for those who persecute you, 45 so that you may be sons of your Father who is in heaven; for he makes his sun rise on the evil and on the good, and sends rain on the just and on the unjust. 46 For if you love those who love you, what reward have you? Do not even the tax collectors do the same? 47 And if you salute only your brethren, what more are you doing than others? Do not even the Gentiles do the same? 48 You, therefore, must be perfect, as your heavenly Father is perfect.

Luke 6:27-31
27 "But I say to you that hear, Love your enemies, do good to those who hate you, 28 bless those who curse you, pray for those who abuse you. 29 To him who strikes you on the cheek, offer the other also; and from him who takes away your coat do not withhold even your shirt.

Love your enemies

**Matthew 5:43-48;
Luke 6:27-31**

Comment

This is another "I say to you" statement.

This time he said they were to love their enemies and pray for those who persecuted and made their lives miserable. He pointed out God sends His rain upon the good and the bad, making clear God's love is equally available for all of His creation. It is creation's responsibility to respond to the love of God.

Jesus made this audacious statement, "You are to be perfect," as His Heavenly Father is perfect. This means they were to fulfill who they were to be according to God's will. An illustration would be a hammer is used for driving nails, not to saw wood. A hammer is perfect when used for the job it was designed to accomplish. Human beings are perfect in God's eyes when they revere Him, serve Him, and love Him.

Jesus opposed the instruments of violence.

30 Give to every one who begs from you; and of him who takes away your goods do not ask them again. 31 And as you wish that men would do to you, do so to them.

Luke captures part of Jesus' "I say to you," concept restating the same admonitions found in Matthew. However, he adds what is known as the Golden Rule, "Do unto others as you would have them do unto you."

In modern times we have corrupted this concept. Frequently we hear this paraphrase, "Those who have the gold make the rules." While this is a truism it is alien to the spirit of Jesus.

Even sinners love those who love them

Luke 6:32-36

32 "If you love those who love you, what credit is that to you? For even sinners love those who love them. 33 And if you do good to those who do good to you, what credit is that to you? For even sinners do the same. 34 And if you lend to those from whom you hope to receive, what credit is that to you? Even sinners lend to sinners, to receive as much again. 35 But love your enemies, and do good, and lend, expecting nothing in return; and your reward will be great, and you will be sons of the Most High; for he

Even sinners love those who love them

Luke 6:32-36

Comment

The main lesson is to unite, not separate into classes of clean, unclean, worthy, unworthy, respectable, and unrespectable. The heavenly reign undercuts the insatiable appetite for material possession and social class. Christians however, are not excluded from the duty of all human beings to be just in all their interactions. The Kingdom's reign goes far beyond earthly conventions and is kind to the ungrateful and the selfish. 36 Be merciful, even as your Father is merciful.

treats the lowest outcast as if he were Jesus.

Practicing your piety

Matthew 6:1

1 "Beware of practicing your piety before men in order to be seen by them; for then you will have no reward from your Father who is in heaven.

Practicing your piety

Matthew 6:1

Comment

Piety is a good word. It connotes positive religious beliefs and practices. Even good things can become perverted when done for the wrong reasons. In this instance Jesus said if you do good deeds for the purpose of attracting attention and praise from others the value of your works is meaningless to God.

When you give alms

Matthew 6:2-4

2 "Thus, when you give alms, sound no trumpet before you, as the hypocrites do in the synagogues and in the streets, that they may be praised by men. Truly, I say to you, they have received their reward. 3 But when you give alms, do not let your left hand know what your right hand is doing, 4 so that your alms may be in secret; and your Father who sees in secret will reward you.

When you give alms

Matthew 6:2-4

Comment

Giving alms was an act of generosity. All who gave to the poor in the highest sense of alms gained stature in the Jewish community. It was a gift that came from the heart not seeking recognition. Jesus counseled against making an ostentatious show of giving. Some persons were notorious for their crass displays accompanying alms giving. One who wished to be seen by the crowd would hire a trumpeter to blast away to call attention to their dropping coins into the treasury or into the hands of a beggar.

Jesus said when you give, give liberally do not give with the thought of what other people will think. In essence, let your right hand be independent of your left. When you give a free will offering do not count the amount before you give it away.

And when you pray

Matthew 6:5-6

5 "And when you pray, you must not be like the hypocrites; for they love to stand and pray in the synagogues and at the street corners, that they may be seen by men. Truly, I say to you, they have received their reward. 6 But when you pray, go into your room and shut the door and pray to your Father who is in secret; and your Father who sees in secret will reward you.

And when you pray

Matthew 6:5-6

Comment

Jesus did many things that offended the religious hierarchy. Chief among them was his opposition to formalism of worship. He believed fervently in prayer and practiced it constantly. He had harsh words for those who abused the privilege of prayer. He called them pretenders, actors on the stage of life knowing the formalities of prayer but not the spirit.

God knows before you pray

**Matthew 6:7-8;
Luke 18:9-14**

Matthew 6:7-8

7 "And in praying do not heap up empty phrases as the Gentiles do; for they think that they will be heard for their many words. 8 Do not be like them, for your Father knows what you need before you ask him.

Luke 18:9-14

9 He also told this parable to some who trusted in themselves that they were righteous and despised others: 10 "Two men went up into the temple to pray, one a Pharisee and the other a tax collector. 11 The Pharisee stood and prayed thus with himself, 'God, I thank thee that I am not like other men, extortioners, unjust, adulterers, or even like this tax collector. 12 I fast twice a week, I give tithes of all that I get.' 13 But the tax collector, standing far off, would not even lift up his eyes to heaven, but beat his breast, saying, 'God, be merciful to me a sinner!' 14 I tell you, this man went down to his house justified rather than the other; for every one who exalts himself will be humbled, but he who humbles himself will be exalted."

God knows before you pray

**Matthew 6:7-8;
Luke 18:9-14**

Comment

Empty phrases may be illustrated as repeating things over and over. To offer a string of words or sounds that convey no sensible meaning becomes boring to the hearer.

Luke expresses his opinion in the introduction of the parable saying, "Jesus told this parable to some who trusted in themselves thinking they were righteous and despised others." The parable describes two men who went up to pray, one a Pharisee the other a sinner.

The Pharisee was illustrative of the religious community. The tax collector represented everyone else. The Pharisee gave thanks to God that he was not like other men. He then recited his list of those he was glad he is not like. He continued by telling God, as though God did not see or know, about his fasting and tithing but says nothing about his attitude.

| | The second man was quite different. He was keenly aware of his many flaws and sins. He did not enumerate them nor did he have any proud moments of which he could boast. He simply hung his head and said, "Oh God be merciful to me a sinner." |

The Lord's Prayer

**Matthew 6:9-13;
Luke 11:1-4**

Matthew 6:9-13	**Comment**
9 Pray then like this: Our Father who art in heaven, Hallowed be thy name. 10 Thy kingdom come. Thy will be done, On earth as it is in heaven. 11 Give us this day our daily bread; 12 And forgive us our debts, As we also have forgiven our debtors; 13 And lead us not into temptation, But deliver us from evil.	This is known as the Lord's Prayer and contains five petitions.

1) Acknowledges the holiness of God.

2) Seeks the full existence of God's rule on earth comparable to His rule in heaven.

3) Recognizes the human need for food. Not a storehouse of food but for food on a daily basis. |
| **Luke 11:1-4**
1 He was praying in a certain place, and when he ceased, one of his disciples said to him, "Lord, teach us to pray, as John taught his disciples." 2 And he | 4) Human beings are worthy of forgiveness only after they forgive others who have wronged them. |

said to them, "When you pray, say: "Father, hallowed be thy name. Thy kingdom come. 3 Give us each day our daily bread; 4 and forgive us our sins, for we ourselves forgive every one who is indebted to us; and lead us not into temptation."

5) Acknowledges the ever present entrapment of temptation. And requests deliverance from the influence of all evil.

The jeopardy of forgiveness

Matthew 6:14-15
14 For if you forgive men their trespasses, your heavenly Father also will forgive you; 15 but if you do not forgive men their trespasses, neither will your Father forgive your trespasses.

The jeopardy of forgiveness

Matthew 6:14-15

Comment

Jesus elaborates on the petitions he has just given. He gives special emphasis to the danger of being unwilling to forgive others. To do so is to prohibit God from forgiving the petitioner.

Do not make a bad face While fasting

Matthew 6:16-18
16 "And when you fast, do not look dismal, like the hypocrites, for they disfigure their faces that their fasting may be seen by men. Truly, I say to you, they have received their reward. 17 But when you fast, anoint your head and wash your face, 18 that

Do not make a bad face While fasting

Matthew 6:16-18

Comment

Some who fasted called attention to themselves by trying to look as pitiful as possible. When others commented on how brave and pious they were

your fasting may not be seen by men but by your Father who is in secret; and your Father who sees in secret will reward you.

in their suffering, they received their instant gratification.

The person who fasted as a religious exercise abstained from food and drink: either entirely, if the fast lasted but a single day, or from customary and choice nourishment, if it continued several days.

Treasure in heaven

**Matthew 6:19-21;
Luke 12:32-34**

Treasure in heaven

**Matthew 6:19-21;
Luke 12:32-34**

Matthew 6:19-21
19 "Do not lay up for yourselves treasures on earth, where moth and rust consume and where thieves break in and steal, 20 but lay up for yourselves treasures in heaven, where neither moth nor rust consumes and where thieves do not break in and steal. 21 For where your treasure is, there will your heart be also.

Luke 12:32-34
32 "Fear not, little flock, for it is your Father's good pleasure to give you the kingdom. 33 Sell your possessions, and give alms; provide yourselves with purses that do not grow old, with a treasure in the heavens

Comment

The places where goods and precious things were collected and stored could be a casket, coffer, or other receptacle. Wherever things were stored for safe keeping was a treasury. The inherent danger was thieves could dig through mud walls and steal the goods. If thieves were not the danger, the lowly moth could feast on the woolen garments. If, on the other hand, the goods were stored in heaven no thief could steal or destroy them.

This is a continuation of the teaching on the treasure in

that does not fail, where no thief approaches and no moth destroys. 34 For where your treasure is, there will your heart be also.

heaven. Matthew's motivation for transferring one's treasure was fear. Luke espouses a motivation of extravagant sharing.

Jesus called for a radical commitment to total dependence on God. He said sell everything you have and give it away as a charitable gift to others. Those willing to sacrifice at this level will have purses that will not grow old.

The eye is the lamp of the body

Matthew 6:22-23

22 "The eye is the lamp of the body. So, if your eye is sound, your whole body will be full of light; 23 but if your eye is not sound, your whole body will be full of darkness. If then the light in you is darkness, how great is the darkness!

The eye is the lamp of the body

Matthew 6:22-23

Comment

Jesus said one's personal outlook is a reflection of their inner being. One who looks at the world and people around them seeing only the bad and spiteful represents what they harbor in their soul. On the other hand, those who see the same people with the same conditions and see opportunity for good is a reflection of what they harbor in their soul.

Two bosses are one too many	*Two bosses are one too many*
Matthew 6:24 24 "No one can serve two masters; for either he will hate the one and love the other, or he will be devoted to the one and despise the other. You cannot serve God and mammon.	**Matthew 6:24** **Comment** It is a reality one cannot serve two masters when they are diverse and lead in different directions. One will be loved the other will be despised. That is the way it is with commitment, you cannot serve God while seeking gain for yourself. Seeking God results in storing up treasure in heaven, seeking wealth, fame and power, stores up nothing in heaven.
Do not be anxious **Matthew 6:25-33;** **Luke 12:22-31**	*Do not be anxious* **Matthew 6:25-33;** **Luke 12:22-31**
Matthew 6:25-33 25 "Therefore I tell you, do not be anxious about your life, what you shall eat or what you shall drink, nor about your body, what you shall put on. Is not life more than food, and the body more than clothing? 26 Look at the birds of the air: they neither sow nor reap nor gather into barns, and yet your heavenly Father 31 Therefore do not be anxious,	**Comment** Indeed this is another hard teaching of Jesus. He points out the obvious, life is more than eating or the clothes we wear. God takes care of the animal kingdom so they have no worry about clothing and they can find their food in abundance in the places God has provided. Jesus continued telling the people

saying, 'What shall we eat?' or 'What shall we drink?' or 'What shall we wear?' 32 For the feeds them. Are you not of more value than they? 27 And which of you by being anxious can add one cubit to his span of life? 28 And why are you anxious about clothing? Consider the lilies of the field, how they grow; they neither toil nor spin; 29 yet I tell you, even Solomon in all his glory was not arrayed like one of these. 30 But if God so clothes the grass of the field, which today is alive and tomorrow is thrown into the oven, will he not much more clothe you, O men of little faith? Gentiles seek all these things; and your heavenly Father knows that you need them all. 33 But seek first his kingdom and his righteousness, and all these things shall be yours as well.

Luke 12:22-31

22 And he said to his disciples, "Therefore I tell you, do not be anxious about your life, what you shall eat, nor about your body, what you shall put on. 23 For life is more than food, and the body more than clothing. 24 Consider the ravens: they neither sow nor reap, they have neither storehouse nor barn, and yet God feeds them. Of how much more

worrying will not increase their life; in fact it will diminish and shorten their lives.

Again Jesus pointed to the flowers of the field and praised their beauty that exceeds the beauty of Solomon in his greatest glory.

Jesus summed up this teaching saying, "Understand you are more than what you eat, drink and wear." All the nations of the world seek ample food and good garments. God knows we need food, shelter and clothing, and when we allow His governance to rule our lives all of these things are provided.

value are you than the birds! 25 And which of you by being anxious can add a cubit to his span of life? 26 If then you are not able to do as small a thing as that, why are you anxious about the rest? 27 Consider the lilies, how they grow; they neither toil nor spin; yet I tell you, even Solomon in all his glory was not arrayed like one of these. 28 But if God so clothes the grass which is alive in the field today and tomorrow is thrown into the oven, how much more will he clothe you, O men of little faith! 29 And do not seek what you are to eat and what you are to drink, nor be of anxious mind. 30 For all the nations of the world seek these things; and your Father knows that you need them. 31 Instead, seek his kingdom, and these things shall be yours as well.

Do not be anxious about tomorrow

Matthew 6:34
34 "Therefore do not be anxious about tomorrow, for tomorrow will be anxious for itself. Let the day's own trouble be sufficient for the day.

Do not be anxious About tomorrow

Matthew 6:34

Comment

Plainly stated, Jesus recognized each day brought its own measure of challenges and fears. We debilitate ourselves with fears of the future that in all probability will never become reality.

Consider the things that you worry about. Worry will not make one live longer. When it comes to clothes most of us cannot find what we want to wear because our closets are so full.

The word *kingdom* means rule. It is the law, it is the standard, therefore seek to know and be obedient to God, said Jesus.

Judging

**Matthew 7:1-5;
Luke 6:41-42;
Luke 6:37-38**

Matthew 7:1-5

1 "Judge not, that you be not judged. 2 For with the judgment you pronounce you will be judged, and the measure you give will be the measure you get. 3 Why do you see the speck that is in your brother's eye, but do not notice the log that is in your own eye? 4 Or how can you say to your brother, 'Let me take the speck out of ur eye,' when there is the log in your own eye? 5 You hypocrite, first take the log out of your own eye, and then you will see clearly to take the speck out of your brother's eye.

Judging

**Matthew 7:1-5;
Luke 6:41-42;
Luke 6:37-38**

Comment

In the human realm there is a graphic difference between judgments and decisions. Decisions include staying in bed or getting out, what to eat, what to wear and a myriad of other such choices.

Judgment means making a determination that affects others for good or bad. Jesus gave a mixture of judgments and decisions to illustrate the point of earthly and heavenly situations. He spoke of judging

Luke 6:41-42
41 Why do you see the speck that is in your brother's eye, but do not notice the log that is in your own eye? 42 Or how can you say to your brother, 'Brother, let me take out the speck that is in your eye,' when you yourself do not see the log that is in your own eye? You hypocrite, first take the log out of your own eye, and then you will see clearly to take out the speck that is in your brother's eye.

Luke 6:37-38
37 "Judge not, and you will not be judged; condemn not, and you will not be condemned; forgive, and you will be forgiven; 38 give, and it will be given to you; good measure, pressed down, shaken together, running over, will be put into your lap. For the measure you give will be the measure you get back."

versus not judging, giving or receiving, criticism and self-examination, do not condemn and you will not be condemned, forgive and you will be forgiven, and what goes around comes around. These are among the many give and takes that populate every day.

All three of these passages carry the same meaning. Here is a beautiful example of the humor of Jesus, imagine the absurd comparison of the speck and the log. Jesus used absurd humor to disclose universal problems. Most humans are alert to see the fault of someone else, while they are blind to their own. Jesus said you can only see clearly, when you have removed the obstacle from your vision.

Don't give dogs holy things

Matthew 7:6
6 "Do not give dogs what is holy; and do not throw your pearls before swine, lest they trample them under foot and turn to attack you.

Don't give dogs holy things

Matthew 7:6

Comment

To understand this passage we must first look individually at the four primary words.

"Holy" includes everything pertaining to God.

	"Dogs" signifies a person of impure mind, or impudence.
	"Pearl" is a proverbial word for something of great value.
	"Swine" this word does not appear in the O.T. but as used here implies that which is lowly or worthless.

People who reject God and His Son Jesus

Unfortunately, there are people who reject God and His Son Jesus. To these individuals Jesus spoke bluntly, "You will have as much success, engaging a dog in conversation about God as you will the person who rejects God. Your time and your effort will be wasted as significantly as if you took a string of pearls and threw them into the hog lot."

Ask, seek, knock, and receive	*Ask, seek, knock, and receive*
Matthew 7:7-12; Luke 11:5-13	Matthew 7:7-12; Luke 11:5-13
Matthew 7:7-12 7 "Ask, and it will be given you; seek, and you will find; knock, and it will be opened to you. 8 For every one who asks receives, and he who seeks finds, and to him who knocks it will be opened. 9 Or what man of you, if his son asks him for bread, will give him a stone? 10 Or if he asks for a fish, will give him	**Comment** Jesus promised those who ask, seek, knock would receive what they yearn for. The faithful loving parent will give to their child those things which are good for them, not those that will hurt them. We are God's children and how much more will He do for us!

a serpent? 11 If you then, who are evil, know how to give good gifts to your children, how much more will your Father who is in heaven give good things to those who ask him! 12 So whatever you wish that men would do to you, do so to them; for this is the law and the prophets.

Luke 11:5-13

5 And he said to them, "Which of you who has a friend will go to him at midnight and say to him, 'Friend, lend me three loaves; 6 for a friend of mine has arrived on a journey, and I have nothing to set before him'; 7 and he will answer from within, 'Do not bother me; the door is now shut, and my children are with me in bed; I cannot get up and give you anything'? 8 I tell you, though he will not get up and give him anything because he is his friend, yet because of his importunity he will rise and give him whatever he needs. 9 And I tell you, Ask, and it will be given you; seek, and you will find; knock, and it will be opened to you. 10 For every one who asks receives, and he who seeks finds, and to him who knocks it will be opened. 11 What father among you, if his son asks for a fish, will instead of a fish give him a serpent; 12 or if

Verse nine is an allusion back to the temptations of Satan, while Jesus was in the wilderness.

The closing verse is better known to us as the Golden rule.

he asks for an egg, will give him a scorpion? 13 If you then, who are evil, know how to give good gifts to your children, how much more will the heavenly Father give the Holy Spirit to those who ask him!"

The narrow gate

Matthew 7:13-14

13 "Enter by the narrow gate; for the gate is wide and the way is easy, that leads to destruction, and those who enter by it are many. 14 For the gate is narrow and the way is hard, that leads to life, and those who find it are few.

The narrow gate

Matthew 7:13-14

Comment

Jesus used profound contrast speaking of the narrow gate that leads to the path of life that is good, honorable, and demanding. The good life is experienced by those who live with integrity, honor, and concern for others. By way of contrast he spoke of the wide gate that was easy to go through, and leads to the problematic life.

Beware of false prophets

Matthew 7:15-20

15 "Beware of false prophets, who come to you in sheep's clothing but inwardly are ravenous wolves. 16 You will know them by their fruits. Are grapes gathered from thorns, or

Beware of false prophets

Matthew 7:15-20

Comment

False prophets in every age look good and sound good, but are like shallow streams making a

figs from thistles? ^{17} So, every sound tree bears good fruit, but the bad tree bears evil fruit. ^{18} A sound tree cannot bear evil fruit, nor can a bad tree bear good fruit. ^{19} Every tree that does not bear good fruit is cut down and thrown into the fire. ^{20} Thus you will know them by their fruits.

lot of noise unlike deep water that runs quietly. False prophets disguise themselves to appear trustworthy. Unfortunately, they are more like the proverbial fox who was appointed guard of the henhouse. Once more Jesus employed contrast, as he spoke of good and bad fruit.

Not every one will enter the kingdom of heaven

Not every one will enter the kingdom of heaven

Matthew 7:21-23

^{21} "Not every one who says to me, 'Lord, Lord,' shall enter the kingdom of heaven, but he who does the will of my Father who is in heaven. ^{22} On that day many will say to me, 'Lord, Lord, did we not prophesy in your name, and cast out demons in your name, and do many mighty works in your name?' ^{23} And then will I declare to them, 'I never knew you; depart from me, you evildoers.'

Matthew 7:21-23

Comment

What did Jesus mean when he said "Lord, Lord?" In the time of Jesus this was a powerful affirmation. The affirmation itself has multiple meanings, but there is one over arching definition uniting them. It means one who has control, as a master over a slave, or a ruler over a kingdom.

When Jesus referred to the "Kingdom of heaven" or the "Kingdom of God" he did not have in mind a geographical location but the over arching authority and power of God to make the rules and to enforce them. For Jesus the 'Kingdom

	of God' or the "Kingdom of Heaven" was here and now. You became a member of the "Kingdom" by accepting God as the only "Lord!"
	Obedience to the Heavenly Father is the criteria for entering the Kingdom of God. No matter how lengthy the list of good works may be they alone are not sufficient to achieve entrance into the Kingdom of Heaven.

"Lord" had a very special meaning

As Jesus used the term, "Lord" it had two primary meanings. First, the Jewish community used the term "Lord" in a very specific way referring to God. After Jesus' resurrection and ascension the term was equally applied to him as "Jesus Christ is Lord."

Second, the word was exceptionally well known throughout all of the Mediterranean area proclaiming, "Caesar is Lord." This affirmation was required of all subjects of the empire who wished to stay out of trouble with the Roman legal system. The Lord of the Roman Empire was the Emperor.

House built upon the rock

**Matthew 7:24-27;
Luke 6:46-49**

Matthew 7:24-27

24 "Every one then who hears these words of mine and does them will be like a wise man who built his house upon the rock; 25 and the rain fell, and the floods came, and the winds blew and beat upon that house, but it did not fall, because it had been founded on the rock. 26 And every one who hears these words of mine and does not do them will be like a foolish man who built his house upon the sand; 27 and the rain fell, and the floods came, and the winds blew and beat against that house, and it fell; and great was the fall of it."

Luke 6:46-49

46 "Why do you call me 'Lord, Lord,' and not do what I tell you? 47 Every one who comes to me and hears my words and does them, I will show you what he is like: 48 he is like a man building a house, who dug deep, and laid the foundation upon rock; and when a flood arose, the stream broke against that house, and could not shake it, because it had

House built upon the rock

**Matthew 7:24-27;
Luke 6:46-49**

Comment

Again Jesus drew a contrast between the wise and foolish builders. In my home state of Tennessee, mighty oak trees are renowned for their beauty and strength, but can in their mature years rot at the core. An ever present possibility of the future of the mighty oak is that it may look strong and stable, but it may be weak and vulnerable.

Those listening to Jesus understood immediately the contrast of building on sand, as opposed to building on rock. In Judea there is a sharp contrast between rock and sand. In the dry regions rain is sparse, but when it comes it comes in torrents. The home built on the rock requires more work, labor, and talent. The home built on sand is easy and quick. The difference becomes terribly conspicuous when the rains fall, and only one home remains.

been well built. ⁴⁹ But he who hears and does not do them is like a man who built a house on the ground without a foundation; against which the stream broke, and immediately it fell, and the ruin of that house was great."	
Jesus spoke with Authority	***Jesus spoke with Authority***
Matthew 7:28-29 ²⁸ And when Jesus finished these sayings, the crowds were astonished at his teaching, ²⁹ for he taught them as one who had authority, and not as their scribes.	**Matthew 7:28-29** **Comment** Jesus spoke with authority, because he was grounded in his relationship with God. The scribes were good at their craft, speaking "of" God and His will but never speaking from the position of a personal relationship.

Chapter 13

Following the Sermon on the Mount, Jesus learned that John the Baptist was dead.

<u>*Execution of John*</u>

**Mark 6:21-29;
Matthew 14:6-12**

Mark 6:21-29
21 But an opportunity came when Herod on his birthday gave a banquet for his courtiers and officers and the leading men of Galilee. 22 For when Hero'di-as' daughter came in and danced, she pleased Herod and his guests; and the king said to the girl, "Ask me for whatever you wish, and I will grant it." 23 And he vowed to her, "Whatever you ask me, I will give you, even half of my kingdom." 24 And she went out, and said to her mother, "What shall I ask?" And she said, "The head of John the baptizer." 25 And she came in immediately with haste to the king, and asked, saying, "I want you to give me at once the head of John the Baptist on a platter." 26 And the <u>king</u> was exceedingly

Following the Sermon on the Mount, Jesus learned that John the Baptist was dead.

<u>*Execution of John*</u>

**Mark 6:21-29;
Matthew 14:6-12**

Comment

The birthday party and death of John the Baptist are not included by Luke and John.

It was Herod Antipas' birthday and he decided to give himself a royal banquet. Everybody who was anybody was invited; the men of influence, the nobles, City Chiefs, military officers at the rank of commander or higher, and of course their Ladies fair.

The banquet was sumptuous with enormous quantities of food and drink to be consumed. The feature entertainment that night was Herod Antipas' beautiful step-daughter. At the appropriate time, after everyone

sorry; but because of his oaths and his guests he did not want to break his word to her. ²⁷ And immediately the king sent a soldier of the guard and gave orders to bring his head. He went and beheaded him in the prison, ²⁸ and brought his head on a platter, and gave it to the girl; and the girl gave it to her mother. ²⁹ When his disciples heard of it, they came and took his body, and laid it in a tomb.

Matthew 14:6-12
⁶ But when Herod's birthday came, the daughter of Hero'dias danced before the company, and pleased Herod, ⁷ so that he promised with an oath to give her whatever she might ask. ⁸ Prompted by her mother, she said, "Give me the head of John the Baptist here on a platter." ⁹ And the king was sorry; but because of his oaths and his guests he commanded it to be given; ¹⁰ he sent and had John beheaded in the prison, ¹¹ and his head was brought on a platter and given to the girl, and she brought it to her mother. ¹² And his disciples came and took the body and buried it; and they went and told Jesus.

had plenty to drink, she entered the room and performed an exotic dance. The aroused, drunken Antipas let his mouth out run his wit. He foolishly promised to give her up to half of his kingdom for such a beautiful performance. The girl was stunned. What should she ask for? Mom would know!

Mark indicates Herodias was not present for the dance or the foolish reward offered by Antipas. The girl ran to her mother for advice. Herodias was thrilled, she had never dreamed of such an unexpected turn of events. Now she would settle the score with John the Baptist once and for all and on her terms!

In a short time the girl returned. Antipas waited, his foggy mind whirling at the possibilities, what would she ask for? Antipas never sobered more quickly in all his life. Her words stunned him, "I want the head of John the Baptist on a platter!" This was the most unlikely request Antipas could possibly have imagined. What could he do? He was afraid to kill John but it was more important to him to fulfill his pledge given in the presence of his guests. His pride was at stake!

Antipas was exceedingly sorry, but not sorry enough to spare John's life. So he sent his guards to carry out the deed. When the guard returned, he brought John's head on a platter. The party was over! This was an ending no one would have scripted.

When John's disciples learned of his execution, they took his body and buried him. Then they went to tell Jesus what had happened.

Jesus' fame is spreading

**Mark 6:14-16;
Matthew 14:1-2;
Luke 9:7-9**

Mark 6:14-16
14 King Herod heard of it; for Jesus' name had become known. Some said, "John the baptizer has been raised from the dead; that is why these powers are at work in him." 15 But others said, "It is Eli'jah." And others said, "It is a prophet, like one of the prophets of old." 16 But when Herod heard of it he said, "John, whom I beheaded, has been raised."

Matthew 14:1-2
1 At that time Herod the tetrarch

Jesus' fame is spreading

**Mark 6:14-16;
Matthew 14:1-2;
Luke 9:7-9**

Comment

Mark refers to Antipas as "King Herod," it is quite true he wanted to be a king but Rome never bestowed the title upon him. Matthew and Luke refer to him by his correct title "Tetrarch." (cf. in chapter 4)

The fame of Jesus continued to spread in spite of his attempts at anonymity. The crowds had grown larger and larger. Antipas could see this as he gazed from

heard about the fame of Jesus; 2 and he said to his servants, "This is John the Baptist, he has been raised from the dead; that is why these powers are at work in him."

Luke 9:7-9
7 Now Herod the tetrarch heard of all that was done, and he was perplexed, because it was said by some that John had been raised from the dead, 8 by some that Eli'jah had appeared, and by others that one of the old prophets had risen. 9 Herod said, "John I beheaded; but who is this about whom I hear such things?" And he sought to see him.

his palace across the Sea of Galilee. He could clearly see the crowds gathering on the far side. To determine just who these people were Antipas had ordered Scribes, Pharisees, and Herodians to mix among the crowds and report to him everything that was said and who said it.

With the death of John and the emergence of Jesus many people believed John the Baptist had been raised from the dead. Others believed the power of John had been transferred to this man called Jesus the Nazarene. Still others contended it was Elijah, while some believed it must have been one of the prophets of old.

Luke records a different variation of this story. Antipas knew John had been executed because he had ordered it. What Antipas did not know was the identity of this individual emerging on the far side of the lake drawing large crowds. Luke seems to be saying Antipas had heard little or nothing about Jesus until now or he had paid no attention to him previously.

Alabaster Jar and the Woman of the Street

Luke 7:36-50

36 One of the Pharisees asked him to eat with him, and he went into the Pharisee's house, and took his place at table. 37 And behold, a woman of the city, who was a sinner, when she learned that he was at table in the Pharisee's house, brought an alabaster flask of ointment, 38 and standing behind him at his feet, weeping, she began to wet his feet with her tears, and wiped them with the hair of her head, and kissed his feet, and anointed them with the ointment. 39 Now when the Pharisee who had invited him saw it, he said to himself, "If this man were a prophet, he would have known who and what sort of woman this is who is touching him, for she is a sinner." 40 And Jesus answering said to him, "Simon, I have something to say to you." And he answered, "What is it, Teacher?" 41 "A certain creditor had two debtors; one owed five hundred denarii, and the other fifty. 42 When they could not pay, he forgave them both. Now which of them will love him more?" 43 Simon answered, "The one, I suppose, to whom he forgave more." And

Alabaster Jar and the Woman of the Street

Luke 7:36-50

Comment

This is an independent story found only in Luke.

Luke gives a polite introduction for a prostitute, "A woman from the city a sinner," entered during the meal. How did she get in? The custom of the day allowed outsiders to enter another's home if a notable guest was present. It was assumed such an uninvited guest would remain quietly inconspicuous listening to what the famous person had to say. This visitor remained quiet but not inconspicuous!

She made her way to a position behind Jesus who was reclining on a couch with the other guest eating their meal. His feet were extended behind him and the woman began to weep. Her tears fell on Jesus' feet. She then let down her hair to be used as a makeshift towel. The Pharisee could not believe what he was seeing. He said to

he said to him, "You have judged rightly." **44** Then turning toward the woman he said to Simon, "Do you see this woman? I entered your house, you gave me no water for my feet, but she has wet my feet with her tears and wiped them with her hair. **45** You gave me no kiss, but from the time I came in she has not ceased to kiss my feet. **46** You did not anoint my head with oil, but she has anointed my feet with ointment. **47** Therefore I tell you, her sins, which are many, are forgiven, for she loved much; but he who is forgiven little, loves little." **48** And he said to her, "Your sins are forgiven." **49** Then those who were at table with him began to say among themselves, "Who is this, who even forgives sins?" **50** And he said to the woman, "Your faith has saved you; go in peace."

himself, "How could this man be a Prophet and not know the kind of woman who is touching him?" It was unconscionable that she would let her hair down in public! Only one kind of woman would do that!

Then she brought out an alabaster flask of expensive perfume and poured it on Jesus' feet. Jesus fully aware of the Pharisees' horror and disgust asked him, "Simon, which was a common name in Jesus' day, do you see this woman?" How could Simon not see her? She was physically standing in his dining room.

The question implied a deeper level of perception. Jesus knew Simon saw her as a sinner, a person who would never have been invited into his home. Jesus was saying, "Do you see a woman who God loves and cares about?"

Knowing forgiveness was a stranger to Simon's relational skills, Jesus told him a parable. The parable was about two men who owed sums of money to a creditor and when neither could pay the creditor forgave their debt. Simon answered correctly the man with the larger debt was more grateful than the other.

Jesus then called everyone's attention to the breech of "hospitality" committed by the Pharisee. "You did not bother to offer water to wash my feet, no kiss of friendship, no oil for my head," said Jesus. A heavy silence engulfed the room. Jesus continued, "This woman whose sins are many is forgiven!"

The room suddenly came alive with the buzz of audible yet whispered comments. "Who is this man who can forgive sin?" they asked.

Are these the same story?

Some interpreters believe this is the same story found in the Gospels of Mark, Matthew, and John. I believe Luke is referring to a different time and place. The references in, Mark 14:3-4; Matthew 26:7-12 and John 12:1-8 all take place in conjunction with Holy Week and after Jesus raised Lazarus from the dead. In this story Luke tells of a judgmental Simon the *Pharisee* and does not mention Judas in the story as do the others in their stories. The woman of Luke's story is later identified in John 11:2 as Mary the sister of Lazarus.

Women who followed Jesus

Luke 8:1-3

1 Soon afterward he went on through cities and villages, preaching and bringing the good news of the kingdom of God. And the twelve were with him, 2 and also some women who had been healed of evil spirits and infirmities: Mary, called Mag'dalene, from whom seven demons had gone out, 3 and Joan'na, the wife of Chuza, Herod's steward, and Susanna, and many others, who provided for them out of their means.

Women who followed Jesus

Luke 8:1-3

Comment

This is an independent statement of Luke.

Mary Magdalene is mentioned in each of the four gospels. She has been referred to as a prostitute by many commentators. Jesus healed her casting out seven demons. How this demonic condition manifested itself, is unknown.

Luke calls her "Mary Mag'dalene." Did her friends call her Mag'dalene? Mary Magdalene's name identifies her as being "of Magdala," thus distinguishing her from the other women named Mary referred to throughout the New Testament. Magdala (meaning "watchtower") is located on the western shore of the Sea of Galilee about three miles northeast of Tiberias. Josephus refers to Magdala by its Greek name *Tarichaea*, meaning "drying and salting." Archaeological work has revealed the remains of a small synagogue from New Testament times at this location.

It is assumed she was from a wealthy family, because she helped support Jesus and his disciples supposedly from her personal wealth. There is no mention of her being married leaving us to wonder if she was single, or perhaps a widow. Her devotion to Jesus was clearly affirmed by Luke's inclusion of her name in this list.

She not only traveled with Jesus and the Inner-Circle throughout Galilee, she was also present in Jerusalem at his crucifixion and resurrection. She was one of those who followed Jesus because her life had been so remarkably changed by his healing power.

Joan'na the wife of Chuza, Herod's steward is also mentioned in the 24th chapter of Luke's Gospel, as one of the women who went to the sepulcher early Easter Sunday morning. Joanna apparently had been miraculously healed of "evil spirits and infirmities." We have no clue as to the nature of her illness.

Susanna was healed of some type of disease. Obviously she had a source of wealth at

Feeding of the five thousand

**Mark 6:33-44;
Matthew 14:15-21;
Luke 9:11-17;
John 6:1-14**

Mark 6:33-44
33 Now many saw them going, and knew them, and they ran there on foot from all the towns, and got there ahead of them. 34 As he went ashore he saw a great throng, and he had compassion on them, because they were like sheep without a shepherd; and he began to teach them many things. 35 And when it grew late, his disciples came to him and said, "This is a lonely place, and the hour is now late; 36 send them away, to go into the country and villages round about and buy themselves something to eat." 37 But he answered them, "You give them something to eat." And they said to him, "Shall we go and buy two hundred denarii worth of bread, and give it to them to eat?" 38 And he said to them, "How many loaves have

---

her disposal. Whether from gratitude or love she was willing to help support the itinerancy of Jesus and the Inner-Circle.

Feeding of the five thousand

**Mark 6:33-44;
Matthew 14:15-21;
Luke 9:11-17;
John 6:1-14**

Comment

All four evangelists include this story. There are some variations between Mark, Matthew, and Luke, while John offers information not found in the others.

The watchful crowd saw Jesus and the Inner-Circle enter a boat and start for the other side. This is a favorite comment of the Gospel writers and tells us the movement back and forth across the Sea of Galilee was a common occurrence. John refers to it as the Sea of Tiberius, recognizing Herod Antipas claimed ownership of the lake. The Sea of Galilee is only seven miles wide at its widest and thirteen miles long from its

you? Go and see." And when they had found out, they said, "Five, and two fish." ³⁹ Then he commanded them all to sit down by companies upon the green grass. ⁴⁰ So they sat down in groups, by hundreds and by fifties. ⁴¹ And taking the five loaves and the two fish he looked up to heaven, and blessed, and broke the loaves, and gave them to the disciples to set before the people; and he divided the two fish among them all. ⁴² And they all ate and were satisfied. ⁴³ And they took up twelve baskets full of broken pieces and of the fish. ⁴⁴ And those who ate the loaves were five thousand men.

Matthew 14:15-21
¹⁵ When it was evening, the disciples came to him and said, "This is a lonely place, and the day is now over; send the crowds away to go into the villages and buy food for themselves." ¹⁶ Jesus said, "They need not go away; you give them something to eat." ¹⁷ They said to him, "We have only five loaves here and two fish." ¹⁸ And he said, "Bring them here to me." ¹⁹ Then he ordered the crowds to sit down on the grass; and taking the five loaves and the two fish he looked up to heaven, and blessed, and

north to south tips. Therefore, it was quite easy for the crowd to see Jesus' movements and to guess where he was headed.

Realizing he was headed for the "other side" they ran ahead to be there when he landed. When Jesus came ashore he looked at the crowd and had compassion on them. To Jesus they resembled a flock of sheep without a shepherd. Throughout the day, he taught many things, and according to Luke he performed healings.

It was a lonely place, and evening was approaching. There is some discrepancy between the writers concerning just how the issue of time and food was addressed. Mark says the disciples came to Jesus suggesting he send the crowd home because of the late hour. Rather than send them home hungry Jesus said to the disciples, "You give them something to eat." The bewildered response was that 200 denarii would not suffice for more than a slight taste of bread. A denarii was the equivalent of a day's wage for a laborer, 200 denarii would amount to about

broke and gave the loaves to the disciples, and the disciples gave them to the crowds. 20 And they all ate and were satisfied. And they took up twelve baskets full of the broken pieces left over. 21 And those who ate were about five thousand men, besides women and children.

Luke 9:11-17
11 When the crowds learned it, they followed him; and he welcomed them and spoke to them of the kingdom of God, and cured those who had need of healing. 12 Now the day began to wear away; and the twelve came and said to him, "Send the crowd away, to go into the villages and country round about, to lodge and get provisions; for we are here in a lonely place." 13 But he said to them, "You give them something to eat." They said, "We have no more than five loaves and two fish—unless we are to go and buy food for all these people." 14 For there were about five thousand men. And he said to his disciples, "Make them sit down in companies, about fifty each." 15 And they did so, and made them all sit down. 16 And taking the five loaves and the two fish he looked up to heaven, and blessed and broke them, and gave them

66 percent of a year's wage.

Jesus asked, "How many loaves do you have?" A loaf was similar to a piece of today's pita bread. It was round, a quarter inch thick and made from wheat or barley. They also found two fish probably the size of an average man's hand. These fish were prolific in the Sea of Galilee. Jesus ordered the people to sit on the grass. This is a clue to the location of this event. Jesus left from the western shoreline to go to the other side, which would be the eastern shoreline. The only area that would provide grass for seating would be Batanea, the land of Herod Philip. Jesus exhibited an excellent understanding of crowd control ordering the people be seated in groups of 50 and 100.

Jesus took the bread and the fish, blessed them, giving thanks to God, and broke the bread. Breaking the bread would be tearing it apart not cutting it. Then he divided the fish meaning it was cut into pieces. Everyone ate to their satisfaction.

After the meal was finished

to the disciples to set before the crowd. ¹⁷ And all ate and were satisfied. And they took up what was left over, twelve baskets of broken pieces.

John 6:1-14

¹ After this Jesus went to the other side of the Sea of Galilee, which is the Sea of Tiber'i-as. ² And a multitude followed him, because they saw the signs which he did on those who were diseased. ³ Jesus went up on the mountain, and there sat down with his disciples. ⁴ Now the Passover, the feast of the Jews, was at hand. ⁵ Lifting up his eyes, then, and seeing that a multitude was coming to him, Jesus said to Philip, "How are we to buy bread, so that these people may eat?" ⁶ This he said to test him, for he himself knew what he would do. ⁷ Philip answered him, "Two hundred denarii would not buy enough bread for each of them to get a little." ⁸ One of his disciples, Andrew, Simon Peter's brother, said to him, ⁹ "There is a lad here who has five barley loaves and two fish; but what are they among so many?" ¹⁰ Jesus said, "Make the people sit down." Now there was much grass in the place; so the men sat down, in number about five thousand. ¹¹ Jesus then took the loaves, and

Jesus ordered the disciples to take up all of the leftovers and bring them to him. They gathered up twelve baskets full of bread and fish. The word used for baskets describes a type of wicker basket. Later, at the feeding of the 4000, the basket is described as a reed basket.

John's version contains significant differences from the other three evangelists. John says Jesus arrived before the crowd. According to John, the people came because they had seen the many signs or miracles Jesus had done in healing people. He also mentions the Passover, the feast of the Jews, was at hand. According to John, Jesus turned to Philip and said, "How are we going to buy bread for this great crowd?" John states this was a test. Philip had no idea it was a test, and said in exasperation 200 denarii would not buy enough bread for all to have a small taste. Andrew said he had found five barley loaves, meaning bread baked of barley which was considered a poor person's fare, because it wasn't made from wheat.

John's crowning touch came after the people experiencing

when he had given thanks, he distributed them to those who were seated; so also the fish, as much as they wanted. 12 And when they had eaten their fill, he told his disciples, "Gather up the fragments left over, that nothing may be lost." 13 So they gathered them up and filled twelve baskets with fragments from the five barley loaves, left by those who had eaten. 14 When the people saw the sign which he had done, they said, "This is indeed the prophet who is to come into the world!"

Walking on the sea

**Mark 6:45-52;
Matthew 14:22-33;
John 6:15-21**

Mark 6:45-52
45 Immediately he made his disciples get into the boat and go before him to the other side, to Beth-sa'ida, while he dismissed the crowd. 46 And after he had taken leave of them, he went up on the mountain to pray. 47 And when evening came, the boat was out on the sea, and he was alone on the land. 48 And he saw that they were making headway painfully, for the wind was against

the feeding said, "This is indeed the prophet the one who is to come."

Walking on the sea

**Mark 6:45-52;
Matthew 14:22-33;
John 6:15-21**

Comment

Luke makes no mention of this event.

Mark and Matthew render the same account of what happened after the feeding of the 5,000. According to their account, Jesus ordered the Inner-Circle to get into the boat and leave for Bethsaida, where he intended to meet them later. Then Jesus

them. And about the fourth watch of the night he came to them, walking on the sea. He meant to pass by them, ^{49} but when they saw him walking on the sea they thought it was a ghost, and cried out; ^{50} for they all saw him, and were terrified. But immediately he spoke to them and said, "Take heart, it is I; have no fear." ^{51} And he got into the boat with them and the wind ceased. And they were utterly astounded, ^{52} for they did not understand about the loaves, but their hearts were hardened.

Matthew 14:22-33

^{22} Then he made the disciples get into the boat and go before him to the other side, while he dismissed the crowds. ^{23} And after he had dismissed the crowds, he went up on the mountain by himself to pray. When evening came, he was there alone, ^{24} but the boat by this time was many furlongs distant from the land, beaten by the waves; for the wind was against them. ^{25} And in the fourth watch of the night he came to them, walking on the sea. ^{26} But when the disciples saw him walking on the sea, they were terrified, saying, "It is a ghost!" And they cried out for fear. ^{27} But immediately he spoke to them,

dismissed the crowd. With the crowd dispersing Jesus went up the mountain alone to pray.

At this point in the story John takes a huge departure from Mark and Matthew. Only John tells us that Jesus realized the crowd was ready to take him by force and make him their king. Before the crowd could implement their thoughts Jesus dismissed them, and with his Inner-Circle went up the mountain to be alone. After dark, Jesus told the Inner-Circle to meet him later at Capernaum.

For the Inner-Circle to leave Jesus behind is hard for moderns to grasp. However, it was perfectly within reason for Jesus to stay behind. He wanted time to be alone and pray. It would have been no more than a few miles from where he was to Capernaum.

At this juncture, Mark, Matthew, and John pick up the same threads of the story. While the Inner-Circle was rowing toward their destination a storm came up. The roaring winds caused the Sea of Galilee to become turbulent. It was midnight and the ship had gone many furlongs * when Jesus

saying, "Take heart, it is I; have no fear." 28 And Peter answered him, "Lord, if it is you, bid me come to you on the water." 29 He said, "Come." So Peter got out of the boat and walked on the water and came to Jesus; 30 but when he saw the wind, he was afraid, and beginning to sink he cried out, "Lord, save me." 31 Jesus immediately reached out his hand and caught him, saying to him, "O man of little faith, why did you doubt?" 32 And when they got into the boat, the wind ceased. 33 And those in the boat worshiped him, saying, "Truly you are the Son of God."

John 6:15-21
15 Perceiving then that they were about to come and take him by force to make him king, Jesus withdrew again to the mountain by himself. 16 When evening came, his disciples went down to the sea, 17 got into a boat, and started across the sea to Caper'na-um. It was now dark, and Jesus had not yet come to them. 18 The sea rose because a strong wind was blowing. 19 When they had rowed about three or four miles, they saw Jesus walking on the sea and drawing near to the boat. They were frightened, 20 but he said to them, "It is I; do not be

came walking across the water. He intended to pass them unseen, but when they saw him they were terrified. Jesus heard the panic in their voices and said, "Do not be afraid it is me."

Matthew makes a powerful insertion into the story at this point. When Peter realized it was Jesus walking on the water he became bold saying, "Lord if it is you bid me to come." Jesus responded, "Come." Peter got out of the boat and began to walk across the water. The magnitude of the waves caused him to become afraid and he began to sink. His voice filled with panic, he cried save me Lord. Jesus asked, "Why did you become afraid?"

Then Jesus and Peter got into the boat and all were amazed at what had happened.

* A furlong is about 220 yards.

afraid." 21 Then they were glad to take him into the boat, and immediately the boat was at the land to which they were going.

The strong winds caused them to land at Gennesaret

Mark 6:53-56;
Matthew 14:34-36

Mark 6:53-56
53 And when they had crossed over, they came to land at Gennes'aret, and moored to the shore. 54 And when they got out of the boat, immediately the people recognized him, 55 and ran about the whole neighborhood and began to bring sick people on their pallets to any place where they heard he was. 56 And wherever he came, in villages, cities, or country, they laid the sick in the market places, and besought him that they might touch even the fringe of his garment; and as many as touched it were made well.

Matthew 14:34-36
34 And when they had crossed over, they came to land at Gennesaret. 35 And when the men of that place recognized him, they sent round to all that region

The strong winds caused them to land at Gennesaret

Mark 6:53-56;
Matthew 14:34-36

Comment

Their original destination had been Beth-sa'ida but the storm had blown them off course. As soon as the locals saw Jesus they spread the word that Jesus had come to their town and people began to arrive from far and near. Jesus healed many and even those who managed to touch his garments were cured. There was no attempt at numbering how many were healed. Numbers were of no concern; it was the act of healing that was written indelibly in their memory.

and brought to him all that were sick, 36 and besought him that they might only touch the fringe of his garment; and as many as touched it were made well.

More Bread

John 6:22-24

22 On the next day the people who remained on the other side of the sea saw that there had been only one boat there, and that Jesus had not entered the boat with his disciples, but that his disciples had gone away alone. 23 However, boats from Tiber'i-as came near the place where they ate the bread after the Lord had given thanks. 24 So when the people saw that Jesus was not there, nor his disciples, they themselves got into the boats and went to Caper'na-um, seeking Jesus.

More Bread

John 6:22-24

Comment

Some of the crowd decided not to go home when Jesus dismissed them. Perhaps they noticed Jesus had not gone with the Inner-Circle and they hoped to be with him for another day. Some may have thought he would perform more miracles and they might receive another free meal. Whatever their reason their morning search turned up nothing. So they got into their boats and headed for Capernaum.

The Bread of Life

John 6:25-34

25 When they found him on the other side of the sea, they said to him, "Rabbi, when did you come here?" 26 Jesus answered them, "Truly, truly, I say to you, you seek me, not because you saw

The Bread of Life

John 6:25-34

Comment

Their interest was in the possibility of an inexhaustible supply of food Jesus might

signs, but because you ate your fill of the loaves. 27 Do not labor for the food which perishes, but for the food which endures to eternal life, which the Son of man will give to you; for on him has God the Father set his seal." 28 Then they said to him, "What must we do, to be doing the works of God?" 29 Jesus answered them, "This is the work of God, that you believe in him whom he has sent." 30 So they said to him, "Then what sign do you do, that we may see, and believe you? What work do you perform? 31 Our fathers ate the manna in the wilderness; as it is written, 'He gave them bread from heaven to eat.'" 32 Jesus then said to them, "Truly, truly, I say to you, it was not Moses who gave you the bread from heaven; my Father gives you the true bread from heaven. 33 For the bread of God is that which comes down from heaven, and gives life to the world." 34 They said to him, "Lord, give us this bread always."

provide. Obviously they were not ready to accept Jesus as the Son of God. They had not been convinced by the first miracle, but were bold enough to ask for yet another sign.

Jesus' point is the manna was not from Moses, it was a gift from God.

The Manna, reference:
31 Now the house of Israel called its name manna; it was like coriander seed, white, and the taste of it was like wafers made with honey. 32 And Moses said, "This is what the LORD has commanded: 'Let an omer of it be kept throughout your generations, that they may see the bread with which I fed you in the wilderness, when I brought you out of the land of Egypt.'" 33 And Moses said to Aaron, "Take a jar, and put an omer of manna in it, and place it before the LORD, to be kept throughout your generations." 34 As the LORD commanded Moses, so Aaron placed it before the testimony, to be kept. 35 And the people of Israel ate the manna forty years, till they came to a habitable land; they ate the manna, till they came to the border of the land of Canaan.

36 (An omer is the tenth part of an ephah.) Exodus 16:31-36

Strong's Hebrew Number 6016
Omer: a dry measure of 1/10 ephah (about 2 liters)

I am the bread of life

John 6:35-40

Comment

Jesus stated unequivocally He was the sustenance of life. He was the bread and the water, the two most essential elements to sustain life. The problem was they were thinking of their belly and Jesus was talking about their spirit.

They had seen Jesus, had been with him, had experienced one of his miracles, yet they still did not believe.

I am the bread of life

John 6:35-40

35 Jesus said to them, "I am the bread of life; he who comes to me shall not hunger, and he who believes in me shall never thirst. 36 But I said to you that you have seen me and yet do not believe. 37 All that the Father gives me will come to me; and him who comes to me I will not cast out. 38 For I have come down from heaven, not to do my own will, but the will of him who sent me; 39 and this is the will of him who sent me, that I should lose nothing of all that he has given me, but raise it up at the last day. 40 For this is the will of my Father, that every one who sees the Son and believes in him should have eternal life; and I will raise him up at the last day."

The Jews then murmured at him

John 6:41-52

⁴¹ The Jews then murmured at him, because he said, "I am the bread which came down from heaven." ⁴² They said, "Is not this Jesus, the son of Joseph, whose father and mother we know? How does he now say, 'I have come down from heaven'?" ⁴³ Jesus answered them, "Do not murmur among yourselves. ⁴⁴ No one can come to me unless the Father who sent me draws him; and I will raise him up at the last day. ⁴⁵ It is written in the prophets, 'And they shall all be taught by God.' Every one who has heard and learned from the Father comes to me. ⁴⁶ Not that any one has seen the Father except him who is from God; he has seen the Father. ⁴⁷ Truly, truly, I say to you, he who believes has eternal life. ⁴⁸ I am the bread of life. ⁴⁹ Your fathers ate the manna in the wilderness, and they died. ⁵⁰ This is the bread which comes down from heaven, that a man may eat of it and not die. ⁵¹ I am the living bread which came down from heaven; if any one eats of this bread, he will live for ever; and the bread which I shall give for the life of the

The Jews then murmured at him

John 6:41-52

Comment

Nazareth is only twenty-two miles from Capernaum, and among those arriving at the beach some were childhood neighbors of Jesus.

Many of us understand it is nearly impossible to change the feelings of people we have grown up with, no matter what one's later accomplishment may be.

Jesus was offering them eternal life, the door was open, but they must choose to go through it. They asked the wrong question. We can only guess at the outcome had they asked Jesus how were they to eat his flesh? The crowd heard the literal, while Jesus spoke of the spiritual.

The reference Jesus made in verse forty-five loosely fits Psalms 119:102 and Jeremiah 32:32.

world is my flesh." 52 The Jews then disputed among themselves, saying, "How can this man give us his flesh to eat?"

Eat the flesh of the Son of man and drink his blood

John 6:53-59
53 So Jesus said to them, "Truly, truly, I say to you, unless you eat the flesh of the Son of man and drink his blood, you have no life in you; 54 he who eats my flesh and drinks my blood has eternal life, and I will raise him up at the last day. 55 For my flesh is food indeed, and my blood is drink indeed. 56 He who eats my flesh and drinks my blood abides in me, and I in him. 57 As the living Father sent me, and I live because of the Father, so he who eats me will live because of me. 58 This is the bread which came down from heaven, not such as the fathers ate and died; he who eats this bread will live for ever." 59 This he said in the synagogue, as he taught at Caper'na-um.

Eat the flesh of the Son of man and drink his blood

John 6:53-59

Comment

Jesus continued to pound the truth. He did not attempt to lead them to ask the right questions. To ask the right questions was their responsibility.

The sixth chapter of John is filled with wide swings of emotion. It was the morning after Jesus had fed the multitudes. His boat landed on the shore of Capernaum, Jesus stepped out and was greeted by a throng of happy followers.

Jesus instantly understood they were there in the hope of free food. First they asked him how he got there from the other side. When Jesus said, "I am the bread of life," a sense of utter confusion over-shadowed them. They immediately thought he was speaking in literal terms.

	They never comprehended Jesus was speaking in spiritual terms. Full understanding would not occur until after his resurrection for most of them. John gives us the exact location of this teaching, it was at Capernaum.
<u>**Conflict with believers at Capernaum**</u> **John 6:60-71** 60 Many of his disciples, when they heard it, said, "This is a hard saying; who can listen to it?" 61 But Jesus, knowing in himself that his disciples murmured at it, said to them, "Do you take offense at this? 62 Then what if you were to see the Son of man ascending where he was before? 63 It is the spirit that gives life, the flesh is of no avail; the words that I have spoken to you are spirit and life. 64 But there are some of you that do not believe." For Jesus knew from the first who those were that did not believe, and who it was that would betray him. 65 And he said, "This is why I told you that no one can come to me unless it is granted him by the Father."	<u>**Conflict with believers at Capernaum**</u> **John 6:60-71** **Comment** At the conclusion of Jesus' statements, many of the disciples (these were not the Inner-Circle) found it difficult to accept what he had said. They could not imagine how they were to "Eat his flesh or drink his blood." These disgruntled disciples said, "These are hard sayings, who can accept this?" Jesus realized what they were thinking and said to them, "Do you take offense at me? It is the spirit that gives life the flesh is of no avail." Then many of the disciples chose to follow Jesus no longer.

⁶⁶ After this many of his disciples drew back and no longer went about with him. ⁶⁷ Jesus said to the twelve, "Do you also wish to go away?" ⁶⁸ Simon Peter answered him, "Lord, to whom shall we go? You have the words of eternal life; ⁶⁹ and we have believed, and have come to know, that you are the Holy One of God." ⁷⁰ Jesus answered them, "Did I not choose you, the twelve, and one of you is a devil?" ⁷¹ He spoke of Judas the son of Simon Iscariot, for he, one of the twelve, was to betray him.	Disheartened and hurt by the actions of many Jesus turned to the Inner-Circle and said to them, "Do you want to leave also?" Peter's heart ached as he said, "To whom shall we go master you have the words of eternal life." Jesus had chosen the twelve and one of them was a devil. John explains that Judas was the one who betrayed Jesus.

Chapter 14

Jesus and his brothers in conflict

Conflict between Jesus and his brothers

John 7:1-9

¹ After this Jesus went about in Galilee; he would not go about in Judea, because the Jews sought to kill him. ² Now the Jews' feast of Tabernacles was at hand. ³ So his brothers said to him, "Leave here and go to Judea, that your disciples may see the works you are doing. ⁴ For no man works in secret if he seeks to be known openly. If you do these things, show yourself to the world." ⁵ For even his brothers did not believe in him. ⁶ Jesus said to them, "My time has not yet come, but your time is always here. ⁷ The world cannot hate you, but it hates me because I testify of it that its works are evil. ⁸ Go to the feast yourselves; I am not going up to this feast, for my time has not yet fully come." ⁹ So saying, he remained in Galilee.

Conflict between Jesus and his brothers

John 7:1-9

Comment

Jesus remained in Galilee, where he felt free to move about. It was no longer safe for him to travel in Judea. The Jews now stated openly they wanted to kill him.

A new conflict with his brothers occurred over when to go to Jerusalem for the feast of the Tabernacles. The brothers implied Jesus was more concerned with making a name for himself, than about his message. The brothers did not believe he was anything special. Jesus responded, "My time has not yet come, your time is always here." Here is a veiled illusion to the two calendars that were operative in Jesus' day. For Jesus there

	was only one right time to go to Jerusalem to celebrate the feast, and that was according to the Essene calendar.

Feast of Tabernacles

The Feast of Tabernacles was the final and most important holiday of the year. It was a weeklong festival that signaled the end of the harvest time. Observance of this feast is commanded in Leviticus (23:39-44), *39 "On the fifteenth day of the seventh month, when you have gathered in the produce of the land, you shall keep the feast of the LORD seven days; on the first day shall be a solemn rest, and on the eighth day shall be a solemn rest. 40 And you shall take on the first day the fruit of goodly trees, branches of palm trees, and boughs of leafy trees, and willows of the brook; and you shall rejoice before the LORD your God seven days. 41 You shall keep it as a feast to the LORD seven days in the year; it is a statute for ever throughout your generations; you shall keep it in the seventh month. 42 You shall dwell in booths for seven days; all that are native in Israel shall dwell in booths, 43 that your generations may know that I made the people of Israel dwell in booths when I brought them out of the land of Egypt: I am the LORD your God." 44 Thus Moses declared to the people of Israel the appointed feasts of the LORD.*

After his brothers had gone up	*After his brothers had gone up*
John 7:10-13	**John 7:10-13**
10 But after his brothers had gone up to the feast, then he also went up, not publicly but in private. 11 The Jews were looking for him at the feast, and saying, "Where is he?" 12 And there was much muttering about him among the	**Comment** Jesus said he was not going to the feast at the same time with his brothers. He went to the feast according to his calendar.

people. While some said, "He is a good man," others said, "No, he is leading the people astray." 13 Yet for fear of the Jews no one spoke openly of him.

John makes no mention of anyone going with Jesus. Again we see the matter of the two calendars in play.

The Jews, meaning the orthodox religious leaders, were seriously watching for Jesus, their intention was to kill him. Not all the Jews wanted Jesus harmed but they were the silent majority, being afraid to voice their position.

Middle of the feast

John 7:14-24

14 About the middle of the feast Jesus went up into the temple and taught. 15 The Jews marveled at it, saying, "How is it that this man has learning, when he has never studied?" 16 So Jesus answered them, "My teaching is not mine, but his who sent me; 17 if any man's will is to do his will, he shall know whether the teaching is from God or whether I am speaking on my own authority. 18 He who speaks on his own authority seeks his own glory; but he who seeks the glory of him who sent him is true, and in him there is no falsehood. 19 Did not Moses give you the law? Yet none of you keeps the law.

Middle of the feast

John 7:14-24

Comment

This is the continuation of the two calendar affect that Jesus lived with (v. 14).

Soon after arrival Jesus was found in the Temple teaching, this is a glaring example of his fearlessness. The Jews, the general population, marvel at his teaching. They were impressed knowing he had no formal education and coming from the Galilee.

Jesus told them his power to teach came from God as did his

Why do you seek to kill me?" 20 The people answered, "You have a demon! Who is seeking to kill you?" 21 Jesus answered them, "I did one deed, and you all marvel at it. 22 Moses gave you circumcision (not that it is from Moses, but from the fathers), and you circumcise a man upon the sabbath. 23 If on the sabbath a man receives circumcision, so that the law of Moses may not be broken, are you angry with me because on the sabbath I made a man's whole body well? 24 Do not judge by appearances, but judge with right judgment."	message. Jesus made it clear he did not speak on his own authority. He was not seeking glory. Here was the rebuttal to the accusation made by his brothers that he was seeking glory for himself. Jesus made it clear he intended to glorify no one but God. Jesus reminded his listeners the law came from Moses, and still none of them keep it. Then the bold question, "Why do you seek to kill me?" The Pharisees responded he had a demon and denied anyone was seeking to kill him. Jesus said, "You circumcise on the Sabbath," Sabbath circumcision was preformed to avoid violating Moses' Law. The Law required the boy child be circumcised on the eighth day after birth. Circumcision is a rite instituted by God upon Abraham and his male descendants as a sign of the covenant with Him, (Gen. 17). Jesus continued his rebuttal reminding them he made a man's body whole and wanted to know, "Why are you angry with me?" "Do not judge by appearances but judge with right judgment,"

Is not this the man whom they seek to kill

John 7:25-31

25 Some of the people of Jerusalem therefore said, "Is not this the man whom they seek to kill? 26 And here he is, speaking openly, and they say nothing to him! Can it be that the authorities really know that this is the Christ? 27 Yet we know where this man comes from; and when the Christ appears, no one will know where he comes from." 28 So Jesus proclaimed, as he taught in the temple, "You know me, and you know where I come from? But I have not come of my own accord; he who sent me is true, and him you do not know. 29 I know him, for I come from him, and he sent me." 30 So they sought to arrest him; but no one laid hands on him, because his hour had not yet come. 31 Yet many of the people believed in him; they said, "When the Christ appears, will he do more signs than this man has done?"

said Jesus. This statement opened a wide arena of thinking. Everyone is called to think before pronouncing judgment on another.

Is not this the man whom they seek to kill

John 7:25-31

Comment

Among those who listened to Jesus were those who knew the authorities planned to kill him. Unbelievably Jesus was speaking openly and the authorities made no move to arrest him. Did this mean the authorities knew he was the Christ? Or were they afraid he was the Christ?

Those who rejected Jesus offered their rebuttal claiming everyone knows where the Christ will come from, Bethlehem, and this man came from the Galilee. Jesus responded, "You think you know where I come from, I have not come on my own accord, I am here because God sent me." He continued saying he knew why God had sent him and they did not know God.

	While they wanted to arrest him they were fearful to lay hands on him. The writer, John, says the reason they did not attempt to arrest him was because God would not allow it. According to God's timetable it was not the time for Jesus to be arrested.
	Once more those supporting Jesus spoke up asking, "When the Christ comes can he do greater things than this man is doing?"
<u>Chief Priest and Pharisees send Officers to arrest Jesus</u>	**<u>Chief Priest and Pharisees send Officers to arrest Jesus</u>**
John 7:32-36	**John 7:32-36**
32 The Pharisees heard the crowd thus muttering about him, and the chief priests and Pharisees sent officers to arrest him. 33 Jesus then said, "I shall be with you a little longer, and then I go to him who sent me; 34 you will seek me and you will not find me; where I am you cannot come." 35 The Jews said to one another, "Where does this man intend to go that we shall not find him? Does he intend to go to the Dispersion among the Greeks and teach the Greeks? 36 What does he mean by saying, 'You will seek me and you will	**Comment** The Pharisees listened to the crowd's mutterings. To put it another way, they heard what the people said to each other as though they were trying to keep secret their conversations about Jesus. Word of the argument among the Jews reached the chief priests and the Pharisees. They determined it was time to have Jesus arrested. While the officers were on their way to arrest

not find me,' and, 'Where I am you cannot come'?"

him, Jesus continued speaking, "I will go away and you will look for me but you will not be able to find me." The crowd wondered, "Where did he intend to go?" Some even consider he might go into the Dispersion to meet the Greeks and teach them. (Mention of the dispersion was a reference to the Israelites that lived in other Gentile nations.) They were bewildered by his statement and could not imagine where he could go that they could not find him.

The last day of the feast

John 7:37-39

37 On the last day of the feast, the great day, Jesus stood up and proclaimed, "If any one thirst, let him come to me and drink. 38 He who believes in me, as the scripture has said, 'Out of his heart shall flow rivers of living water.'" 39 Now this he said about the Spirit, which those who believed in him were to receive; for as yet the Spirit had not been given, because Jesus was not yet glorified.

The last day of the feast

John 7:37-39

Comment

John refers to the last day as the "great day" of the feast. This was the concluding day of the feast and spirits ran high. At this point Jesus made a bold and bewildering statement saying, "If anyone thirst let them come to me and drink." He pointed out if they believed the Scripture, "From the heart shall flow rivers of living water," they would have believed in him. John makes it clear Jesus was talking about believers receiving

	the Holy Spirit. But since the Holy Spirit had not yet come, the audience was bewildered and could not understand what this meant. John goes on to say Jesus had not been glorified yet, meaning the resurrection had not yet occurred.

References of Jesus

The exact reference Jesus made cannot be found, but here are three that convey the meaning:

1) *8 On that day living waters shall flow out from Jerusalem, half of them to the eastern sea and half of them to the western sea; it shall continue in summer as in winter.* (Zech. 14:8)

2) *11 The mouth of the righteous is a fountain of life, but the mouth of the wicked conceals violence.* (Prov. 10:11)

3) *4 The words of a man's mouth are deep waters; the fountain of wisdom is a gushing stream.* (Prov. 18:4)

Is the Christ to come from Galilee?	*Is the Christ to come from Galilee?*
John 7:40-44	**John 7:40-44**
40 When they heard these words, some of the people said, "This is really the prophet." 41 Others said, "This is the Christ." But some said, "Is the Christ to come from Galilee? 42 Has not the scripture said that the Christ	**Comment** The reference in verse forty refers to Moses promising God will send a prophet, much like himself.

is descended from David, and comes from Bethlehem, the village where David was?" 43 So there was a division among the people over him. 44 Some of them wanted to arrest him, but no one laid hands on him.

15 The LORD thy God will raise up unto thee a Prophet from the midst of thee, of thy brethren, like unto me; unto him ye shall hearken; Deuteronomy 18:15 (KJV)

Others said this man must be the Christ. Still others shouted the Christ could not come from Galilee because he must come from Bethlehem and be a descendent of David their great king of the past. So there continued to be division among the people of Israel.

While some wanted him arrested, no one laid a hand upon him at that moment.

<u>Officers then went back to the chief priests</u>

John 7:45-53
45 The officers then went back to the chief priests and Pharisees, who said to them, "Why did you not bring him?" 46 The officers answered, "No man ever spoke like this man!" 47 The Pharisees answered them, "Are you led astray, you also? 48 Have any of the authorities or of the Pharisees believed in him? 49 But this crowd, who do not know the law,

<u>Officers then went back to the chief priests</u>

John 7:45-53

Comment

When the officers returned to the chief priest they were confronted with a harsh question, "Why do you not have the prisoner?" They explained they had never heard a man speak as this man spoke. The Pharisees in their anger accused

are accursed." 50 Nicode′mus, who had gone to him before, and who was one of them, said to them, 51 "Does our law judge a man without first giving him a hearing and learning what he does?" 52 They replied, "Are you from Galilee too? Search and you will see that no prophet is to rise from Galilee." 53 They went each to his own house,	the officers of becoming followers of Jesus. Angrily the Pharisees challenged the officers declaring none of the Pharisees believed in him and neither did any of the authorities. They called the followers of Jesus a crowd lacking knowledge of the law and accursed. At this point Nicodemus attempted, though meekly, to defend Jesus. He posed a question to his colleagues, "Was it their custom to judge someone without a hearing?" Mockingly they asked, "Are you also from Galilee?" They challenged him to prove through Scripture that any prophet should come from Galilee!

A heated, almost violent, confrontation between Jesus and his adversaries

Chapter 8 of John's Gospel reveals a heated, almost violent, confrontation between Jesus and his adversaries, the Scribes and Pharisees. In this story one comes face to face with the Jesus who is strong, stern, and unafraid. Jesus states God's position clearly in the face of angry disbelievers.

Woman who had been caught in adultery

John 8:1-11

1 but Jesus went to the Mount of Olives. 2 Early in the morning he came again to the temple; all the people came to him, and he sat down and taught them. 3 The scribes and the Pharisees brought a woman who had been caught in adultery, and placing her in the midst 4 they said to him, "Teacher, this woman has been caught in the act of adultery. 5 Now in the law Moses commanded us to stone such. What do you say about her?" 6 This they said to test him, that they might have some charge to bring against him. Jesus bent down and wrote with his finger on the ground. 7 And as they continued to ask him, he stood up and said to them, "Let him who is without sin among you be the first to throw a stone at her." 8 And once more he bent down and wrote with his finger on the ground. 9 But when they heard it, they went away, one by one, beginning with the eldest, and Jesus was left alone with the woman standing before him. 10 Jesus looked up and said to her, "Woman, where are they? Has no one condemned you?" 11 She

Woman who had been caught in adultery

John 8:1-11

Comment

Jesus spent the night on the Mount of Olives. There were caves on the Mount of Olives customarily used by travelers. In one of these caves Jesus spent the night.

Very early the next morning he returned to the temple. Hearing Jesus had returned, many people came and gathered around him. Jesus sat down and taught them, this was the appropriate posture for a rabbi to conduct his teachings. The serenity of the moment was broken as Scribes and Pharisees entered, dragging a woman into their midst. They proudly proclaimed this woman had been taken in the very act of adultery. Their position became obvious as they quoted Moses saying such a person should be stoned. Next they challenged Jesus saying, "What do you say about her?"

The Pharisees quoted Moses but they did not apply the complete

said, "No one, Lord." And Jesus said, "Neither do I condemn you; go, and do not sin again."	reference to their case against the woman. *10 "If a man commits adultery with the wife of his neighbor, both the adulterer and the adulteress shall be put to death. Leviticus 20:10* To apply the Law fully would have required that the man also be brought forward and both would have been stoned. If the Pharisees were referring to this passage: *22 "If a man is found lying with the wife of another man, both of them shall die, the man who lay with the woman, and the woman; so you shall purge the evil from Israel. Deuteronomy 22:22* Here too the standard applied to both the man and the woman. This was to test him hoping to have charges to bring against him based on an incorrect answer. The trap was this: if Jesus said release her, he would be violating the Law of Moses; if He agreed to have her stoned, it would appear to the people that he had no compassion. Jesus bent over and began to write with his

finger in the dust. We have no record of what he wrote. They continue to badger him growing confident they had succeeded in trapping him. Finally, Jesus stood and said, "Let whichever one of you who is without sin throw the first stone at her." Then he knelt down once more and continued writing in the dust with his finger. Soon you could hear the thud of the stones dropping to the ground one by one beginning with the eldest, her accusers began to leave. Jesus stood again, looked at the woman and asked, "Where are your accusers?" She said, "They are gone." Then Jesus made a profound and unexpected statement, "Neither do I accuse you, go and sin no more."

It is noteworthy that Jesus did not challenge or disavow Moses' teaching.

I am the light of the world

John 8:12-20

12 Again Jesus spoke to them, saying, "I am the light of the world; he who follows me will not walk in darkness, but will have the light of life." 13 The Pharisees then said to him, "You

I am the light of the world

John 8:12-20

Comment

After the scribes and Pharisees were silenced concerning the

are bearing witness to yourself; your testimony is not true." 14 Jesus answered, "Even if I do bear witness to myself, my testimony is true, for I know whence I have come and whither I am going, but you do not know whence I come or whither I am going. 15 You judge according to the flesh, I judge no one. 16 Yet even if I do judge, my judgment is true, for it is not I alone that judge, but I and he who sent me. 17 In your law it is written that the testimony of two men is true; 18 I bear witness to myself, and the Father who sent me bears witness to me." 19 They said to him therefore, "Where is your Father?" Jesus answered, "You know neither me nor my Father; if you knew me, you would know my Father also." 20 These words he spoke in the treasury, as he taught in the temple; but no one arrested him, because his hour had not yet come.

woman caught in adultery, Jesus continued his teaching, stating, "I am the light of the world." He said if one walks in darkness there is danger, but if one has light he can avoid many of the pitfalls. The Pharisees immediately pounced upon his statement accusing him of bearing witness to himself, meaning under the law his testimony would be untrue. Jesus responded saying even if he did bear witness to himself his witness was still true. In a commanding tone Jesus told them they did not know where he came from or where he was going. He accused them of judging according to the flesh and told them he judged no one. Almost as an afterthought he said, "But if I do judge my judgment is true." The scribes and the Pharisees challenged him in return, "Where is your father?" Jesus responded, "You do not know me or my father, if you had known either of us you would have known the other."

John gives us the location of this encounter saying, "Jesus spoke in the treasury." Jesus continued to teach in the temple throughout the remainder of

Will he kill himself?

John 8:21-30

^{21} Again he said to them, "I go away, and you will seek me and die in your sin; where I am going, you cannot come." ^{22} Then said the Jews, "Will he kill himself, since he says, 'Where I am going, you cannot come'?" ^{23} He said to them, "You are from below, I am from above; you are of this world, I am not of this world. ^{24} I told you that you would die in your sins, for you will die in your sins unless you believe that I am he." ^{25} They said to him, "Who are you?" Jesus said to them, "Even what I have told you from the beginning. ^{26} I have much to say about you and much to judge; but he who sent me is true, and I declare to the world what I have heard from him." ^{27} They did not understand that he spoke to them of the Father. ^{28} So Jesus said, "When you have lifted up the Son of man, then you will know that I am he, and that I do nothing on my own authority but speak thus as the Father taught me. ^{29} And he who sent me is with me; he has not left me alone, for I always do

the day and no one made any attempt to arrest him.

Will he kill himself?

John 8:21-30

Comment

Again Jesus told them he was going to go away, they would seek him but would not find him and they would die in their sin. The Jews did not understand what Jesus meant and questioned among themselves did Jesus plan to kill himself. Jesus then boldly stated, "You are from below and I am from above." Meaning they were earthly beings while he had one foot in heaven and one foot on earth. He then said, "You will die in your sin unless you believe that I am He," meaning he was the Messiah. Again the Jews, the nonbelievers, failed to understand what Jesus was saying and asked boldly, "Who are you?" In a roundabout way Jesus said I have told you from the beginning who I am.

Jesus concluded his message foretelling of his crucifixion.

what is pleasing to him." ³⁰ As he spoke thus, many believed in him.

Jesus said, "When you have lifted up the Son of Man then you will know." He closed with a very revealing statement, "I do nothing of my own accord but speak as the Father has taught me." Then he told them it was God who sent him and God had never left him alone. Boldly Jesus said, "I always do what is pleasing to the father." John tells us many at that moment believed in Jesus.

The Jews who had believed in him

John 8:31-33
³¹ Jesus then said to the Jews who had believed in him, "If you continue in my word, you are truly my disciples, ³² and you will know the truth, and the truth will make you free." ³³ They answered him, "We are descendants of Abraham, and have never been in bondage to any one. How is it that you say, 'You will be made free'?"

The Jews who had believed in him

John 8:31-33

Comment

Jesus then spoke to those who had believed in him. If they continue to follow his teachings they would prove themselves as true disciples. He told them they would know the truth and the truth would make them free. After Jesus had addressed these new believers, those who did not believe angrily retorted they were descendents of Abraham and considered themselves as free, never having been in bondage to anyone, "What did you mean we will be made free?"

You seek to kill me

John 8:34-38

34 Jesus answered them, "Truly, truly, I say to you, every one who commits sin is a slave to sin. 35 The slave does not continue in the house for ever; the son continues for ever. 36 So if the Son makes you free, you will be free indeed. 37 I know that you are descendants of Abraham; yet you seek to kill me, because my word finds no place in you. 38 I speak of what I have seen with my Father, and you do what you have heard from your father."

You seek to kill me

John 8:34-38

Comment

The dialogue continued between the non-believing Jews and Jesus. Jesus explained his statement of their being in bondage saying, "Everyone who commits sin is a slave to sin." He then drew a distinction between those who believe and those who did not believe saying, "If the Son makes you free you are free indeed, I know you are descendents of Abraham. Why do you seek to kill me?" Then he answered his own question, "It is because you do not believe in me." Jesus reiterates what he has seen in the Father and what he has heard from the Father.

Abraham is our father

John 8:39-47

39 They answered him, "Abraham is our father." Jesus said to them, "If you were Abraham's children, you would do what Abraham did, 40 but now you seek to kill me, a man who has told you the truth which I heard from God; this is

Abraham is our father

John 8:39-47

Comment

The verbal war continued. The nonbelievers continue to tout Abraham as their father. Jesus

not what Abraham did. ^{41} You do what your father did." They said to him, "We were not born of fornication; we have one Father, even God." ^{42} Jesus said to them, "If God were your Father, you would love me, for I proceeded and came forth from God; I came not of my own accord, but he sent me. ^{43} Why do you not understand what I say? It is because you cannot bear to hear my word. ^{44} You are of your father the devil, and your will is to do your father's desires. He was a murderer from the beginning, and has nothing to do with the truth, because there is no truth in him. When he lies, he speaks according to his own nature, for he is a liar and the father of lies. ^{45} But, because I tell the truth, you do not believe me. ^{46} Which of you convicts me of sin? If I tell the truth, why do you not believe me? ^{47} He who is of God hears the words of God; the reason why you do not hear them is that you are not of God."

responded, if they were children of Abraham they would act as Abraham acted. Here the meaning is clear, when God spoke Abraham responded in the affirmative. Jesus spoke the truth to them but they would not hear it. Angrily they responded saying, "We were not born in fornication and we have only one Father and that is God." Jesus rifled back, "If God is your Father you would love me because I come from God." Then, almost in remorse, Jesus said he did not come of his own accord but God had sent him. Jesus became frustrated and exasperated with his challengers, looking them straight in the eye he said, "Why do you not understand what I say?" Then he answered his own question telling them they were children of their father the devil and their actions proved they were following the Devil's plan.

Jesus then gave a vivid picture of the Devil. The Devil was a murderer from his beginning; he had nothing to do with truth because there was no truth in him. Satan lies because that is his nature; he is the father of

You are a Samaritan and have a demon

John 8:48-59

⁴⁸ The Jews answered him, "Are we not right in saying that you are a Samaritan and have a demon?" ⁴⁹ Jesus answered, "I have not a demon; but I honor my Father, and you dishonor me. ⁵⁰ Yet I do not seek my own glory; there is One who seeks it and he will be the judge. ⁵¹ Truly, truly, I say to you, if any one keeps my word, he will never see death." ⁵² The Jews said to him, "Now we know that you have a demon. Abraham died, as did the prophets; and you say, 'If any one keeps my word, he will never taste death.' ⁵³ Are you greater than our father Abraham, who died? And the prophets died! Who do you claim to be?" ⁵⁴ Jesus answered, "If I glorify myself, my glory is nothing; it is my Father who

mission telling them, "I tell you the truth you do not believe me." Then he challenged them in an unbelievable manner asking, "Which of you can convict me of sin?" Again he answered his own question, "The reason you do not hear me is because you are not children of God."

You are a Samaritan and have a demon

John 8:48-59

Comment

The verbal war continued to intensify. The Jews ridiculed Jesus saying he was a Samaritan possessed by a demon. Jesus answered, "I have no demon but I honor my Father and you dishonor me." Once more he said anyone who keeps his word will never see death. The Jews responded we know for sure you have a demon. Abraham died, the prophets died, and you say if anyone keeps your word they will never taste death. You can almost hear the sneers of laughter. Then they challenged Jesus thinking they had the upper hand saying, "Are you

glorifies me, of whom you say that he is your God. 55 But you have not known him; I know him. If I said, I do not know him, I should be a liar like you; but I do know him and I keep his word. 56 Your father Abraham rejoiced that he was to see my day; he saw it and was glad." 57 The Jews then said to him, "You are not yet fifty years old, and have you seen Abraham?" 58 Jesus said to them, "Truly, truly, I say to you, before Abraham was, I am." 59 So they took up stones to throw at him; but Jesus hid himself, and went out of the temple.

greater than Abraham? Who do you claim to be?"

Jesus answered, "Abraham saw my glory and rejoiced." This brought an immediate incredulous response, "You are not yet fifty years old and you claimed to have seen Abraham!" Jesus responded, "Truly, truly I say to you before Abraham was I am." Jesus may have been thinking of the conversation between Moses and God when Moses asked God what His name was, *13 Then Moses said to God, "If I come to the people of Israel and say to them, 'The God of your fathers has sent me to you,' and they ask me, 'What is his name?' what shall I say to them?" 14 God said to Moses, "I AM WHO I AM." And he said, "Say this to the people of Israel, 'I AM has sent me to you.'" Exodus 3:13-14*

If Jesus was thinking about that conversation the Jews did not catch the connection. They felt completely justified in thinking Jesus was a madman making such wild audacious claims. So they began to pick up stones that littered the ground with the intent of stoning him. John says

Jesus hid himself and went out of the temple.

According to Strong's Greek Dictionary Number 2928, the word translated "hid" can mean any of the following: *to hide, conceal, to be hidden, escape notice.*

Who sinned, this man or his parents?

John 9:1-12

Comment

These disciples, not the Inner-Circle, but those in and around Jerusalem, gave voice to a widespread myth. It was commonly believed anyone born with a birth defect was being punished for the sins of the parents.

Verse three is a very troubling comment. Taken at face value it seems to say God intends some persons to come into the world handicapped. Could this be to see how the rest of us are going to respond? This being so it would indicate we as a world of people have failed miserably to

Who sinned, this man or his parents?

John 9:1-12

1 As he passed by, he saw a man blind from his birth. 2 And his disciples asked him, "Rabbi, who sinned, this man or his parents, that he was born blind?" 3 Jesus answered, "It was not that this man sinned, or his parents, but that the works of God might be made manifest in him. 4 We must work the works of him who sent me, while it is day; night comes, when no one can work. 5 As long as I am in the world, I am the light of the world." 6 As he said this, he spat on the ground and made clay of the spittle and anointed the man's eyes with the clay, 7 saying to him, "Go, wash in the pool of Silo'am" (which means Sent). So he went and washed and came back seeing. 8 The neighbors and those who

had seen him before as a beggar, said, "Is not this the man who used to sit and beg?" 9 Some said, "It is he"; others said, "No, but he is like him." He said, "I am the man." 10 They said to him, 'Then how were your eyes opened?" 11 He answered, "The man called Jesus made clay and anointed my eyes and said to me, 'Go to Silo'am and wash'; so I went and washed and received my sight." 12 They said to him, "Where is he?" He said, "I do not know."

correct the problems affecting such persons.

Verse six is more than a homeopathic remedy; here is the awesome power of God at work. Jesus told him to follow the rules, go and wash himself in the pool of Siloam. The man did what he was told to do by Jesus.

He put clay on my eyes

John 9:13-17

13 They brought to the Pharisees the man who had formerly been blind. 14 Now it was a sabbath day when Jesus made the clay and opened his eyes. 15 The Pharisees again asked him how he had received his sight. And he said to them, "He put clay on my eyes, and I washed, and I see." 16 Some of the Pharisees said, "This man is not from God, for he does not keep the sabbath." But others said, "How can a man who is a sinner do such signs?" There was a division among them. 17 So they again said to the blind man, "What do you say about him, since he has opened your eyes?"

He put clay on my eyes

John 9:13-17

Comment

The man, formerly blind, was taken to the Pharisees for interrogation. All of this resulted from Jesus healing the man on the Sabbath. The Pharisees asked the man to describe how Jesus had performed the healing. The man recounted what Jesus had done. He then encountered a hornet's nest with respect to the orthodox religious leaders. The Pharisees proclaimed boldly Jesus could not be from God because he did not keep the Sabbath law. Others disagreed,

He said, "He is a prophet."

saying, "A sinner could not do such a sign as this." It was evident there was division among them. The Pharisees, hoping to strengthen their position, questioned the man again asking, "What do you say about him?" The man astounded them responding that Jesus must be a prophet.

Jews did not believe that he had been blind

John 9:18-23

18 The Jews did not believe that he had been blind and had received his sight, until they called the parents of the man who had received his sight, 19 and asked them, "Is this your son, who you say was born blind? How then does he now see?" 20 His parents answered, "We know that this is our son, and that he was born blind; 21 but how he now sees we do not know, nor do we know who opened his eyes. Ask him; he is of age, he will speak for himself." 22 His parents said this because they feared the Jews, for the Jews had already agreed that if any one should confess him to be Christ, he was to be put out of the synagogue. 23 Therefore his parents said, "He is of age, ask him."

Jews did not believe that he had been blind

John 9:18-23

Comment

Here Jews refers to the Pharisees who did not believe the man was blind from the beginning. To try and prove this they called the parents to come and testify before them. "Is this your son who was born blind?" they challenged. "How then does he now see?" The frightened parents answered, "This is our son and he was born blind. We don't know how he gained his sight." Trembling with fear, they challenged the Pharisees to ask him, saying, he was of age and could answer. Word had already spread that the Jews, Pharisees, had already agreed if anyone

The second time they called the man

John 9:24-34

24 So for the second time they called the man who had been blind, and said to him, "Give God the praise; we know that this man is a sinner." 25 He answered, "Whether he is a sinner, I do not know; one thing I know, that though I was blind, now I see." 26 They said to him, "What did he do to you? How did he open your eyes?" 27 He answered them, "I have told you already, and you would not listen. Why do you want to hear it again? Do you too want to become his disciples?" 28 And they reviled him, saying, "You are his disciple, but we are disciples of Moses. 29 We know that God has spoken to Moses, but as for this man, we do not know where he comes from." 30 The man answered, "Why, this is a marvel! You do not know where he comes from, and yet he opened my eyes. 31 We know that God does not listen to sinners, but if any one is a worshiper of God and does

confessed Jesus to be the Christ that person was to be thrown out of the synagogue.

The second time they called the man

John 9:24-34

Comment

Continuing their effort to discredit the man they recalled him to the witness stand. Their first statement challenged the credibility of the once blind man. They told him to give God the praise because they knew this man who healed him was a sinner. The man responded, "I don't know if he's a sinner or not all I know is I was blind and now I see!" Incensed the Pharisees demand to know how his eyes were opened. The blind man reminded them he had already told them how it all happened, why did they want to hear it again? Then he asked, "Do you want to hear it again so you too can become disciples?" With blood boiling they revile him calling him a disciple of Jesus and affirming their discipleship to Moses. The Pharisees said they knew God

his will, God listens to him. 32 Never since the world began has it been heard that any one opened the eyes of a man born blind. 33 If this man were not from God, he could do nothing." 34 They answered him, "You were born in utter sin, and would you teach us?" And they cast him out.

spoke to Moses but they did not know where this man Jesus came from.

The testimony of the recovered blind man is an outstanding witness to one's experience with Jesus Christ. He said to his accusers, "What a marvel this is that you don't know where he came from but he had the power to open my eyes." The Pharisees again interrupted him and charge that never in all the world has anyone ever heard of a man born blind receiving his sight. The once blind man responded, "If the man was not from God then he could have done nothing." Now, in total frustration, the Pharisees shout at a man, "You were born in utter sin and you would attempt to teach us?" With that they cast him out, he was excommunicated.

Lord, I believe

John 9:35-41

35 Jesus heard that they had cast him out, and having found him he said, 'Do you believe in the Son of man?" 36 He answered, "And who is he, sir, that I may believe in him?" 37 Jesus said to him, "You have seen him, and

Lord, I believe

John 9:35-41

Comment

Later, Jesus heard of the man's excommunication and found him. Jesus asked, "Do you believe in the Son of Man?" The

it is he who speaks to you." ³⁸ He said, "Lord, I believe"; and he worshiped him. ³⁹ Jesus said, "For judgment I came into this world, that those who do not see may see, and that those who see may become blind." ⁴⁰ Some of the Pharisees near him heard this, and they said to him, "Are we also blind?" ⁴¹ Jesus said to them, "If you were blind, you would have no guilt; but now that you say, 'We see,' your guilt remains	man showing his innocence, "Who is he I certainly would believe in him." Jesus says, "You have seen him it is he who speaks to you now." The man joyfully responded, "Lord I believe." Jesus then told him he came into the world to judge the world and those who do not see. Those who truly experience God in their lives shall truly see, while those who think they have a relationship with God but do not will become blind. There were some Pharisees standing nearby and overhearing this conversation challenged Jesus saying, "Are we also blind?" Jesus said, "If you were blind you would be okay but since you have sight and claim to see your guilt is still upon you."

Chapter 15

The Syrophoenician Mother

**Mark 7:24-30;
Matthew 15:21-28**

Mark 7:24-30

24 And from there he arose and went away to the region of Tyre and Sidon. And he entered a house, and would not have any one know it; yet he could not be hid. 25 But immediately a woman, whose little daughter was possessed by an unclean spirit, heard of him, and came and fell down at his feet. 26 Now the woman was a Greek, a Syrophoeni'cian by birth. And she begged him to cast the demon out of her daughter. 27 And he said to her, "Let the children first be fed, for it is not right to take the children's bread and throw it to the dogs." 28 But she answered him, "Yes, Lord; yet even the dogs under the table eat the children's crumbs." 29 And he said to her, "For this saying you may go your way; the demon has left your daughter." 30 And she went home, and found the child lying in bed, and the demon gone.

The Syrophoenician Mother

**Mark 7:24-30;
Matthew 15:21-28**

Comment

According to Mark, the woman was a Greek, a Syrophoenician by birth. Matthew writes she was a Canaanite woman.

According to Strong's Greek dictionary, the word *Syrophoenician* means: 1) the name of a mixed nation, half Phoenicians and half Syrians. The word Canaanite means; 1) the name of the ancient inhabitants of Palestine before the conquest of the Israelites. 2) In Christ's time: a Phoenician.

I take this to mean, the woman was born of Greek parents who were at the time living in Sidon.

Matthew tells us the Inner-Circle wanted Jesus to turn this woman away. Jesus addressed her saying he was sent only to the lost sheep of Israel.

Matthew 15:21-28

21 And Jesus went away from there and withdrew to the district of Tyre and Sidon. 22 And behold, a Canaanite woman from that region came out and cried, "Have mercy on me, O Lord, Son of David; my daughter is severely possessed by a demon." 23 But he did not answer her a word. And his disciples came and begged him, saying, "Send her away, for she is crying after us." 24 He answered, "I was sent only to the lost sheep of the house of Israel." 25 But she came and knelt before him, saying, "Lord, help me." 26 And he answered, "It is not fair to take the children's bread and throw it to the dogs." 27 She said, "Yes, Lord, yet even the dogs eat the crumbs that fall from their masters' table." 28 Then Jesus answered her, "O woman, great is your faith! Be it done for you as you desire." And her daughter was healed instantly.

When Jesus spoke of feeding the children the woman seized upon the fact that crumbs always fell or were wiped from the table falling to the floor. Many homes in Israel possessed dogs either as pets or for protection. No matter what the dogs were free to eat the crumbs that fell from the table.

Since healing was available to the privileged (Jews), why should not children in the presence of the Healer receive healing? Jesus rewarded her faith saying, "So be it."

Return from the region of Tyre

**Mark 7:31-37;
Matthew 15:29-31**

Return from the region of Tyre

**Mark 7:31-37;
Matthew 15:29-31**

Mark 7:31-37
31 Then he returned from the region of Tyre, and went

Comment

Mark goes into detail concerning

through Sidon to the Sea of Galilee, through the region of the Decap'olis. 32 And they brought to him a man who was deaf and had an impediment in his speech; and they besought him to lay his hand upon him. 33 And taking him aside from the multitude privately, he put his fingers into his ears, and he spat and touched his tongue; 34 and looking up to heaven, he sighed, and said to him, "Eph'phatha," that is, "Be opened." 35 And his ears were opened, his tongue was released, and he spoke plainly. 36 And he charged them to tell no one; but the more he charged them, the more zealously they proclaimed it. 37 And they were astonished beyond measure, saying, "He has done all things well; he even makes the deaf hear and the dumb speak."

Matthew 15:29-31

29 And Jesus went on from there and passed along the Sea of Galilee. And he went up on the mountain, and sat down there. 30 And great crowds came to him, bringing with them the lame, the maimed, the blind, the dumb, and many others, and they put them at his feet, and he healed them, 31 so that the throng wondered, when they saw

this healing. Matthew tells of something similar, but in very general terms.

When Jesus left Tyre his destination was the Decapolis. A man of the region was brought to him, who could neither speak nor hear. Jesus took him aside where no one else could hear what he might say to the man. He then put his fingers in the man's ears, spit and touched the man's tongue with his finger. Then Jesus looked heavenward and said, "be opened." The man was healed and the crowd marveled. Jesus ordered him to tell no one, but the man was so filled with joy he ignored the admonition.

Jesus feeds the four thousand

**Mark 8:1-10;
Matthew 15:32-39**

Mark 8:1-10

¹ In those days, when again a great crowd had gathered, and they had nothing to eat, he called his disciples to him, and said to them, ² "I have compassion on the crowd, because they have been with me now three days, and have nothing to eat; ³ and if I send them away hungry to their homes, they will faint on the way; and some of them have come a long way." ⁴ And his disciples answered him, "How can one feed these men with bread here in the desert?" ⁵ And he asked them, "many loaves have you?" They said, "Seven." ⁶ And he commanded the crowd to sit down on the ground; and he took the seven loaves, and having given thanks he broke them and gave them to his disciples to set before the people; and they set them before the crowd. ⁷ And they had a few small fish; and having

Jesus feeds the four thousand

**Mark 8:1-10;
Matthew 15:32-39**

Comment

The people had been with Jesus for three days and he knew they had run out of food. He was reluctant to send them home without feeding them first. The Inner-Circle was bewildered by such a task.

They had located only seven loaves of bread (slices), and a few small fish to feed such a large crowd. Jesus took what was available, blessed it, and had the people sit down. He directed the Inner-Circle to distribute the food among them. When everyone was full, they gathered up seven baskets of left over pieces. Mark says they fed 4,000. Matthew tells us this number did not include women and children, who also were fed.

After feeding the 4,000, Jesus

blessed them, he commanded that these also should be set before them. 8 And they ate, and were satisfied; and they took up the broken pieces left over, seven baskets full. 9 And there were about four thousand people. 10 And he sent them away; and immediately he got into the boat with his disciples, and went to the district of Dalmanu'tha.

Matthew 15:32-39
32 Then Jesus called his disciples to him and said, "I have compassion on the crowd, because they have been with me now three days, and have nothing to eat; and I am unwilling to send them away hungry, lest they faint on the way." 33 And the disciples said to him, "Where are we to get bread enough in the desert to feed so great a crowd?" 34 And Jesus said to them, "How many loaves have you?" They said, "Seven, and a few small fish." 35 And commanding the crowd to sit down on the ground, 36 he took the seven loaves and the fish, and having given thanks he broke them and gave them to the disciples, and the disciples gave them to the crowds. 37 And they all ate and were satisfied; and they took up seven baskets full of the broken pieces left over. 38 Those

departed for Dalmanutha, a small town on the west side of the Sea of Galilee near Magdala, which was located about three miles south of Tiberias.

who ate were four thousand men, besides women and children. 39 And sending away the crowds, he got into the boat and went to the region of Mag'adan.

Ten Lepers

Luke 17:11-19
11 On the way to Jerusalem he was passing along between Sama'ria and Galilee. 12 And as he entered a village, he was met by ten lepers, who stood at a distance 13 and lifted up their voices and said, "Jesus, Master, have mercy on us." 14 When he saw them he said to them, "Go and show yourselves to the priests." And as they went they were cleansed. 15 Then one of them, when he saw that he was healed, turned back, praising God with a loud voice; 16 and he fell on his face at Jesus' feet, giving him thanks. Now he was a Samaritan. 17 Then said Jesus, "Were not ten cleansed? Where are the nine? 18 Was no one found to return and give praise to God except this foreigner?" 19 And he said to him, "Rise and go your way; your faith has made you well."

Ten Lepers

Luke 17:11-19

Comment

This is an independent story of Luke.

The story takes place along the border between Galilee and Samaria. Jesus was moving toward Jerusalem. As he journeyed South he entered a Samaritan village. Here he was met by a wandering band of ten lepers. It would not have been an uncommon thing to find such a group of lepers wandering together. Lepers were prohibited from approaching people known as clean. Lepers were required to call out "unclean, unclean" at the approach of any other person.

Instead of crying out unclean, they cried out, Jesus heal us. Jesus' instantaneous response was "go and show yourself to

	the priest." This very statement means he had healed them. How far they had gone before they realized they had been cleansed isn't stated. The point of the story; however, is that one man realized his cleansing and turned back to say thank you. That one was the "hated" Samaritan. This Scripture took place under the umbrella of circumstances that impacted both Samaritans and Jews. It also explains why Jesus referred to this Samaritan as a foreigner.

Show yourself to the priest

When Jesus said, "Show yourself to the priest," he was referring to Leviticus 14:1-9.

1 The LORD said to Moses, 2 "This shall be the law of the leper for the day of his cleansing. He shall be brought to the priest; 3 and the priest shall go out of the camp, and the priest shall make an examination. Then, if the leprous disease is healed in the leper, 4 the priest shall command them to take for him who is to be cleansed two living clean birds and cedarwood and scarlet stuff and hyssop; 5 and the priest shall command them to kill one of the birds in an earthen vessel over running water. 6 He shall take the living bird with the cedarwood and the scarlet stuff and the hyssop, and dip them and the living bird in the blood of the bird that was killed over the running water; 7 and he shall sprinkle it seven times upon him who is to be cleansed of leprosy; then he shall pronounce him clean, and shall let the living bird go into *the open field. ^{8} And he who is to be cleansed shall wash his clothes, and shave off all his hair, and bathe himself in water, and he shall be clean; and after that he shall come into the camp, but shall dwell outside his tent seven days. ^{9} And on the seventh day he shall shave all his hair off his head; he shall shave off his beard and his eyebrows, all his hair. Then he shall wash his clothes, and bathe his body in water, and he shall be clean.*

<u>**Jesus and giving a Sign**</u>	<u>**Jesus and giving a Sign**</u>
Mark 8:11-13; **Matthew 16:1-4;** **Luke 12:54-56**	**Mark 8:11-13;** **Matthew 16:1-4;** **Luke 12:54-56**
Mark 8:11-13 ^{11} The Pharisees came and began to argue with him, seeking from him a sign from heaven, to test him. ^{12} And he sighed deeply in his spirit, and said, "Why does this generation seek a sign? Truly, I say to you, no sign shall be given to this generation." ^{13} And he left them, and getting into the boat again he departed to the other side. **Matthew 16:1-4** ^{1} And the Pharisees and Sad'ducees came, and to test him they asked him to show them a sign from heaven. ^{2} He answered them, "When it is evening, you say, 'It will be fair weather; for the sky is red.' ^{3} And in the morning, 'It will be stormy today, for the sky is red	**Comment** Asking to see a sign was a way of saying they wanted Jesus to perform a miracle for them. Mark and Matthew combined to tell us the story of the Pharisees and Sadducees coming to test Jesus. They demanded a sign (miracle), but Jesus refused. He said they could read the signs of the weather, but they could not interpret the signs of the time. Matthew describes a confrontation with the scribes and the Pharisees and again refers to the sign of the prophet Jonah. Luke tells almost exactly the same story.

and threatening.' You know how to interpret the appearance of the sky, but you cannot interpret the signs of the times. 4 An evil and adulterous generation seeks for a sign, but no sign shall be given to it except the sign of Jonah." So he left them and departed.

Luke 12:54-56
54 He also said to the multitudes, "When you see a cloud rising in the west, you say at once, 'A shower is coming'; and so it happens. 55 And when you see the south wind blowing, you say, 'There will be scorching heat'; and it happens. 56 You hypocrites! You know how to interpret the appearance of earth and sky; but why do you not know how to interpret the present time?

Galilean blood

Luke 13:1-5
1 There were some present at that very time who told him of the Galileans whose blood Pilate had mingled with their sacrifices. 2 And he answered them, "Do you think that these Galileans were worse sinners than all the other Galileans, because they suffered thus? 3 I tell you, No; but unless you repent you will all likewise

Galilean blood

Luke 13:1-5

Comment

When the moment came to disperse the crowd, the soldiers acted with violence far beyond their orders. The mob consisted of Galileans who were at the Temple to offer sacrifices. When violence broke out the victims'

perish. 4 Or those eighteen upon whom the tower in Silo'am fell and killed them, do you think that they were worse offenders than all the others who dwelt in Jerusalem? 5 I tell you, No; but unless you repent you will all likewise perish."	blood was spilled upon the floor mixing with the blood of the sacrificial animals. One of the towers at the pool of Siloam collapsed killing eighteen people. Very little is known about this incident. Jesus neither praised nor condemned the Galileans. Common wisdom of the day said those who suffered were being punished for their own or their parents' sin while the righteous would be rewarded. Jesus strongly repudiated this common belief. He further challenged the idea that God is the immediate cause of every event. He was thereby introducing the new concept of human freedom. Jesus quickly added that unless the crowd repented, they too would perish. Repentance meant they should conduct their lives and affairs in a manner that they would not be fearful to stand before God when the judgment comes.

Infuriated Galileans

This situation revolved around a decision made by Pontius Pilate. Jerusalem needed its water system improved. Pilate's proposal for handling the problem infuriated the Galileans. The plan called for using monies taken from the Temple to fund the project. When news leaked out mobs began to form in protest. To disperse the mob Pilate instructed his soldiers to disguise themselves and mix with the crowd. The soldiers were ordered to carry clubs, not swords.

Woman with eighteen years of infirmity	*Woman with eighteen years of infirmity*
Luke 13:10-17 10 Now he was teaching in one of the synagogues on the sabbath. 11 And there was a woman who had had a spirit of infirmity for eighteen years; she was bent over and could not fully straighten herself. 12 And when Jesus saw her, he called her and said to her, "Woman, you are freed from your infirmity." 13 And he laid his hands upon her, and immediately she was made straight, and she praised God. 14 But the ruler of the synagogue, indignant because Jesus had healed on the sabbath, said to the people, "There are six days on which work ought to be done; come on those days and be healed, and not on the sabbath day." 15 Then the Lord answered him, "You hypocrites! Does not each of you on the sabbath	**Luke 13:10-17** **Comment** Only Luke contains this story. Infirmity = (Strong's Greek Dictionary) "lack of strength, weakness, infirmity of the body, its native weakness and frailty, feebleness of health or sickness." Eighteen years is a long time. Jesus pronounced her healed and laid his hand on her, he touched her. The Ruler of the Synagogue was extremely displeased. It was the responsibility of the "Ruler of the Synagogue" to insure that everything done in the Synagogue was according to

untie his ox or his ass from the manger, and lead it away to water it? 16 And ought not this woman, a daughter of Abraham whom Satan bound for eighteen years, be loosed from this bond on the sabbath day?" 17 As he said this, all his adversaries were put to shame; and all the people rejoiced at all the glorious things that were done by him.

Forgot to bring bread

**Mark 8:14-21;
Matthew 16:5-12;
Luke 12:1-3**

Mark 8:14-21
14 Now they had forgotten to bring bread; and they had only one loaf with them in the boat. 15 And he cautioned them, saying, "Take heed, beware of the leaven of the Pharisees and the leaven of Herod." 16 And they discussed it with one another, saying, "We have no bread." 17 And being aware of it, Jesus said to them, "Why do you discuss the fact

the Law of Moses.

The Ruler's words sounded as though healing could be done any day of the week, but just don't heal on the Sabbath. Jesus sharply denounced him as being a hypocrite. Then he proceeds to show how the hypocrites do work on the Sabbath.

Jesus explained her infirmity as being held in the bonds of Satan.

Jesus' adversaries were put to shame while the people rejoiced with gladness.

Forgot to bring bread

**Mark 8:14-21;
Matthew 16:5-12;
Luke 12:1-3**

Comment

Matthew's version of the story is somewhat softer than that of Mark. Having just finished feeding the 4,000 the Inner-Circle realized they had forgotten to bring any bread as they make their way across the Sea of Galilee. Jesus told them to be aware of the leaven of the Pharisees and Herod. He was

that you have no bread? Do you not yet perceive or understand? Are your hearts hardened? 18 Having eyes do you not see, and having ears do you not hear? And do you not remember? 19 When I broke the five loaves for the five thousand, how many baskets full of broken pieces did you take up?" They said to him, "Twelve." 20 "And the seven for the four thousand, how many baskets full of broken pieces did you take up?" And they said to him, "Seven." 21 And he said to them, "Do you not yet understand?"

Matthew 16:5-12
5 When the disciples reached the other side, they had forgotten to bring any bread. 6 Jesus said to them, "Take heed and beware of the leaven of the Pharisees and Sad'ducees." 7 And they discussed it among themselves, saying, "We brought no bread." 8 But Jesus, aware of this, said, "O men of little faith, why do you discuss among yourselves the fact that you have no bread? 9 Do you not yet perceive? Do you not remember the five loaves of the five thousand, and how many baskets you gathered? 10 Or the seven loaves of the four thousand, and how many baskets you gathered? 11 How is it that

speaking of the inner driving force of these individuals. The Inner-Circle thought he was talking about bread to eat.

In Mark's version Jesus spoke harshly to the Inner-Circle, asking if they had closed their hearts to understanding. Have their eyes and ears failed them? Matthew, on the other hand, says when Jesus explained the meaning they understood.

you fail to perceive that I did not speak about bread? Beware of the leaven of the Pharisees and Sad'ducees." 12 Then they understood that he did not tell them to beware of the leaven of bread, but of the teaching of the Pharisees and Sad'ducees.

Luke 12:1-3
1 In the meantime, when so many thousands of the multitude had gathered together that they trod upon one another, he began to say to his disciples first, "Beware of the leaven of the Pharisees, which is hypocrisy. 2 Nothing is covered up that will not be revealed, or hidden that will not be known. 3 Therefore whatever you have said in the dark shall be heard in the light, and what you have whispered in private rooms shall be proclaimed upon the housetops.

Spit on his eyes

Mark 8:22-26
22 And they came to Beth-sa'ida. And some people brought to him a blind man, and begged him to touch him. 23 And he took the blind man by the hand, and led him out of the village; and when he had spit on his eyes and laid

Spit on his eyes

Mark 8:22-26

Comment

This is an independent statement found only in Mark.

his hands upon him, he asked him, "Do you see anything?" 24 And he looked up and said, "I see men; but they look like trees, walking." 25 Then again he laid his hands upon his eyes; and he looked intently and was restored, and saw everything clearly. 26 And he sent him away to his home, saying, "Do not even enter the village."	This is the only recorded healing, requiring two stages for completion.

Chapter 16

The Final Preparation

Caesera Philippi

If you want to hear the unvarnished non-sugarcoated message of Jesus, this is where you find it. John does not include this event in his report. Mark begins the story, Matthew adds pertinent factors, but Luke finishes the story with the most unbelievable comment of all.

The Final Preparation	*The Final Preparation*
Caesera Philippi	*Caesera Philippi*
Mark 8:27-28; Matthew 16:13-14; Luke 9:18-19	Mark 8:27-28; Matthew 16:13-14; Luke 9:18-19
Mark 8:27-28	**Comment**
27 And Jesus went on with his disciples, to the villages of Caesare'a Philip'pi; and on the way he asked his disciples, "Who do men say that I am?" 28 And they told him, "John the Baptist; and others say, Eli'jah; and others one of the prophets."	The city of Caesarea Philippi was built by Herod Philip to honor Cesar. Mark indicates many villages surrounded the city and these seem to be the focus of Jesus' visit.
Matthew 16:13-14 13 Now when Jesus came into the district of Caesare'a Philip'pi, he asked his disciples, "Who do men say that the Son of man is?" 14 And they said, "Some	It is here Jesus asked the pivotal question of, "Who do men say that I am?" The Inner-Circle gave a variety of answers.

say John the Baptist, others say Eli'jah, and others Jeremiah or one of the prophets."

Luke 9:18-19
18 Now it happened that as he was praying alone the disciples were with him; and he asked them, "Who do the people say that I am?" 19 And they answered, "John the Baptist; but others say, Eli'jah; and others, that one of the old prophets has risen."

<u>*Who do you say that I am?*</u>

**Mark 8:29-30;
Matthew 16:15-16;
Luke 9:20**

Mark 8:29-30
29 And he asked them, "But who do you say that I am?" Peter answered him, "You are the Christ." 30 And he charged them to tell no one about him.

Matthew 16:15-16
15 He said to them, "But who do you say that I am?" 16 Simon Peter replied, "You are the Christ, the Son of the living God."

Luke 9:20
20 And he said to them, "But who do you say that I am?" And Peter answered, "The Christ of God."

<u>*Who do you say that I am?*</u>

**Mark 8:29-30;
Matthew 16:15-16;
Luke 9:20**

Comment

Jesus called for an individual answer from each man. He bluntly asked, "Who do you say that I am?" Only they could make the decision, no one could do it for them. Only Peter ventures forth with an answer, "You are the Christ."

Blessed are you, Simon Bar-Jona!	*Blessed are you, Simon Bar-Jona!*
Matthew 16:17-19 17 And Jesus answered him, "Blessed are you, Simon Bar-Jona! For flesh and blood has not revealed this to you, but my Father who is in heaven. 18 And I tell you, you are Peter, and on this rock I will build my church, and the powers of death shall not prevail against it. 19 I will give you the keys of the kingdom of heaven, and whatever you bind on earth shall be bound in heaven, and whatever you loose on earth shall be loosed in heaven."	**Matthew 16:17-19** **Comment** This is an independent statement found only in Matthew. Jesus praised Simon Peter, saying God had revealed this to him. Jesus then changed Simon's name to Peter, the rock. Jesus announced he would build his church on this rock. Was he referring to Peter? Or was he referring to the confession Peter had just made? Jesus promised "The powers of death would not prevail against it," the KJV says, "The gates of Hell will not prevail against it." Both versions refer to "it" meaning the church, not Peter. Hell may be considered like a vast prisoner of war concentration camp of the most unimaginable horror.

Who holds the keys?

The Catholic Church holds that the promise was to the man Peter. The remainder of Christ Church holds the promise was to soon be the new church.

Assuming Jesus gave the keys to the kingdom to Peter individually, one might conclude that upon the death of Peter the entrustment would be canceled. However, if the soon to be established church is entrusted with the "Keys," the power would have potentially a life that would last as long as humanity existed.

Tell no one	*Tell no one*
Matthew 16:20; **Luke 9:21**	**Matthew 16:20;** **Luke 9:21**
Matthew 16:20 20 Then he strictly charged the disciples to tell no one that he was the Christ. **Luke 9:21** 21 But he charged and commanded them to tell this to no one,	**Comment** Jesus orders the Inner-Circle to say nothing of this to the public. It would seem the other gospel writers adhered seriously to this admonition having not included this information in their works.
The Son of man must suffer	*The Son of man must suffer*
Mark 8:31-32a; **Matthew 16:21;** **Luke 9:22**	**Mark 8:31-32a;** **Matthew 16:21;** **Luke 9:22**
Mark 8:31-32a 31 And he began to teach them that the Son of man must suffer many things, and be rejected by the elders and the chief priests and the scribes, and be killed, and after three days rise again. 32 And he said this plainly.	**Comment** Luke added to the story that Jesus would suffer rejection, be killed and on the third day be raised from the dead. No one wants to suffer. No one wants to be rejected. We do not deal well with any of these.

Matthew 16:21
21 From that time Jesus began to show his disciples that he must go to Jerusalem and suffer many things from the elders and chief priests and scribes, and be killed, and on the third day be raised.

Luke 9:22
22 saying, "The Son of man must suffer many things, and be rejected by the elders and chief priests and scribes, and be killed, and on the third day be raised."

Peter began to rebuke Jesus

**Mark 8:32b-33;
Matthew 16:22-23**

Mark 8:32b-33
32b And Peter took him, and began to rebuke him. 33 But turning and seeing his disciples, he rebuked Peter, and said, "Get behind me, Satan! For you are not on the side of God, but of men."

Matthew 16:22-23
22 And Peter took him and began to rebuke him, saying, "God forbid, Lord! This shall never happen to you." 23 But he turned and said to Peter, "Get behind me, Satan! You are a hindrance

Peter began to rebuke Jesus

**Mark 8:32b-33;
Matthew 16:22-23**

Comment

Jesus must go to Jerusalem for fulfillment of his words. He tells the Inner-Circle in detail what to expect. He will be rejected by the elders and the chief priest and be put to death. But on the third day he will be raised.

Peter was so disturbed by these comments, that he boldly stated Jesus is wrong. It cannot happen! Jesus turned toward him instantly with temper

to me; for you are not on the side of God, but of men."

flaring. Peter's position mirrors the opposition of Satan himself. Thinking in this manner Peter will be a hindrance rather than a help in the challenge that lies ahead.

Take up your cross

**Mark 8:34-38; 9:1;
Matthew 16:24-28;
Luke 9:23-27**

Take up your cross

**Mark 8:34-38; 9:1;
Matthew 16:24-28;
Luke 9:23-27**

Mark 8:34-38
34 And he called to him the multitude with his disciples, and said to them, "If any man would come after me, let him deny himself and take up his cross and follow me. 35 For whoever would save his life will lose it; and whoever loses his life for my sake and the gospel's will save it. 36 For what does it profit a man, to gain the whole world and forfeit his life? 37 For what can a man give in return for his life? 38 For whoever is ashamed of me and of my words in this adulterous and sinful generation, of him will the Son of man also be ashamed, when he comes in the glory of his Father with the holy angels."

Mark 9:1
1 And he said to them, "Truly,

Comment

Did someone in the crowd ask to travel with Jesus? If it was a question, Jesus wanted to clarify the demands and expectations of following him. It would mean the follower must put his personal desires second to their commitment. The follower would make a daily commitment to follow Jesus. The natural desire is to save one's life, and to live well in the pursuit of earthly treasure. To dedicate one's life to the servant role is to forgo these earthly pleasures.

Jesus then made the bold claim that should one gain the whole world and lose their life in the bargain would be a catastrophe. If one's earthly life was all that

I say to you, there are some standing here who will not taste death before they see that the kingdom of God has come with power."

Matthew 16:24-28
24 Then Jesus told his disciples, "If any man would come after me, let him deny himself and take up his cross and follow me. 25 For whoever would save his life will lose it, and whoever loses his life for my sake will find it. 26 For what will it profit a man, if he gains the whole world and forfeits his life? Or what shall a man give in return for his life? 27 For the Son of man

is to come with his angels in the glory of his Father, and then he will repay every man for what he has done. 28 Truly, I say to you, there are some standing here who will not taste death before they see the Son of man coming in his kingdom."

Luke 9:23-27
23 And he said to all, "If any man would come after me, let him deny himself and take up his cross daily and follow me. 24 For whoever would save his life will lose it; and whoever loses his life for my sake, he will save it.

was at stake it would be worth the goal. But there is more at stake than one's earthly life, there is a second life yet to be experienced, and that would be forfeited in the pursuit of earthly gain.

Jesus further stated those who refuse to follow him he will refuse to receive into the kingdom of heaven.

The Kingdom of God comes when God's perfect will is being followed. On the cross, Jesus was completely engulfed in God's will for him and humanity. The Inner-Circle would witness this in time to come.

25 For what does it profit a man if he gains the whole world and loses or forfeits himself? 26 For whoever is ashamed of me and of my words, of him will the Son of man be ashamed when he comes in his glory and the glory of the Father and of the holy angels. 27 But I tell you truly, there are some standing here who will not taste death before they see the kingdom of God."

The Transfiguration

Mark 9:2;
Matthew 17:1;
Luke 9:28

Mark 9:2
2 And after six days Jesus took with him Peter and James and John, and led them up a high mountain apart by themselves; and he was transfigured before them,

Matthew 17:1
1 And after six days Jesus took with him Peter and James and John his brother, and led them up a high mountain apart.

Luke 9:28
28 Now about eight days after these sayings he took with him

The Transfiguration

Mark 9:2;
Matthew 17:1;
Luke 9:28

Comment

Mark and Matthew tell us, "Six days later" an amazing event took place. Those were an amazing six days and understanding them is the only way we can appreciate what is about to unfold. Luke is less sure of the exact number of days and reports, "About eight days."

The big three were with Jesus, that is, Peter James and John. Once up the mountain the disciples witnessed the

| Peter and John and James, and went up on the mountain to pray. | Transfiguration of Jesus. Perhaps this was on snowcapped Mount Hermon. |

Peter acknowledged Jesus

Peter had acknowledged Jesus as the Messiah. Then he tried to tell him what to do. This resulted in Jesus saying Peter was like Satan to him because he was attempting to divert Jesus from his appointed duty. Following that, a number of events heighten the tension between Jesus and the Inner-Circle.

Glistening garments	*Glistening garments*
Mark 9:3; **Matthew 17:2;** **Luke 9:29**	**Mark 9:3;** **Matthew 17:2;** **Luke 9:29**
Mark 9:3 3 and his garments became glistening, intensely white, as no fuller on earth could bleach them. **Matthew 17:2** 2 And he was transfigured before them, and his face shone like the sun, and his garments became white as light. **Luke 9:29** 29 And as he was praying, the appearance of his countenance was altered, and his raiment became dazzling white.	**Comment** The word translated *glistening* means to flash like lightning, to shine, to be radiant.

Eli'jah with Moses appear

Mark 9:4;
Matthew 17:3;
Luke 9:30-31

Mark 9:4
4 And there appeared to them Eli'jah with Moses; and they were talking to Jesus.

Matthew 17:3
3 And behold, there appeared to them Moses and Eli'jah, talking with him.

Luke 9:30-31
30 And behold, two men talked with him, Moses and Eli'jah, 31 who appeared in glory and spoke of his departure, which he was to accomplish at Jerusalem.

Let us make three booths

Mark 9:5-6;
Matthew 17:4;
Luke 9:32

Mark 9:5-6
5 And Peter said to Jesus, "Master, it is well that we are here; let us make three booths, one for you and one for Moses and one for Eli'jah." 6 For he did

Eli'jah with Moses appear

Mark 9:4;
Matthew 17:3;
Luke 9:30-31

Comment

Luke says the purpose of Elijah and Moses was to discuss with Jesus his pending death and its location.

Let us make three booths

Mark 9:5-6;
Matthew 17:4;
Luke 9:32

Comment

Mark tells us the members of the Inner-Circle were "exceedingly afraid." Luke says Peter, James and John were asleep.

not know what to say, for they were exceedingly afraid.

Matthew 17:4
4 And Peter said to Jesus, "Lord, it is well that we are here; if you wish, I will make three booths here, one for you and one for Moses and one for Eli'jah."

Luke 9:32
32 Now Peter and those who were with him were heavy with sleep, and when they wakened they saw his glory and the two men who stood with him.

Peter, not knowing what to say, asked if Jesus would like him to build three booths for them? The word translated *booth* means something made out of materials found on the mountain; wood or brush, or a tent.

This is a difficult passage to understand. The intent is they would remain on the mountaintop, live out some period if not all of their lives in the place of the Divine Revelation. All who have experienced a mountaintop experience want it to last forever. The reality is life is not lived top of the mountain. Life is lived in the valley of reality.

<u>*My beloved Son; listen to Him*</u>

Mark 9:7-8;
Matthew 17:5-8;
Luke 9:33-36

<u>*My beloved Son; listen to Him*</u>

Mark 9:7-8;
Matthew 17:5-8;
Luke 9:33-36

Mark 9:7-8
7 And a cloud overshadowed them, and a voice came out of the cloud, "This is my beloved Son; listen to him." 8 And suddenly looking around they no longer saw any one with them but Jesus only.

Comment

Matthew follows Mark until the latter part of verse six. Matthew tells us the disciples fell on their faces and were filled with awe. The voice from the cloud said, "This is my son, listen to him."

Matthew 17:5-8
5 He was still speaking, when lo, a bright cloud overshadowed them, and a voice from the cloud said, "This is my beloved Son, with whom I am well pleased; listen to him." 6 When the disciples heard this, they fell on their faces, and were filled with awe. 7 But Jesus came and touched them, saying, "Rise, and have no fear." 8 And when they lifted up their eyes, they saw no one but Jesus only.

Luke 9:33-36
33 And as the men were parting from him, Peter said to Jesus, "Master, it is well that we are here; let us make three booths, one for you and one for Moses and one for Eli'jah"—not knowing what he said. 34 As he said this, a cloud came and overshadowed them; and they were afraid as they entered the cloud. 35 And a voice came out of the cloud, saying, "This is my Son, my Chosen; listen to him!" 36 And when the voice had spoken, Jesus was found alone. And they kept silence and told no one in those days anything of what they had seen.

You can't listen, if you're trying to do all of the talking. Jesus touched them and told them to rise and do not be afraid.

Luke adds the closing comment that they remained silent about what had happened and told no one.

Coming down the mountain

Mark 9:9-13;
Matthew 17:9-13

Mark 9:9-13
9 And as they were coming down the mountain, he charged them to tell no one what they had seen, until the Son of man should have risen from the dead. 10 So they kept the matter to themselves, questioning what the rising from the dead meant. 11 And they asked him, "Why do the scribes say that first Eli'jah must come?" 12 And he said to them, "Eli'jah does come first to restore all things; and how is it written of the Son of man, that he should suffer many things and be treated with contempt? 13 But I tell you that Eli'jah has come, and they did to him whatever they pleased, as it is written of him."

Matthew 17:9-13
9 And as they were coming down the mountain, Jesus commanded them, "Tell no one the vision, until the Son of man is raised from the dead." 10 And the disciples asked him, "Then why do the scribes say that first Eli'jah must come?" 11 He replied, "Eli'jah does come, and he is to restore all things; 12 but I tell you that

Coming down the mountain

Mark 9:9-13;
Matthew 17:9-13

Comment

As they descend the mountain Jesus told them to tell no one that he is to be raised from the dead. To their credit, they told no one perhaps because they did not understand what it meant. The disciples asked why the scribes said Elijah must come before The Messiah. Jesus helped them understand that the spirit of Elijah had been upon John the Baptist.

Eli'jah has already come, and they did not know him, but did to him whatever they pleased. So also the Son of man will suffer at their hands." 13 Then the disciples understood that he was speaking to them of John the Baptist.

At the foot of the mountain

Mark 9:14-29;
Matthew 17:14-20;
Luke 9:37-42

Mark 9:14-29
14 And when they came to the disciples, they saw a great crowd about them, and scribes arguing with them. 15 And immediately all the crowd, when they saw him, were greatly amazed, and ran up to him and greeted him. 16 And he asked them, "What are you discussing with them?" 17 And one of the crowd answered him, "Teacher, I brought my son to you, for he has a dumb spirit; 18 and wherever it seizes him, it dashes him down; and he foams and grinds his teeth and becomes rigid; and I asked your disciples to cast it out, and they were not able." 19 And he answered them, "O faithless generation, how long am I to be with you? How long am I to bear with you?

At the foot of the mountain

Mark 9:14-29;
Matthew 17:14-20;
Luke 9:37-42

Comment

All three Evangelists tell the story, but Mark gives more detail than the others.

We are not told how long they stayed upon the mountain, but obviously it was long enough for a crowd to gather. Jesus noticed there was a group of scribes arguing with the remainder of the Inner-Circle. He inquired as to the issue. The father interceded and told the story of his son and his demon possession. To the humiliation of the disciples, the father told Jesus his disciples were incapable of performing the exorcism. The father then said to

Bring him to me." 20 And they brought the boy to him; and when the spirit saw him, immediately it convulsed the boy, and he fell on the ground and rolled about, foaming at the mouth. 21 And Jesus asked his father, "How long has he had this?" And he said, "From childhood. 22 And it has often cast him into the fire and into the water, to destroy him; but if you can do anything, have pity on us and help us." 23 And Jesus said to him, "If you can! All things are possible to him who believes." 24 Immediately the father of the child cried out and said, "I believe; help my unbelief!" 25 And when Jesus saw that a crowd came running together, he rebuked the unclean spirit, saying to it, "You dumb and deaf spirit, I command you, come out of him, and never enter him again." 26 And after crying out and convulsing him terribly, it came out, and the boy was like a corpse; so that most of them said, "He is dead." 27 But Jesus took him by the hand and lifted him up, and he arose. 28 And when he had entered the house, his disciples asked him privately, "Why could we not cast it out?" 29 And he said to them, "This kind cannot be driven out by anything but prayer."

Jesus, "If you can help." Once more we see a flare of temper as Jesus responded, "What do you mean if I can."

In a roundabout way, Jesus told the Inner-Circle he would not always be there to perform these miracles for them. When they asked privately, why they could not cast out the demon, Jesus told them they did not have enough faith. Using the mustard seed as the example he said, if you had even the tiniest amount of genuine faith you could have done it. He also told them this kind of demon only responded to prayer.

Matthew 17:14-20
14 And when they came to the crowd, a man came up to him and kneeling before him said, 15 "Lord, have mercy on my son, for he is an epileptic and he suffers terribly; for often he falls into the fire, and often into the water. 16 And I brought him to your disciples, and they could not heal him." 17 And Jesus answered, "O faithless and perverse generation, how long am I to be with you? How long am I to bear with you? Bring him here to me." 18 And Jesus rebuked him, and the demon came out of him, and the boy was cured instantly. 19 Then the disciples came to Jesus privately and said, "Why could we not cast it out?" 20 He said to them, "Because of your little faith. For truly, I say to you, if you have faith as a grain of mustard seed, you will say to this mountain, 'Move from here to there,' and it will move; and nothing will be impossible to you."

Luke 9:37-42
37 On the next day, when they had come down from the mountain, a great crowd met him. 38 And behold, a man from the crowd cried, "Teacher, I beg you to look upon my son, for he is my only child; 39 and behold, a spirit

seizes him, and he suddenly cries out; it convulses him till he foams, and shatters him, and will hardly leave him. ^{40} And I begged your disciples to cast it out, but they could not." ^{41} Jesus answered, "O faithless and perverse generation, how long am I to be with you and bear with you? Bring your son here." ^{42} While he was coming, the demon tore him and convulsed him. But Jesus rebuked the unclean spirit, and healed the boy, and gave him back to his father.

The Inner-Circle failed to understand

Luke 9:43-45
^{43} And all were astonished at the majesty of God. But while they were all marveling at everything he did, he said to his disciples, ^{44} "Let these words sink into your ears; for the Son of man is to be delivered into the hands of men." ^{45} But they did not understand this saying, and it was concealed from them, that they should not perceive it; and they were afraid to ask him about this saying.

The Inner-Circle failed to understand

Luke 9:43-45

Comment

The Inner-Circle did not understand what Jesus was trying to tell them and they were afraid to ask. They still felt the sharp rebuke that Peter had received for challenging Jesus saying he must suffer and die.

Jesus returns to Galilee Mark 9:30-32; Matthew 17:22-23 **Mark 9:30-32** 30 They went on from there and passed through Galilee. And he would not have any one know it; 31 for he was teaching his disciples, saying to them, "The Son of man will be delivered into the hands of men, and they will kill him; and when he is killed, after three days he will rise." 32 But they did not understand the saying, and they were afraid to ask him. **Matthew 17:22-23** 22 As they were gathering in Galilee, Jesus said to them, "The Son of man is to be delivered into the hands of men, 23 and they will kill him, and he will be raised on the third day." And they were greatly distressed.	**Jesus returns to Galilee** Mark 9:30-32; Matthew 17:22-23 **Comment** Leaving the area of Caesarea Philippi they entered Galilee, the northern most province of Israel ruled by Herod Antipas. Jesus told the Inner-Circle to tell no one he was there or what he was doing. Why? Two reasons stand out clearly. The first was he was trying to prepare the Inner-Circle for the immediate future. Secondly, he does not want to place his followers in jeopardy with Herod at this moment.
Does Jesus pay taxes? **Matthew 17:24-27** 24 When they came to Caper'na-um, the collectors of the half-shekel tax went up to Peter and said, "Does not your teacher pay the tax?" 25 He said, "Yes." And	**_Does Jesus pay taxes?_** **Matthew 17:24-27** **Comment** This is an independent statement found only in Matthew

when he came home, Jesus spoke to him first, saying, "What do you think, Simon? From whom do kings of the earth take toll or tribute? From their sons or from others?" 26 And when he said, "From others," Jesus said to him, "Then the sons are free. 27 However, not to give offense to them, go to the sea and cast a hook, and take the first fish that comes up, and when you open its mouth you will find a shekel; take that and give it to them for me and for yourself."

These "collectors" were very different from tax collectors like Matthew who collected for the government. The collectors mentioned here are from the Temple. Their job was to collect from each adult Jewish citizen the half shekel Temple tax. This was a compulsory tax for the support of the Temple.

These collectors did not assess the tax they simply collected it. The word implies they came to take the tax. The tax was equal to the Roman denarius, equivalent of a day's wage for a laborer.

The collectors did not go to Jesus directly, but rather to Peter. When asked, Peter affirmed that Jesus did indeed pay the tax. Jesus poses an interesting question to Peter, "Do the kings of the earth take a toll or tribute from their sons or from others?" Peter answered, they take it from others, Jesus rejoined saying the sons were free. Jesus was saying the compulsory Temple tax should not be upon the natural born Jews. Jews by birth were sons of the kingdom and should be exempt. This would imply only

	proselytes should pay the tax. The sons should contribute freely and willingly and not consider it a tax. Jesus did not confront the collectors with this proposition. He fulfilled what he had just said by paying the tax willingly. Certainly the manner of his paying a half shekel tax could only be defined as a miracle of extra ordinary proportions.

Chapter 17

THE MILL STONE

What were you discussing?

Mark 9:33-37;
Matthew 18:1-4;
Luke 9:46-48

Mark 9:33-37

33 And they came to Caper'na-um; and when he was in the house he asked them, "What were you discussing on the way?" 34 But they were silent; for on the way they had discussed with one another who was the greatest. 35 And he sat down and called the

What were you discussing?

Mark 9:33-37;
Matthew 18:1-4;
Luke 9:46-48

Comments

Capernaum became the home base for Jesus after he left Nazareth. Whose house did they enter? It was the house of Simon Peter. Once inside Jesus asked, "What were you talking about?" One can almost hear

twelve; and he said to them, "If any one would be first, he must be last of all and servant of all." 36 And he took a child, and put him in the midst of them; and taking him in his arms, he said to them, 37 "Whoever receives one such child in my name receives me; and whoever receives me, receives not me but him who sent me."

Matthew 18:1-4
1 At that time the disciples came to Jesus, saying, "Who is the greatest in the kingdom of heaven?" 2 And calling to him a child, he put him in the midst of them, 3 and said, "Truly, I say to you, unless you turn and become like children, you will never enter the kingdom of heaven. 4 Whoever humbles himself like this child, he is the greatest in the kingdom of heaven.

Luke 9:46-48
46 And an argument arose among them as to which of them was the greatest. 47 But when Jesus perceived the thought of their hearts, he took a child and put him by his side, 48 and said to them, "Whoever receives this child in my name receives me, and whoever receives me receives him who sent me; for he

the Inner-Circle thinking, "O man we have messed up again."

Jesus sat down, which was the posture of a rabbi when he was ready to teach, and told them to take a seat. We can only imagine how uncomfortable they felt knowing Jesus was going to talk to them about what they had been talking about.

Jesus then said, "Here is what it takes for you who want to be first, you must be servant of all."

This was a revolutionary thought!

Jesus placed a child in the middle of them. Why didn't he choose another adult for this purpose? Adults do not qualify because they no longer possess the innocence or a simple trusting faith. Jesus' point was the child did represent innocence. Their seeking personal power represented the loss of innocence.

On other occasions, Peter, James and John had argued over which of them would be greatest in Jesus' kingdom. In Luke's account he uses the plural

who is least among you all is the one who is great."

mean the entire Inner-Circle was engaged in this argument. We can only wonder which of the disciples Jesus thought would ultimately be qualified as the least.

Others casting out demons

**Mark 9:38-41;
Luke 9:49-50**

Mark 9:38-41
38 John said to him, "Teacher, we saw a man casting out demons in your name, and we forbade him, because he was not following us." 39 But Jesus said, "Do not forbid him; for no one who does a mighty work in my name will be able soon after to speak evil of me. 40 For he that is not against us is for us. 41 For truly, I say to you, whoever gives you a cup of water to drink because you bear the name of Christ, will by no means lose his reward.

Luke 9:49-50
49 John answered, "Master, we saw a man casting out demons in your name, and we forbade him, because he does not follow with us." 50 But Jesus said to him, "Do not forbid him; for he that is not against you is for you."

Others casting out demons

**Mark 9:38-41;
Luke 9:49-50**

Comments

Upon first reading this passage looks to be out of place. It seems to be totally inconsistent with what has gone before it and what follows. Here is one possible explanation for this apparent interruption in the narrative. Perhaps John was trying to change the subject. He may have felt very uncomfortable being asked to reveal the discussion about who would be first in the kingdom.

John's concern about others casting out demons was altogether plausible. He told Jesus of seeing a stranger who cast out demons in his name, "but we put a stop to that," he said proudly. Perhaps he thought this would even bring a commendation from Jesus. Jesus knew John meant well but he did not realize those who work in Jesus' cause were doing a good work.

Millstone around your neck

**Mark 9:42-50;
Matthew 18:5-6;
Luke 17:1-4**

Millstone around your neck

**Mark 9:42-50;
Matthew 18:5-6;
Luke 17:1-4**

Mark 9:42-50

42 "Whoever causes one of these little ones who believe in me to sin, it would be better for him if a great millstone were hung round his neck and he were thrown into the sea. 43 And if your hand causes you to sin, cut it off; it is better for you to enter life maimed than with two hands to go to hell, to the unquenchable fire. 45 And if your foot causes you to sin, cut it off; it is better for you to enter life lame than with two feet to be thrown into hell. 47 And if your eye causes you to sin, pluck it out; it is better for you to enter the kingdom of God with one eye than with two eyes to be thrown into hell, 48 where their worm does not die, and the fire is not quenched. 49 For every one will be salted with fire. 50 Salt is good; but if the salt has lost its

Comments

Following John's interruption, Jesus returns to the matters at hand.

Mark records these hard sayings of Jesus. We know Jesus did not condone any form of self-mutilation. So what does Jesus mean? To eliminate anything causing one to sin, even to the extent of one's hand, leg, foot, or eye would be better than letting one's appendages keep one out of the kingdom.

Verse forty-eight is even more obscure. The word translated as "worm" is also translated as "maggot." The obscurity is removed when we realize Jesus is quoting from the prophet Isaiah. Isaiah in relating what

saltness, how will you season it? Have salt in yourselves, and be at peace with one another."

Matthew 18:5-6
5 "Whoever receives one such child in my name receives me; 6 but whoever causes one of these little ones who believe in me to sin, it would be better for him to have a great millstone fastened round his neck and to be drowned in the depth of the sea.

Luke 17:1-4
1 And he said to his disciples, "Temptations to sin are sure to come; but woe to him by whom they come! 2 It would be better for him if a millstone were hung round his neck and he were cast into the sea, than that he should cause one of these little ones to sin. 3 Take heed to yourselves; if your brother sins, rebuke him, and if he repents, forgive him; 4 and if he sins against you seven times in the day, and turns to you seven times, and says, 'I repent,' you must forgive him."

God plans in His new creation, His new heaven and new earth, when people from all the present nations will gather before Him. *"And they shall go forth and look on the dead bodies of the men that have rebelled against me; for their worm shall not die, their fire shall not be quenched, and they shall be an abhorrence to all flesh." Isaiah 66:24*

In verses forty-nine to fifty, the Old Testament says sacrifices were salted before being burned. Salt was very valuable for preserving meats and fish. When applying the concept of salt to Christians, the issues are accountability and discipline. For a Christian to lose his saltiness would mean he had committed apostasy, that is to renounce Jesus as Lord and Savior.

Angels watch over them

Matthew 18:10-14
10 "See that you do not despise one of these little ones; for I tell

Angels watch over them

Matthew 18:10-14

Comment

you that in heaven their angels always behold the face of my Father who is in heaven. 12 What do you think? If a man has a hundred sheep, and one of them has gone astray, does he not leave the ninety-nine on the mountains and go in search of the one that went astray? 13 And if he finds it, truly, I say to you, he rejoices over it more than over the ninety-nine that never went astray. 14 So it is not the will of my Father who is in heaven that one of these little ones should perish.

This is an independent statement of Matthew.

Jesus sternly warned them not to hold children in contempt. Child abusers would do well to read this passage! Jesus upheld the concept of angels, saying a child's Angel is ever before God. He further asserted God does not wish one of His children to perish.

Jesus is ready to go to Jerusalem

Luke 9:51-56

51 When the days drew near for him to be received up, he set his face to go to Jerusalem. 52 And he sent messengers ahead of him, who went and entered a village of the Samaritans, to make ready for him; 53 but the people would not receive him, because his face was set toward Jerusalem. 54 And when his disciples James and John saw it, they said, "Lord, do you want us to bid fire come down from heaven and consume them?" 55 But he turned and rebuked them. 56 And they went on to another village.

Jesus is ready to go to Jerusalem

Luke 9:51-56

Comment

Leaving Capernaum Jesus turned south to head back toward Jerusalem. When Jesus' messengers, presumably James and John, reached the Samaritan village the inhabitants refused Jesus entry into their city. James and John angrily reported the incident to Jesus, asking permission to bring down fire from Heaven upon these impertinent foreigners. Jesus crushes their idea with a stern rebuke.

Reason for the rejection of Jesus

The reason for the rejection was because Jesus was heading toward Jerusalem. Earlier in John's Gospel, you will remember, Jesus was warmly greeted by the Samaritans after talking to the woman at the well. The difference in acceptance and rejection revolves around which direction Jesus was traveling. Coming from Jerusalem he was accepted, going toward Jerusalem he was rejected.

The issue was where was the proper place to worship God, Jerusalem or Mount Gerizim?

I will follow you wherever you go	*I will follow you wherever you go*
Luke 9:57-62	**Luke 9:57-62**
57 As they were going along the road, a man said to him, "I will follow you wherever you go." 58 And Jesus said to him, "Foxes have holes, and birds of the air have nests; but the Son of man has nowhere to lay his head." 59 To another he said, "Follow me." But he said, "Lord, let me first go and bury my father." 60 But he said to him, "Leave the dead to bury their own dead; but as for you, go and proclaim the kingdom of God." 61 Another said, "I will follow you, Lord; but let me first say farewell to those at my home." 62 Jesus said to him, "No one who puts his hand to the plow and looks back is fit for the kingdom of God."	**Comment** This is an independent statement found only in Luke. Luke tells us of a second would-be disciple. In this case the man wants to go and bury his father. This statement implies the father is still alive, and the son wanted to wait until his death before becoming a disciple. Jesus' answer seems to be harsh indeed. Jesus knows the demands of discipleship will be much harder than giving up the opportunity to bury one's loved one. Jesus refuses to set a person in the position where he is doomed to fail.

Sending out the seventy

Luke 10:1-12

1 After this the Lord appointed seventy others, and sent them on ahead of him, two by two, into every town and place where he himself was about to come. 2 And he said to them, "The harvest is plentiful, but the laborers are few; pray therefore the Lord of the harvest to send out laborers into his harvest. 3 Go your way; behold, I send you out as lambs in the midst of wolves. 4 Carry no purse, no bag, no sandals; and salute no one on the road. 5 Whatever house you enter, first say, 'Peace be to this house!' 6 And if a son of peace is there, your peace shall rest upon him; but if not, it shall return to you. 7 And remain in the same house, eating and drinking what they provide, for the laborer deserves his wages; do not go from house to house. 8 Whenever you enter a town and they receive you, eat what is set before you; 9 heal the sick in it and say to them, 'The kingdom of God has come near to you.' 10 But whenever you enter a town and they do not receive you, go into its streets and say, 11 'Even the dust of your town that clings to our feet, we wipe off

Sending out the seventy

Luke 10:1-12

Comment

This is an independent statement found only in Luke's Gospel.

After the success of the two by two expedition, Jesus now planned to send out seventy more volunteers. He planned to follow them shortly after their departure. The clarion call for their mission is his comment, "The harvest is plentiful, but the laborers are few."

The Lord of the harvest is Jesus, the harvesters are the seventy. They will be like lambs in the midst of wolves. Jesus could hardly have used a more descriptive comment on their precarious position in society. Like the group before them, they will carry no purse, meaning they will have no money with them.

When they were welcomed into a private home they were to say, "Peace be upon this house!" If the householder was of a like mind they were welcomed to

against you; nevertheless know this, that the kingdom of God has come near.' 12 I tell you, it shall be more tolerable on that day for Sodom than for that town.

stay. On the other hand, if he was not of like mind their peace would return to them.

Virtually the same instructions were given to those who went out two by two. They were to heal the sick and say to the people the kingdom of God has come near. If the people would not accept their words they were to shake the dust off of their feet and move on to the next village. For those who reject their message their fate would be more disastrous than that of the residents of Sodom.

Woe to Capernaum and Chorazin

**Matthew 11:20-24;
Luke 10:13-16**

Matthew 11:20-24
20 Then he began to upbraid the cities where most of his mighty works had been done, because they did not repent. 21 "Woe to you, Chora'zin! woe to you, Beth-sa'ida! for if the mighty works done in you had been done in Tyre and Sidon, they would have repented long ago in sackcloth and ashes.

Woe to Capernaum and Chorazin

**Matthew 11:20-24;
Luke 10:13-16**

Comment

"Upbraid" is used only three times in the New Testament. It means strong reproach that is well deserved. In other words, the cities well deserved the strong words Jesus spoke against them. It should be realized Jesus did not say this from wrath, he spoke them from sorrow.

22 But I tell you, it shall be more tolerable on the day of judgment for Tyre and Sidon than for you. 23 And you, Caper'na-um, will you be exalted to heaven? You shall be brought down to Hades. For if the mighty works done in you had been done in Sodom, it would have remained until this day. 24 But I tell you that it shall be more tolerable on the day of judgment for the land of Sodom than for you."

Luke 10:13-16
13 "Woe to you, Chora'zin! woe to you, Beth-sa'ida! for if the mighty works done in you had been done in Tyre and Sidon, they would have repented long ago, sitting in sackcloth and ashes. 14 But it shall be more tolerable in the judgment for Tyre and Sidon than for you. 15 And you, Caper'na-um, will you be exalted to heaven? You shall be brought down to Hades. 16 "He who hears you hears me, and he who rejects you rejects me, and he who rejects me rejects him who sent me."

The Seventy Return

Luke 10:17-20
17 The seventy returned with

The Seventy Return

Luke 10:17-20

joy, saying, "Lord, even the demons are subject to us in your name!" 18 And he said to them, "I saw Satan fall like lightning from heaven. 19 Behold, I have given you authority to tread upon serpents and scorpions, and over all the power of the enemy; and nothing shall hurt you. 20 Nevertheless do not rejoice in this, that the spirits are subject to you; but rejoice that your names are written in heaven."

Comment

This is independent statement found only in Luke.

The returnees were ecstatic! They could hardly wait to tell Jesus, the demons had obeyed because of his name. Jesus sharing in their joy said, "I saw Satan fall like lightning from heaven." Jesus warned them about getting the "big head" over their success. Jesus expected no less, because he had given them authority even to step on the heads of serpents and scorpions, should that be called for.

Their names were written in heaven. The word written is the same word used to describe those things which were written in sacred books.

Jesus gives thanks

**Matthew 11:25-30;
Luke 10:21-24**

Matthew 11:25-30
25 At that time Jesus declared, "I thank thee, Father, Lord of heaven and earth, that thou hast hidden these things from the wise

Jesus gives thanks

**Matthew 11:25-30;
Luke 10:21-24**

Comment

Jesus uses an impressive array of verbs in this short passage: "Wise" means skill in letters,

and understanding and revealed them to babes; 26 yea, Father, for such was thy gracious will. 27 All things have been delivered to me by my Father; and no one knows the Son except the Father, and no one knows the Father except the Son and any one to whom the Son chooses to reveal him. 28 Come to me, all who labor and are heavy laden, and I will give you rest. 29 Take my yoke upon you, and learn from me; for I am gentle and lowly in heart, and you will find rest for your souls. 30 For my yoke is easy, and my burden is light."	a cultivated person with education. "Babes" is a word used to describe an infant or small child, a minor at best. The seventy were not skilled or writers learned in letters. They were indeed in their faith like infants or small children and willing to follow and learn.
	Jesus then invited the masses to come to him, because all were truly burdened with heavy loads. From his carpenter background Jesus knew that an ill fitting yoke would chafe and create sores. Jesus offers his yoke to be a perfect fit. Everyone will have to do something to get through life, doing the will of God provides the perfect path.
Luke 10:21-24 21 In that same hour he rejoiced in the Holy Spirit and said, "I thank thee, Father, Lord of heaven and earth, that thou hast hidden these things from the wise and understanding and revealed them to babes; yea, Father, for such was thy gracious will. 22 All things have been delivered to me by my Father; and no one knows who the Son is except the Father, or who the Father is except the Son and any one to whom the Son chooses to reveal him." 23 Then turning to the disciples he said privately, "Blessed are	

Parable of the Good Samaritan

Luke 10:25-37

the eyes which see what you see! 24 For I tell you that many prophets and kings desired to see what you see, and did not see it, and to hear what you hear, and did not hear it."

25 And behold, a lawyer stood up to put him to the test, saying, "Teacher, what shall I do to inherit eternal life?" 26 He said to him, "What is written in the law? How do you read?" 27 And he answered, "You shall love the Lord your God with all your heart, and with all your soul, and with all your strength, and with all your mind; and your neighbor as yourself." 28 And he said to him, "You have answered right; do this, and you will live." 29 But he, desiring to justify himself, said to Jesus, "And who is my neighbor?"

30 Jesus replied, "A man was going down from Jerusalem to Jericho, and he fell among robbers, who stripped him and beat him, and departed, leaving him half dead. 31 Now by chance a priest was going down

Parable of the Good Samaritan

Luke 10:25-37

Comment

This is an independent statement found only in Luke.

The Lawyer was an authority in the Law of Moses. He intended to test Jesus with the intention of trapping him. Jesus knew the answer to the question, and so did the lawyer. It was a profound question, and many people struggle with it to this day, "What shall I do to inherit eternal life?"

The Jericho road is very narrow and runs a twisting, tortured course at the base of large mountains on either side. It begins at Jerusalem and winds its way to the town of Jericho, which is near the Dead Sea. It drops some 3,600 feet from

that road; and when he saw him he passed by on the other side. ³² So likewise a Levite, when he came to the place and saw him, passed by on the other side. ³³ But a Samaritan, as he journeyed, came to where he was; and when he saw him, he had compassion, ³⁴ and went to him and bound up his wounds, pouring on oil and wine; then he set him on his own beast and brought him to an inn, and took care of him. ³⁵ And the next day he took out two denarii and gave them to the innkeeper, saying, 'Take care of him; and whatever more you spend, I will repay you when I come back.' ³⁶ Which of these three, do you think, proved neighbor to the man who fell among the robbers?" ³⁷ He said, "The one who showed mercy on him." And Jesus said to him, "Go and do likewise."

Jerusalem to Jericho. Every foot of this road was a dangerous lair for robbers.

The identity of the victim can only be surmised from the story itself. He was a Jew, probably a merchant, who was carrying either expensive goods or money on his person.

The priest may have been making his way from Jericho to Jerusalem, to do service at the Temple. If the man was dead and he touched him, it would make him unclean and therefore unfit for service in the Temple.

The Levite was a member of the Hebrew tribe of Levi. The Levites were the only tribe that received cities but no tribal land when Joshua led the people of Israel into the land of Canaan. The Levites preformed particular religious duties for the Israelites. In return, the landed tribes were expected to give the tithe to the Levites.

The Jews hated the Samaritans. They did not want to step on Samaritan territory, nor did they want to hold conversations with them. The Jew looked down on

the laborer deserves his wages; do not go from house to house. 8 Whenever you enter a town and they receive you, eat what is set before you; 9 heal the sick in it and say to them, 'The kingdom of God has come near to you.' 10 But whenever you enter a town and they do not receive you, go into its streets and say, 11 'Even the dust of your town that clings to our feet, we wipe off against you; nevertheless know this, that the kingdom of God has come near.' 12 I tell you, it shall be more tolerable on that day for Sodom than for that town.	a Samaritan in every aspect of life. Only the hated Samaritan stopped and helped the injured man. Oil and wine were used to cleanse the wounds. Next he managed to get the man on his "beast" and transported him to the inn at the juncture of the road. The Samaritan gave the innkeeper an amount of money equal to two days wages for a laborer. He went even further by committing himself to pay all of the expenses incurred for helping the victim. The Innkeeper trusted the Samaritan.

The Samaritan

This story would have been exceptionally distressful to every Jew listening to Jesus. The priest and the Levite held exalted positions in the Jewish religious community. The hated and despised Samaritan was the only person who showed compassion for the injured man. Putting the injured man on his own beast of burden placed himself at risk. He would have to travel much slower through this dangerous territory. When he reached the inn, he was not at the end of his commitment of compassion. He committed himself to an unknown amount of money for the full recovery of the victim. The innkeeper probably knew and trusted the Samaritan.

Martha, Martha

Luke 10:38-42

38 Now as they went on their way, he entered a village; and a woman named Martha received him into her house. 39 And she had a sister called Mary, who sat at the Lord's feet and listened to his teaching. 40 But Martha was distracted with much serving; and she went to him and said, "Lord, do you not care that my sister has left me to serve alone? Tell her then to help me."

41 But the Lord answered her, "Martha, Martha, you are anxious and troubled about many things; 42 one thing is needful. Mary has chosen the good portion, which shall not be taken away from her."

Martha, Martha

Luke 10:38-42

Comment

The village was without a doubt Bethany. Martha had a sister named Mary and a brother named Lazarus. Martha was a works oriented individual. Mary was more interested in hearing and being with Jesus. The scene irritated Martha greatly, so she went to Jesus, believing he would tell Mary to help with getting the meal ready. Jesus made it absolutely clear Mary had made the better choice.

Chapter 18

This man receives sinners and eats with them	*This man receives sinners and eats with them*
Luke 15:1-2 ¹ Now the tax collectors and sinners were all drawing near to hear him. ² And the Pharisees and the scribes murmured, saying, "This man receives sinners and eats with them."	**Luke 15:1-2** **Comment** This is an independent statement found only in Luke. The scribes and Pharisees were at a loss for words to express their disdain for Jesus allowing tax collectors and sinners to come near him. To eat with them was absolutely revolting.

Lost – of Great Value

Chapter 15 in Luke's Gospel is unparalleled for its significance and beauty. The stories are exclusive to Luke, found nowhere else in the entire Bible. These four stories, while different, are companions with each other, because each deals with something precious having been lost.

Lost sheep

Luke 15:3-7

3 So he told them this parable: 4 "What man of you, having a hundred sheep, if he has lost one of them, does not leave the ninety-nine in the wilderness, and go after the one which is lost, until he finds it? 5 And when he has found it, he lays it on his shoulders, rejoicing. 6 And when he comes home, he calls together his friends and his neighbors, saying to them, 'Rejoice with me, for I have found my sheep which was lost.' 7 Just so, I tell you, there will be more joy in heaven over one sinner who repents than over ninety-nine righteous persons who need no repentance.

Lost coin

Luke 15:8-10

8 "Or what woman, having ten silver coins, if she loses one coin, does not light a lamp and sweep the house and seek diligently until she finds it? 9 And when she has found it, she calls together her friends and neighbors, saying, 'Rejoice with me, for I have found the coin

---

Lost sheep

Luke 15:3-7

Comment

Story number one deals with a lost sheep. Jesus knew there was not a man in the audience who would not understand what he was about to say. He knew beyond a doubt they would leave the ninety-nine and hunt for the lost sheep. A sheep was a valuable asset to any family. Once the lost sheep was found, the man returned home. He was joyous, and his neighbors celebrated his success. Jesus then stated the purpose of the story. There will be even more rejoicing in heaven over one lost sinner who repents.

Lost coin

Luke 15:8-10

Comment

Story number two concerns a woman who has lost one of her ten coins.

A woman lost one coin, so what is the big deal? Why

which I had lost.' ^{10} Just so, I tell you, there is joy before the angels of God over one sinner who repents."

would Jesus tell a story about the loss of a single coin? Most of us today are rather contemptuous of the thought of being concerned about losing a single coin. How many pieces of our furniture in the average home are laden with dimes and quarters that have slipped out of unsuspecting pockets?

In the first place, she only had ten coins to her name. She could not afford the loss of even one. It was so important she lit a lamp to provide adequate light for her search. Failing to find it she swept her entire dwelling clean looking for the coin. When at last she found it she called her neighbors to share in her joy.

If you lost 10 percent of your total assets, would you just shrug it off?

Lost Son

Luke 15:11-24

^{11} And he said, "There was a man who had two sons; ^{12} and the younger of them said to his father, 'Father, give me the share of property that falls to me.' And he divided his living between them. ^{13} Not many days later,

Lost Son

Luke 15:11-24

Comment

Story number three is one of the best-known and most loved stories of all literature.

the younger son gathered all he had and took his journey into a far country, and there he squandered his property in loose living. 14 And when he had spent everything, a great famine arose in that country, and he began to be in want. 15 So he went and joined himself to one of the citizens of that country, who sent him into his fields to feed swine. 16 And he would gladly have fed on the pods that the swine ate; and no one gave him anything. 17 But when he came to himself he said, 'How many of my father's hired servants have bread enough and to spare, but I perish here with hunger! 18 I will arise and go to my father, and I will say to him, "Father, I have sinned against heaven and before you; 19 I am no longer worthy to be called your son; treat me as one of your hired servants."' 20 And he arose and came to his father. But while he was yet at a distance, his father saw him and had compassion, and ran and embraced him and kissed him. 21 And the son said to him, 'Father, I have sinned against heaven and before you; I am no longer worthy to be called your son.' 22 But the father said to his servants, 'Bring quickly the best robe, and put it on him; and put a ring on his hand, and shoes on

The primary subject of this story is a younger brother who wants to go find his fortune in the world and the father who allows him to go. Before leaving the younger brother asked his father for his share of the inheritance. This would be the smaller of the inheritances with his older brother receiving the larger share. This request would signify his intention never to return. The father does not try to dissuade his son. Fully aware of the implications and dangers the young man will soon face it makes his heart indeed heavy.

The inheritance is a light load for the young man's soaring dreams. Within a few days, he bid his father farewell and launched his journey. We are compelled to feel empathy for the father as he watched his son disappear over the nearest hill.

As long as his money lasted there were friends abound. When his money was gone so were his new found friends. When no one offered him any assistance, he was forced to slop hogs for one of the residents of that country. Finally, the indignity of his lifestyle broke through to him. Considering

his feet; 23 and bring the fatted calf and kill it, and let us eat and make merry; 24 for this my son was dead, and is alive again; he was lost, and is found.' And they began to make merry.	himself he realized his father's hired help, lived better than he. Belatedly, he determined to tell his father that he did not deserve to continue being his son but would he please hire him as a slave?

Homeward bound he rehearsed his speech, infinitely. His father saw him a long distance away. The father ran to him and threw his arms around him and hugged him and rejoiced saying my son who was dead, has been found. He called one of his servants and told him to bring a family signet ring * for his finger. Bring a fine cloak for his raiment, ** and shoes *** for his feet. A son of the wealthy must have shoes. Now go and kill the fatted calf for the feast honoring my returned son.

* The signet ring was used to impress the wax seal of a legally binding agreement such as a purchase.

** **Strong's Greek Number 4749**
a loose outer garment for men extending to the feet, worn by kings, priests, and persons of rank

*** **Strong's Greek Number 5266**
what is bound under, a sandal, a sole fastened to the foot with thongs

Lost second son

Luke 15:25-32

25 "Now his elder son was in the field; and as he came and drew near to the house, he heard music and dancing. 26 And he called one of the servants and asked what this meant. 27 And he said to him, 'Your brother has come, and your father has killed the fatted calf, because he has received him safe and sound.' 28 But he was angry and refused to go in. His father came out and entreated him, 29 but he answered his father, 'Lo, these many years I have served you, and I never disobeyed your command; yet you never gave me a kid, that I might make merry with my friends. 30 But when this son of yours came, who has devoured your living with harlots, you killed for him the fatted calf!' 31 And he said to him, 'Son, you are always with me, and all that is mine is yours. 32 It was fitting to make merry and be glad, for this your brother was dead, and is alive; he was lost, and is found.'"

Lost second son

Luke 15:25-32

Comment

When the elder son heard the sound of music it was like the wailing of an Emergency alarm! His desperate hope was the servant would allay his fears. The servant told him what he did not want to hear.

The older brother could not control his rising anger. The Greek word (anger) implies "an intended provocation." The Greek word (refused) implies "a powerful no or rejection to a question believed to be answered in the affirmative."

The Greek word for "entreat" means "to strive, to tease another person." The Elder brother's words seethed with anger. The Greek word for "served" means "to be a slave, to serve to do service." This brother never felt he was a son! The Greek word for "disobeying" means he "never neglected or transgressed his father's word." The Greek word for "Command" means "a prescribed rule in accordance with that which is to be done." Never mind the fact that the father had feed him, clothed him, and housed him all the days of his life.

The father said, "I am so proud of you. There has never been a moment in my life, when you were not foremost in my thinking and my heart." He spoke reassuring words, telling him the younger son had no claim on his, the elder son's, inheritance. The word "fitting" means "necessity brought on by circumstances, or by the conduct of others toward us." The father said, "You break my heart with your anger toward your brother. I am devastated to learn, that your love for me rested on what you would receive from me."

<u>The fourth story</u>

The fourth story concerns the elder brother. This is perhaps the least appreciated of the stories. One reason is both stories concerning the boys are too real and make us uncomfortable. Who can say that was not exactly what Jesus had in mind by telling the stories?

Hear the anger in the older son's voice. How did he know what his younger brother had done with his inheritance? Could it be that this is secretly what he would have done? The word *devour* can mean "to forcibly appropriate a widow's property." What a vicious interpretation of his younger brother.

The traditional interpretation of the parable follows this formula. The younger brother is identified with sinners and becomes a ritually unclean person. In due time he comes to recognize that he had squandered the gifts of God. He repented and sought God's forgiveness, and received it.

The older brother represents the Pharisees, the scribes, and the religious orthodoxy. In their eyes, they have never disobeyed God's command. They critically looked down upon everyone else in the society. The parable ends with the elder brother refusing to join the party. The parable is deliberately left open ended allowing each listener/reader to reach their personal conclusion.

Dishonest Steward	*Dishonest Steward*
Luke 16:1-2; **Luke 16:3-7;** **Luke 16:8-9**	**Luke 16:1-2;** **Luke 16:3-7;** **Luke 16:8-9**
Luke 16:1-2 1 He also said to the disciples, "There was a rich man who had a steward, and charges were brought to him that this man was wasting his goods. 2 And he called him and said to him, 'What is this that I hear about you? Turn in the account of your stewardship, for you can no longer be steward.' **Luke 16:3-7** 3 And the steward said to himself, 'What shall I do, since my master is taking the stewardship away from me? I am not strong enough to dig, and I am ashamed	**Comment** This is an independent story found only in Luke. This wealthy man hired a manager for his business. He expected him to be honest and dependable. At a point well into the servant's career, someone brought charges against him, accusing him of miss-management. The rich man demanded the steward give a full accounting and dismissed him in the same breath. Having been discovered the

to beg. ⁴ I have decided what to do, so that people may receive me into their houses when I am put out of the stewardship.' ⁵ So, summoning his master's debtors one by one, he said to the first, 'How much do you owe my master?' ⁶ He said, 'A hundred measures of oil.' And he said to him, 'Take your bill, and sit down quickly and write fifty.' ⁷ Then he said to another, 'And how much do you owe?' He said, 'A hundred measures of wheat.' He said to him, 'Take your bill, and write eighty.'	servant then considered his future. He was too old or too weak to dig ditches, and too proud to beg. He decided his best course of action was to engage in more "creative accounting." He next contacted all his master's debtors and told each to alter his bill downward.
Luke 16:8-9 ⁸ The master commended the dishonest steward for his shrewdness; for the sons of this world are more shrewd in dealing with their own generation than the sons of light. ⁹ And I tell you, make friends for yourselves by means of unrighteous mammon so that when it fails they may receive you into the eternal habitations.	This parable has a strange conclusion. Taken at face value, it seems to praise the dishonest servant for his misconduct, thievery and cunning. Jesus' comment of "sons of this world," and "sons of light," give a glimpse of the Essene influence in his life. The Essenes referred to themselves as the "sons of light" and all others as "sons of darkness." Jesus makes a clear declaration that in the end dishonest conduct will lead to the destruction of the individual.

White collar crime

This story is about a dishonest servant who commits what we today would call a white collar crime.

However, many of the words that appear to be flattery also have a negative meaning. Shrewdness in this context can also mean conceited. Unrighteous also means wrongfulness of character, and unjust. Mammon can also mean avarice or defiled. Habitation can mean a tent or a cloth hut.

Therefore, I believe Jesus was issuing condemnation in the strongest terms possible. This conceited "white collar criminal" had exposed his character as one who could not be trusted. His greed for stolen money and his "creative accounting" tactics can at best, provide hope that he will be welcome in the homes and company of like-minded individuals.

Can't serve God and mammon	*Can't serve God and mammon*
Luke 16:10-13	**Luke 16:10-13**
10 "He who is faithful in a very little is faithful also in much; and he who is dishonest in a very little is dishonest also in much. 11 If then you have not been faithful in the unrighteous mammon, who will entrust to you the true riches? 12 And if you have not been faithful in that which is another's, who will give you that which is your own? 13 No servant can serve two masters; for either he will hate the one and love the other, or he will be devoted to the one and despise the other. You cannot serve God and mammon."	**Comment** This is an independent comment found only in the Gospel of Luke. This is Jesus' commentary on the story he had just told about the dishonest servant. He stated, "One who is faithful over small things will be faithful over large things as well. One who is dishonest about small matters will be dishonest in large matters." One judged to be a liar and a thief will never have great responsibilities entrusted to him. Jesus assured all, no one can serve two masters, one he will love the other he will hate.

Lovers of money

Luke 16:14-15
14 The Pharisees, who were lovers of money, heard all this, and they scoffed at him. 15 But he said to them, "You are those who justify yourselves before men, but God knows your hearts; for what is exalted among men is an abomination in the sight of God.

Lovers of money

Luke 16:14-15

Comment

This is an independent statement found only in Luke's Gospel.

This is another scathing condemnation by Jesus of the Pharisees. He supported his charge by saying they are the people who justify themselves before men, but forget that God reads the heart. The Pharisees who arrayed themselves against Jesus were conditioned by their positions of power, wealth, and property.

Law and the Prophets

Luke 16:16-17
16 "The law and the prophets were until John; since then the good news of the kingdom of God is preached, and every one enters it violently. 17 But it is easier for heaven and earth to pass away, than for one dot of the law to become void.

Law and the Prophets

Luke 16:16-17

Comment

Before John the Baptist and Jesus, the Law and the prophets were the final word on all things legal concerning God. Jesus introduced the good news about the kingdom of God. His proclamation opened the way of entrance to the Kingdom of God for those who had been considered outcast, sinners, and unredeemable.

The Gospel of Jesus cut through the clutter of ceremonial Law that was entrenched in the Orthodox mind. Jesus carefully articulated the good news in a manner that did not in any way abridge the Law of Moses.

Increase of faith

Luke 17:5-6

5 The apostles said to the Lord, "Increase our faith!" 6 And the Lord said, "If you had faith as a grain of mustard seed, you could say to this sycamine tree, 'Be rooted up, and be planted in the sea,' and it would obey you.

Increase of faith

Luke 17:5-6

Comment

Faith is not an ingredient that can be measured out and administered like a liquid medicine. Faith and trust are the same. If one trusts God's power without question God will grant the petition if it does not offend the righteousness of God.

We have only to reflect over the worlds of medicine and science covering the last 100 years to see the validation of this concept. Where once the position was, "It can't be done," pioneers turned the concept by saying, "Why can't it be done?"

Doing your duty, nothing more

Luke 17:7-10

7 "Will any one of you, who has a servant plowing or keeping sheep, say to him when he has come in from the field, 'Come at once and sit down at table'? 8 Will he not rather say to him, 'Prepare supper for me, and gird yourself and serve me, till I eat and drink; and afterward you shall eat and drink'? 9 Does he thank the servant because he did what was commanded? 10 So you also, when you have done all that is commanded you, say, 'We are unworthy servants; we have only done what was our duty.'"

Doing your duty, nothing more

Luke 17:7-10

Comment

The working-class understood their day was from sun up to sun down. Their job was to fulfill every need of their employer/master. They understood their place, to prepare the meal, never to expect one to be prepared for them. No one ever expected a thank you for their labors. Having done all one was commanded to do one earned the right to consider himself a worthy servant.

You will look for Me but ...

Luke 17:22-37

22 And he said to the disciples, "The days are coming when you will desire to see one of the days of the Son of man, and you will not see it. 23 And they will say to you, 'Lo, there!' or 'Lo, here!' Do not go, do not follow them. 24 For as the lightning flashes and lights up the sky from one side to the other, so will the Son of man be in his day. 25 But first he must suffer many things and be rejected by this generation.

You will look for Me but ...

Luke 17:22-37

Comment

This is an independent statement found only in Luke.

This is an apocalyptic message from Jesus. The disciples he is referring to are numerous. The times will be such that they will long for the message of the Son of man. But the time for seeing him will have passed.

26 As it was in the days of Noah, so will it be in the days of the Son of man. 27 They ate, they drank, they married, they were given in marriage, until the day when Noah entered the ark, and the flood came and destroyed them all. 28 Likewise as it was in the days of Lot—they ate, they drank, they bought, they sold, they planted, they built, 29 but on the day when Lot went out from Sodom fire and sulphur rained from heaven and destroyed them all— 30 so will it be on the day when the Son of man is revealed. 31 On that day, let him who is on the housetop, with his goods in the house, not come down to take them away; and likewise let him who is in the field not turn back. 32 Remember Lot's wife. 33 Whoever seeks to gain his life will lose it, but whoever loses his life will preserve it. 34 I tell you, in that night there will be two in one bed; one will be taken and the other left. 35 There will be two women grinding together; one will be taken and the other left." 37 And they said to him, "Where, Lord?" He said to them, "Where the body is, there the eagles will be gathered together."

Jesus warned them that when they were told he is here or he is there, not to believe them. Do not follow them.

Before this can happen Jesus must suffer the crucifixion. The sign of this coming will be when the world lives as it did in the days of Noah and Lot. Death and destruction shall descend on the nonbelievers who have made a debauchery of God's love. Wherever you are on that day do not make haste to save what you have accumulated, wait for the Lord. This judgment will bring recognition between believers and nonbelievers.

When asked, "When this would take place," Jesus in a roundabout way, said, "When God's time is ready and not before."

Judge who feared neither God nor regarded man

Luke 18:1-8

¹ And he told them a parable, to the effect that they ought always to pray and not lose heart. ² He said, "In a certain city there was a judge who neither feared God nor regarded man; ³ and there was a widow in that city who kept coming to him and saying, 'Vindicate me against my adversary.' ⁴ For a while he refused; but afterward he said to himself, 'Though I neither fear God nor regard man, ⁵ yet because this widow bothers me, I will vindicate her, or she will wear me out by her continual coming.'" ⁶ And the Lord said, "Hear what the unrighteous judge says. ⁷ And will not God vindicate his elect, who cry to him day and night? Will he delay long over them? ⁸ I tell you, he will vindicate them speedily. Nevertheless, when the Son of man comes, will he find faith on earth?"

Judge who feared neither God nor regarded man

Luke 18:1-8

Comment

This is an independent statement found only in Luke.

The purpose of this parable is stated in verse one. One should continue to pray and never lose heart.

There are two major characters in this story; the fearless judge and the widow. The judge is described as one who has no fear of God and who could care less about the status of man. The widow is the most persistent person the judge had ever encountered. Relentlessly she petitioned the judge to vindicate her from her adversary.

There are multiple definitions for this word, vindicate: 1) it can mean to defend a person or protect them from aggression of others; 2) it can mean to receive justice; 3) or punishment of the wrongdoer. Perhaps all of these apply to the widow's request. The word adversary equally has more than one potential

	meaning: 1) it can refer to one's enemy; 2) it can mean one's opponent in a lawsuit. The persistent widow finally wore the judge down and he realized the only way he would ever be rid of her was to give her what she wanted.
	In verse six, Jesus refers to the judge as unrighteous. Once more we encounter a word that can be used in more than one way. It is possible Jesus is accusing him of violating the law that he has sworn to uphold by rendering incorrect verdicts. Jesus then stated God would vindicate the elect who cried to Him for relief.
	The closing statement in this passage is confusing. It seems to ask when the Son of man returns to earth will he find people of faith?
If your brother sins against you	***If your brother sins against you***
Matthew 18:15-20 15 "If your brother sins against you, go and tell him his fault, between you and him alone. If he listens to you, you have gained your brother. 16 But if he does not listen, take one or two others along with you, that every word	**Matthew 18:15-20** **Comment** This is an independent statement found only in Matthew. Jesus said talk to your brother

may be confirmed by the evidence of two or three witnesses. 17 If he refuses to listen to them, tell it to the church; and if he refuses to listen even to the church, let him be to you as a Gentile and a tax collector. 18 Truly, I say to you, whatever you bind on earth shall be bound in heaven, and whatever you loose on earth shall be loosed in heaven. 19 Again I say to you, if two of you agree on earth about anything they ask, it will be done for them by my Father in heaven. 20 For where two or three are gathered in my name, there am I in the midst of them."	in private and the two of you try to reach a settlement. If you can settle your quarrel each of you will have regained his brother. But if you cannot reach agreement have two or three witnesses meet with you to confirm exactly what was said. If that does not work tell it to the church. Jesus is not talking about a Christian assembly for worship. The Greek word (ek-klay-see'-ah) means any group of men who are called to a public place for the purpose of settling disputes.

<u>If your brother sins against you</u>

Jesus said specifically, "If your brother sins against you ..." In verse twenty-one, Peter asked how many times should he forgive his brother if his brother sins against him? Is it possible that Peter had more than one brother? However, the only brother we know is Andrew. Perhaps Jesus' comment was specifically aimed at some controversy between these two brothers.

Matthew first used this word in Matthew 16:18-19 and then again here. These are the only references to the word "church" used in the Gospels.

Peter said, "Lord, How often shall my Brother sin against me?"

Matthew 18:21-22

21 Then Peter came up and said to him, "Lord, how often shall my brother sin against me, and I forgive him? As many as seven times?" 22 Jesus said to him, "I do not say to you seven times, but seventy times seven.

Kingdom of heaven is like ... A king settling accounts

Matthew 18:23-27

23 "Therefore the kingdom of heaven may be compared to a king who wished to settle accounts with his servants. 24 When he began the reckoning, one was brought to him who owed him ten thousand talents; 25 and as he could not pay, his lord ordered him to be sold, with his wife and children and all that he had, and payment to be made. 26 So the servant fell on his knees, imploring him, 'Lord, have patience with me, and I will pay you everything.' 27 And out of pity for him the lord of that servant released him and forgave him the debt.

Peter said, "Lord, How often shall my Brother sin against me?"

Matthew 18:21-22

Comment

Jesus said continue to forgive your brother, until it really takes hold.

Kingdom of heaven is like ... A king settling accounts

Matthew 18:23-27

Comment

This parable is found only in Matthew's Gospel.

The servant owes the king 10,000 talents. We realize this is a big sum, but just how big?
  6000 denarii = 1 talent
  1 denarii = a day's wages

6000 x 10,000 = 60,000,000 days of labor = 164,383+ years

Turn this into terms of salaries and debt on today's terms: Assume an annual salary per year of $100,000.

	$60,000,000 = $ Debt Pay off in 600 years And that does not include interest. Such an incredible amount would leave the man hopelessly in debt. The servant fell on his knees and begged his master for mercy. The King was moved with compassion and forgave the entire debt.
Fellow servants who owed him **Matthew 18:28-31** 28 But that same servant, as he went out, came upon one of his fellow servants who owed him a hundred denarii; and seizing him by the throat he said, 'Pay what you owe.' 29 So his fellow servant fell down and besought him, 'Have patience with me, and I will pay you.' 30 He refused and went and put him in prison till he should pay the debt. 31 When his fellow servants saw what had taken place, they were greatly distressed, and they went and reported to their lord all that had taken place.	***Fellow servants who owed him*** **Matthew 18:28-31** **Comment** Shortly after leaving the presence of the King, this servant encountered someone who owed him money. His fellow servant owed him 100 denarii, (less than four months wage for a day laborer). The unmerciful servant demanded immediate payment. The man could not pay. He begged for time to make restitution. The unmerciful servant had him put into jail.

Wicked servant, have you no mercy?	*Wicked servant, have you no mercy?*
Matthew 18:32-35 32 Then his lord summoned him and said to him, 'You wicked servant! I forgave you all that debt because you besought me; 33 and should not you have had mercy on your fellow servant, as I had mercy on you?' 34 And in anger his lord delivered him to the jailers, till he should pay all his debt. 35 So also my heavenly Father will do to every one of you, if you do not forgive your brother from your heart."	**Matthew 18:32-35** **Comment** Other servants witnessed this injustice and reported the incident to the King. This angered the King and he ordered the unmerciful servant to be brought to him at once. The King was dismayed at the servant who had received such mercy and who was absolutely unmerciful with one who owed him. The King was so angry he ordered him thrown into jail until he was able to repay his debt!

King revoked amnesty

It is interesting the King revoked the amnesty previously granted and imposed a new sentence of life imprisonment.

Could it be Jesus is saying salvation can be removed? We are reminded of the words of the Lord's Prayer, "Forgive us our debts as we forgive our debtors." It also reminds us Jesus once said we should "Do unto others as we would have them do unto us."

One should remember forgiving does not imply the loss of memory. Remembering serves the dual purpose of protecting one from committing the same wrong again, and at the same time preventing the perpetrator from repeatedly committing the same sin.

I am the door for the sheep	***I am the door for the sheep***
John 10:1-6 ¹ "Truly, truly, I say to you, he who does not enter the sheepfold by the door but climbs in by another way, that man is a thief and a robber; ² but he who enters by the door is the shepherd of the sheep. ³ To him the gatekeeper opens; the sheep hear his voice, and he calls his own sheep by name and leads them out. ⁴ When he has brought out all his own, he goes before them, and the sheep follow him, for they know his voice. ⁵ A stranger they will not follow, but they will flee from him, for they do not know the voice of strangers." ⁶ This figure Jesus used with them, but they did not understand what he was saying to them.	**John 10:1-6** **Comment** For one to enter the sheepfold another way means simply to climb over the wall, wherever one would choose. Anyone entering this way would be there for mischief. This person would wait for the darkest part of the night. Shepherds do have to sleep sometime. So when the time was right the thief would step over the wall, grab a lamb and escape. The people understood the role of a shepherd. What they did not understand was Jesus was speaking of himself.

What door to the sheepfold?

Why would Jesus talk about the door to the sheepfold? He and everyone else knew there was no door, at least what we think of as part of a house. The sheepfold was often simply an area of ground enclosed by picking up the loose stones and stacking them upon each other, making a wall maybe two feet high. The door of the sheepfold was in reality an opening in the wall. The gate keeper and the door are one and the same, the "shepherd."

Several flocks would generally occupy a single sheepfold. When daylight came each shepherd would call his sheep. As the sheep's name was called it would arise and go to him. All the other sheep would stay in place. They would wait for their shepherd.

Shepherds lead their sheep, they do not drive them. None of that "do as I say and not as I do" business. The sheep trust the shepherd implicitly and are frightened by a strange voice.

I am the good shepherd	*I am the good shepherd*
John 10:7-18	**John 10:7-18**
7 So Jesus again said to them, "Truly, truly, I say to you, I am the door of the sheep. 8 All who came before me are thieves and robbers; but the sheep did not heed them. 9 I am the door; if any one enters by me, he will be saved, and will go in and out and find pasture. 10 The thief comes only to steal and kill and destroy; I came that they may have life, and have it abundantly. 11 I am the good shepherd. The good shepherd lays down his life for the sheep. 12 He who is a hireling and not a shepherd, whose own the sheep are not, sees the wolf coming and leaves the sheep and flees; and the wolf snatches them and scatters them. 13 He flees because he is a hireling and cares nothing for the sheep. 14 I am the good shepherd; I know my own and my own know me, 15 as the Father knows me and I	**Comment** Jesus defined himself as the "door" not a door, but "the" door. It is important to note He said "by" me not "through" me. I take this to mean one must enter by the true meaning of Messiah and not by the human person of Jesus the man. Jesus contrasts his role to that of a thief. This word, like many others, has more than one meaning. The most common application is to one who steals or takes what does not belong to him. Later it came to include teachers who were more interested in their personal gain, than imparting knowledge to their students. Jesus asserts, the thief comes to steal, but is willing to kill and destroy in

know the Father; and I lay down my life for the sheep. 16 And I have other sheep, that are not of this fold; I must bring them also, and they will heed my voice. So there shall be one flock, one shepherd. 17 For this reason the Father loves me, because I lay down my life, that I may take it again. 18 No one takes it from me, but I lay it down of my own accord. I have power to lay it down, and I have power to take it again; this charge I have received from my Father."

the process. He contrasts this with his goal of bringing life abundant to those who follow him.

Next, Jesus compares the good shepherd to the hireling. If need be, the good Shepherd will lay down his life to protect the sheep.

The sheep do not belong to the hireling and he will not run the risk of harm, whether they are protected or not. When danger approaches, he abandons his responsibility.

In verse sixteen, Jesus made a revealing statement of prophecy. He said he has sheep that are not of this flock.

A more clear way of saying this is Jesus had followers who were not Jewish. To the Pharisees this was a horrible concept. He further enforced the point saying he must bring them along so there will be only one flock and one shepherd.

This bold new concept of God's kingdom was pleasing to God. Jesus' emphasis is upon his laying his life down, and his promise that he will pick it up again.

Division among the Jews

John 10:19-21

19 There was again a division among the Jews because of these words. 20 Many of them said, "He has a demon, and he is mad; why listen to him?" 21 Others said, "These are not the sayings of one who has a demon. Can a demon open the eyes of the blind?"

Division among the Jews

John 10:19-21

Comment

The running battle between the blind man who had received his sight and the Pharisees left a huge division among the Jews. Those who remained unconvinced still believed Jesus was possessed by a demon. (Demons were believed to be spirits superior to men but inferior to God.) The opposition continued to advise no one should listen to Jesus. Those who became believers retorted that what Jesus said were not the ravings of a demon possessed person and demons could not open the eyes of the blind.

Feast of the Dedication

John 10:22-30

22 It was the feast of the Dedication at Jerusalem; 23 it was winter, and Jesus was walking in the temple, in the portico of Solomon. 24 So the Jews gathered round him and said to him, "How long will you keep us in suspense? If you are the

Feast of the Dedication

John 10:22-30

Comment

The feast of the dedication was an annual feast celebrated for eight days, beginning the twenty-fifth of the month that corresponds with our month of December. It was instituted by

Christ, tell us plainly." ²⁵ Jesus answered them, "I told you, and you do not believe. The works that I do in my Father's name, they bear witness to me; ²⁶ but you do not believe, because you do not belong to my sheep. ²⁷ My sheep hear my voice, and I know them, and they follow me; ²⁸ and I give them eternal life, and they shall never perish, and no one shall snatch them out of my hand. ²⁹ My Father, who has given them to me, is greater than all, and no one is able to snatch them out of the Father's hand. ³⁰ I and the Father are one."	Judas Maccabaeus in memory of the cleansing of the temple. Jesus was in Jerusalem at the temple in the portico of Solomon. The Jews, (nonbelievers) gathered around him and asked him straightforwardly, "Are you the Christ? How long will you keep us in suspense before you say?" Jesus said, "I told you but you didn't believe me. The works that I do bear witness to who I am." Jesus made it clear the nonbelievers were not part of his flock, meaning they were not his followers, they would not listen to his voice and they would not follow. But to those who belonged to him he gave eternal life that they should never perish and no one would have the ability to snatch them out of his hand. Then he made another inflammatory statement, "I and the father are one," thus proclaiming equality with God.

It was winter

John 10:22, "And it was winter and it was the feast of the dedication (Chanukah) and Jesus walked in the portico of Solomon."

Jesus celebrated Chanukah sometimes traveling many difficult miles from Galilee over mountains and through valleys. His journey went through spans of desert leading him to the old Jericho road. The weather at this time of the year could be rainy, cold, and sometimes snowy. The long journey would culminate in the city of Jerusalem and the Temple.

Jesus age thirty-two

Assuming Jesus was born in the winter months, this Feast of Dedication could be an indication his birthday was about this season.

Stone him!	*Stone him!*
John 10:31-39	**John 10:31-39**
	Comment
31 The Jews took up stones again to stone him. 32 Jesus answered them, "I have shown you many good works from the Father; for which of these do you stone me?" 33 The Jews answered him, "It is not for a good work that we stone you but for blasphemy; because you, being a man, make yourself God." 34 Jesus answered them, "Is it not written in your law, 'I said, you are gods'? 35 If he called them gods to whom the word of God came (and scripture cannot be broken), 36 do you say of him whom the Father consecrated and sent into the world, 'You are blaspheming,' because I said, 'I am the Son of God'? 37 If I am not doing the works of my Father, then do not believe me;	The Jews (nonbelievers) took up stones intending to stone Jesus. Jesus said to them, "I have done the good works of the Father so which of these is the reason you desire to stone me?" "It is not a matter of what you did in the way of good works it is that you have committed blasphemy," they said. "Is it not written in your law 'I said you are gods?'" Jesus asked. (Ps. 82:6) Jesus challenged their thinking stating if he was not doing the work of the Father then they would be right to not believe him, but if he was doing the

38 but if I do them, even though you do not believe me, believe the works, that you may know and understand that the Father is in me and I am in the Father." 39 Again they tried to arrest him, but he escaped from their hands.

good works of the Father then why do they not believe him? Then as a last hope of winning them over, Jesus said, "Even if you can not believe me then believe the evidence of the work that I do in God's name because the Father and I are one." The Jews (nonbelievers) had heard all they could stand and now tried to arrest him, but he escaped out of their hands.

Judea and beyond the Jordan

**Mark 10:1;
Matthew 19:1-2;
John 10:40-42**

Judea and beyond the Jordan

**Mark 10:1;
Matthew 19:1-2;
John 10:40-42**

Mark 10:1

1 And he left there and went to the region of Judea and beyond the Jordan, and crowds gathered to him again; and again, as his custom was, he taught them.

Matthew 19:1-2

1 Now when Jesus had finished these sayings, he went away from Galilee and entered the region of Judea beyond the Jordan; 2 and large crowds followed him, and he healed them there.

Comment

Jesus moved further south into Judea. As always, people came to him. He taught them, healed them and befriended them. Many remembered what John the Baptist had said about Jesus and now they believed in him too.

John 10:40-42

40 He went away again across the Jordan to the place where John at first baptized, and there he remained. 41 And many came to him; and they said, "John did no sign, but everything that John said about this man was true." 42 And many believed in him there.

Chapter 19

Jesus teaching on divorce

Mark 10:2-9;
Matthew 19:3-9;
Luke 16:18

Mark 10:2-9
2 And Pharisees came up and in order to test him asked, "Is it lawful for a man to divorce his wife?" 3 He answered them, "What did Moses command you?" 4 They said, "Moses allowed a man to write a certificate of divorce, and to put her away." 5 But Jesus said to them, "For your hardness of heart he wrote you this commandment. 6 But from the beginning of creation, 'God made them male and female.' 7 'For this reason a man shall leave his father and mother and be joined to his wife, 8 and the two shall become one flesh.' So they are no longer two but one flesh. 9 What therefore God has joined together, let not man put asunder."

Matthew 19:3-9
3 And Pharisees came up to him and tested him by asking, "Is

Jesus teaching on divorce

Mark 10:2-9;
Matthew 19:3-9;
Luke 16:18

Comment

Moses' writ of divorce is covered in detail in chapter 12 under the Sermon on the Mount (Refer to Matt. 5:31-32).

Perhaps these Pharisees had not heard Jesus' earlier comments on divorce. As stated before, this was a hot button issue. The Pharisees were confident their confronting Jesus on this issue would damage his reputation. The Pharisees proudly reminded Jesus, that Moses permitted divorce. Jesus responded it was because of their hardness of heart that Moses had accepted it.

Jesus then explained to them God's purpose for creating man and woman. Men and women are different and are intended to be joined together as husband

it lawful to divorce one's wife for any cause?" 4 He answered, "Have you not read that he who made them from the beginning made them male and female, 5 and said, 'For this reason a man shall leave his father and mother and be joined to his wife, and the two shall become one flesh'? 6 So they are no longer two but one flesh. What therefore God has joined together, let not man put asunder." 7 They said to him, "Why then did Moses command one to give a certificate of divorce, and to put her away?" 8 He said to them, "For your hardness of heart Moses allowed you to divorce your wives, but from the beginning it was not so. 9 And I say to you: whoever divorces his wife, except for unchastity, and marries another, commits adultery."

Luke 16:18
18 "Every one who divorces his wife and marries another commits adultery, and he who marries a woman divorced from her husband commits adultery.

and wife. As husband and wife they are joined together in the bond that results in the two becoming one.

Both Mark and Matthew assert that no man should put asunder (break) this bond. Put asunder means to leave one's husband or wife, such as to divorce, or simply walk away with no intention of returning.

Matthew quotes Jesus as saying the only exception for divorce is the act of unchastity. The act of unchastity covers a wide list of situations. For example: a) any form of illicit sexual intercourse such as adultery, homosexuality, lesbianism, intercourse with animals or sexual intercourse with close relatives; (Lev. 18) and especially sexual intercourse with a divorced man or woman, which is also defined as adultery.

The man who divorces for any other reason, and remarries, makes his new wife an adulteress. Luke adds that any man who marries a divorced woman commits adultery.

Marriage is the union of one man and one woman

Some may consider it politically improper to make the following statement. Jesus is crystal clear marriage consists of the union of one man and one woman.

Eunuchs	*Eunuchs*
Matthew 19:10-12	**Matthew 19:10-12**
10 The disciples said to him, "If such is the case of a man with his wife, it is not expedient to marry." 11 But he said to them, "Not all men can receive this saying, but only those to whom it is given. 12 For there are eunuchs who have been so from birth, and there are eunuchs who have been made eunuchs by men, and there are eunuchs who have made themselves eunuchs for the sake of the kingdom of heaven. He who is able to receive this, let him receive it."	**Comment** The response of the disciples was, "If such is the case it is not expedient to marry." Jesus responded, "It is not an easy saying and all men could not accept it." At last, Jesus gives us a clue as he mentions eunuchs. A eunuch is defined as a man who has been emasculated either by natural incapacitation or at the hands of others rendering them incapable of sexual intercourse. When Jesus said, "There are eunuchs who have made themselves eunuchs for the sake of the kingdom of heaven," He was referring to celibacy, the voluntarily abstinence of sexual activity. Reaffirming the difficulty of this choice Jesus said, "He who is able to receive this, let him receive it."

Eunuchs

Eunuchs filled very special roles in ancient times. They were considered ideal for protecting the bed chamber of the wealthy. Philip encountered the Ethiopian eunuch mentioned in Acts 8:27-39, also Nehemiah in the Old Testament was a eunuch. The word eunuch is mentioned eight times in the entire Bible with five of these occurrences found in the passage under consideration.

Inner-Circle asked him again	*Inner-Circle asked him again*

Mark 10:10-12
10 And in the house the disciples asked him again about this matter. 11 And he said to them, "Whoever divorces his wife and marries another, commits adultery against her; 12 and if she divorces her husband and marries another, she commits adultery."
	Mark 10:10-12
	
	Comment
	
	The aim of *Jesus and the Gospel Timeline* is to see exactly what Jesus had to say and not to add to or take away from it. Those who would like to do further research on the subject of divorce may find the following references of interest.
	    Deuteronomy 24:1-4
	    Isaiah 2
	    Matthew 1:18-25
	    Matthew 5:31
	
	For more on the subject of divorce confer with *Jesus and the Gospel Timeline, chapter 12.*

Let the children come to me Mark 10:13-16; Matthew 19:13-15; Luke 18:15-17	*Let the children come to me* Mark 10:13-16; Matthew 19:13-15; Luke 18:15-17

Mark 10:13-16 13 And they were bringing children to him, that he might touch them; and the disciples rebuked them. 14 But when Jesus saw it he was indignant, and said to them, "Let the children come to me, do not hinder them; for to such belongs the kingdom of God. 15 Truly, I say to you, whoever does not receive the kingdom of God like a child shall not enter it." 16 And he took them in his arms and blessed them, laying his hands upon them. **Matthew 19:13-15** 13 Then children were brought to him that he might lay his hands on them and pray. The disciples rebuked the people; 14 but Jesus said, "Let the children come to me, and do not hinder them; for to such belongs the kingdom of heaven." 15 And he laid his hands on them and went away. **Luke 18:15-17** 15 Now they were bringing even infants to him that he might touch them; and when the disciples saw it, they rebuked them. 16 But Jesus called them to him, saying, "Let the children come to me, and do not hinder them; for to such belongs the kingdom of God.	**Comment** The disciples were trying hard to preserve Jesus' precious time. They felt the children were an unnecessary distraction for him. When Jesus saw what was taking place he was very displeased. He let it be understood clearly, that he would receive children of any age even infants.

17 Truly, I say to you, whoever does not receive the kingdom of God like a child shall not enter it."

What can I do to Inherit eternal life?

**Mark 10:17-22:
Matthew 19:16-22;
Luke 18:18-23**

Mark 10:17-22
17 And as he was setting out on his journey, a man ran up and knelt before him, and asked him, "Good Teacher, what must I do to inherit eternal life?" 18 And Jesus said to him, "Why do you call me good? No one is good but God alone. 19 You know the commandments: 'Do not kill, Do not commit adultery, Do not steal, Do not bear false witness, Do not defraud, Honor your father and mother.'" 20 And he said to him, "Teacher, all these I have observed from my youth." 21 And Jesus looking upon him loved him, and said to him, "You lack one thing; go, sell what you have, and give to the poor, and you will have treasure in heaven; and come, follow me." 22 At that saying his countenance fell, and he went away sorrowful; for he had great possessions.

What can I do to Inherit eternal life?

**Mark 10:17-22:
Matthew 19:16-22;
Luke 18:18-23**

Comment

Why do we call this story "The Rich Young Ruler?" Mark says, "a man"; Matthew says, "one came up"; Luke says, "a ruler." Mark and Matthew say, "great possessions." Luke says, "He was very rich."

No one makes mention of the man's age. Luke refers to him as a "ruler." This implies one who has reached levels of advancement within his sphere and community. To have the title of "ruler" implies a person of respectable age, probably middle adulthood or older.

This man seeking eternal life had always attempted to live up to the intent of the Ten Commandments. Yet he still felt

Matthew 19:16-22

16 And behold, one came up to him, saying, "Teacher, what good deed must I do, to have eternal life?" 17 And he said to him, "Why do you ask me about what is good? One there is who is good. If you would enter life, keep the commandments." 18 He said to him, "Which?" And Jesus said, "You shall not kill, You shall not commit adultery, You shall not steal, You shall not bear false witness, 19 Honor your father and mother, and, You shall love your neighbor as yourself." 20 The young man said to him, "All these I have observed; what do I still lack?" 21 Jesus said to him, "If you would be perfect, go, sell what you possess and give to the poor, and you will have treasure in heaven; and come, follow me." 22 When the young man heard this he went away sorrowful; for he had great possessions.

Luke 18:18-23

18 And a ruler asked him, "Good Teacher, what shall I do to inherit eternal life?" 19 And Jesus said to him, "Why do you call me good? No one is good but God alone. 20 You know the commandments: 'Do not commit adultery, Do not kill, Do not steal, Do not bear

there was something missing in his quest. Jesus told him the void could be filled only by disposing of all of his goods and giving the proceeds to the poor.

Jesus was testing the level of his commitment. A test always implies the risk of failure. Was he willing to rid himself of the cause of his disability or did his wealth have the greater control?

Perhaps Jesus was thinking of the test God had given Abraham centuries earlier. God wanted to know whom Abraham loved the most; his precious son Isaac or his God. When Abraham raised the knife to sacrifice his son God had the answer and called a halt to the test.

The rich ruler preferred keeping his wealth rather than gaining the sought after eternal life.

false witness, Honor your father and mother.'" 21 And he said, "All these I have observed from my youth." 22 And when Jesus heard it, he said to him, "One thing you still lack. Sell all that you have and distribute to the poor, and you will have treasure in heaven; and come, follow me." 23 But when he heard this he became sad, for he was very rich.

Rich man and Lazarus

Luke 16:19-31

19 "There was a rich man, who was clothed in purple and fine linen and who feasted sumptuously every day. 20 And at his gate lay a poor man named Laz'arus, full of sores, 21 who desired to be fed with what fell from the rich man's table; moreover the dogs came and licked his sores. 22 The poor man died and was carried by the angels to Abraham's bosom. The rich man also died and was buried; 23 and in Hades, being in torment, he lifted up his eyes, and saw Abraham far off and Laz'arus in his bosom. 24 And he called out, 'Father Abraham, have mercy upon me, and send Laz'arus to dip the end of his finger in water and cool

Rich man and Lazarus

Luke 16:19-31

Comment

Here is a beautiful story told by Jesus that carries enormous impact when we listen carefully to it. The story is of a rich man clothed in expensive garments made of fine linen dyed purple, he dined sumptuously every day. Outside his house, at the gate, there lay a poor man whose name was Lazarus. His body was racked with pain and he was full of sores. Lazarus dreamed of being able to feed on the crumbs that fell from the rich man's table, but unfortunately he was never offered even a crust of bread. Lazarus was in such miserable condition that he

my tongue; for I am in anguish in this flame.' 25 But Abraham said, 'Son, remember that you in your lifetime received your good things, and Laz'arus in like manner evil things; but now he is comforted here, and you are in anguish. 26 And besides all this, between us and you a great chasm has been fixed, in order that those who would pass from here to you may not be able, and none may cross from there to us.' 27 And he said, 'Then I beg you, father, to send him to my father's house, 28 for I have five brothers, so that he may warn them, lest they also come into this place of torment.' 29 But Abraham said, 'They have Moses and the prophets; let them hear them.' 30 And he said, 'No, father Abraham; but if some one goes to them from the dead, they will repent.' 31 He said to him, 'If they do not hear Moses and the prophets, neither will they be convinced if some one should rise from the dead.'"

could not prevent the dogs from licking his sores.

At last Lazarus died and was carried to Abraham's bosom, meaning he went to heaven. Soon the rich man died and instead of going to heaven he went to a place called Hades, a place of torment.

As the rich man looked at his surroundings, far off he could see Abraham with Lazarus close beside him. The rich man cried out for Abraham to have mercy upon him. The irony of this story is that even now he looked at Lazarus as a servant saying, "Father Abraham send Lazarus to dip his finger in the water and place it on my tongue for I am in anguish in the flames." Abraham reminded him that during their life on earth he had everything, all the good stuff, while Lazarus had nothing. But now the tables were turned; Lazarus has everything and the rich man had nothing.

Abraham told the rich man that a great chasm had been placed between Heaven and Hades so that no one could traverse in either direction. But the rich man did not give up, he begs

	Abraham to send a witness to his father's house to warn his five brothers that they also are headed for this place of torment unless they change. Abraham answered that they have Moses and the prophets to guide them. The rich man responded saying they don't believe Moses or the prophets, but if someone comes from the dead they will believe him. Abraham answered that since they won't believe Moses and the prophets neither will they believe one who has been raised from the dead. Luke intended this as a graphic commentary upon those Jews who refused to accept Jesus as the Son of God. We could easily replace the word Jew saying all of humanity that refuses to acknowledge Jesus as the son of God.
Hard time for the rich **Mark 10:23-25;** **Matthew 19:23-24;** **Luke 18:24-25**	**_Hard time for the rich_** **Mark 10:23-25;** **Matthew 19:23-24;** **Luke 18:24-25**
Mark 10:23-25 23 And Jesus looked around and said to his disciples, "How hard it	**Comment** Peter and the other Disciples

will be for those who have riches to enter the kingdom of God!" 24 And the disciples were amazed at his words. But Jesus said to them again, "Children, how hard it is to enter the kingdom of God! 25 It is easier for a camel to go through the eye of a needle than for a rich man to enter the kingdom of God."

Matthew 19:23-24
23 And Jesus said to his disciples, "Truly, I say to you, it will be hard for a rich man to enter the kingdom of heaven. 24 Again I tell you, it is easier for a camel to go through the eye of a needle than for a rich man to enter the kingdom of God."

Luke 18:24-25
24 Jesus looking at him said, "How hard it is for those who have riches to enter the kingdom of God! 25 For it is easier for a camel to go through the eye of a needle than for a rich man to enter the kingdom of God."

accepted the old idea that God blessed the wealthy, and something was inferior about poor and handicapped people. So when Jesus said the rich would have a hard time getting into heaven it was for them a frightening comment.

The reign or rule of the Kingdom is a dynamic process, not a place or structure. It is not two things, one present and one to come. It is one process that is unfolding all the time.

That is why Jesus spoke of the reign as already active among his followers. Untold numbers would ultimately join their ranks in the future. Unfortunately, not everyone would gain entrance.

Who then can be saved?

Mark 10:26-31;
Matthew 19:25-30

Mark 10:26-31

Who then can be saved?

Mark 10:26-31;
Matthew 19:25-30

Comment

26 And they were exceedingly astonished, and said to him, "Then who can be saved?" 27 Jesus looked at them and said, "With men it is impossible, but not with God; for all things are possible with God." 28 Peter began to say to him, "Lo, we have left everything and followed you." 29 Jesus said, "Truly, I say to you, there is no one who has left house or brothers or sisters or mother or father or children or lands, for my sake and for the gospel, 30 who will not receive a hundredfold now in this time, houses and brothers and sisters and mothers and children and lands, with persecutions, and in the age to come eternal life. 31 But many that are first will be last, and the last first."

Matthew 19:25-30
25 When the disciples heard this they were greatly astonished, saying, "Who then can be saved?" 26 But Jesus looked at them and said to them, "With men this is impossible, but with God all things are possible." 27 Then Peter said in reply, "Lo, we have left everything and followed you. What then shall we have?" 28 Jesus said to them, "Truly, I say to you, in the new world, when the Son of man shall sit

The listeners were "astonished." The Greek word for this conveys a much different meaning. It conveys the reaction of the person "to be struck with terror."

So when the onlooker asked, who can be saved? It was asked from a posture of fear of losing what they thought they already possessed. Jesus responded, that man alone, cannot achieve this. While it is impossible for man it is no problem for God.

Peter began to plead his case, "We left everything and followed you. Isn't that worth a basket full of brownie points?"

Jesus responded, don't worry, everyone who has sacrificed the comforts of home and family will be rewarded a hundred fold.

This reward is found in the fellowship of faith within the community of believers. As the community grows in love and mutual respect, previously unknown person become brothers and sisters through their relationship to Jesus Christ.

Many persons who enjoyed the bounty of power, position, and wealth would find themselves

on his glorious throne, you who have followed me will also sit on twelve thrones, judging the twelve tribes of Israel. 29 And every one who has left houses or brothers or sisters or father or mother or children or lands, for my name's sake, will receive a hundredfold, and inherit eternal life. 30 But many that are first will be last, and the last first.	accepted or rejected on a new level of understanding of who they were, rather than what they had been. Matthew adds this comment to the writings of Mark: but when Jesus assumes his throne there will be twelve additional thrones. The Inner-Circle will sit as judges of the tribes of Israel. Matthew includes Judas as one of the future judges.

God is in control

God is in control of who is saved and who isn't. This fact is of great comfort to me personally.

The Kingdom of God will have representatives from the four corners of the earth **Luke 18:26-30;** **Luke 13:22-30**	***The Kingdom of God will have representatives from the four corners of the earth*** **Luke 18:26-30;** **Luke 13:22-30**
Luke 18:26-30 26 Those who heard it said, "Then who can be saved?" 27 But he said, "What is impossible with men is possible with God." 28 And Peter said, "Lo, we have left our homes and followed you." 29 And he said query handling to them, "Truly, I say	**Comment** Jesus continued his march toward Jerusalem. He continued to encounter persons who wanted assurance of eternal life. To this particular inquirer Jesus said, you must enter by the narrow door. Do not be like

to you, there is no man who has left house or wife or brothers or parents or children, for the sake of the kingdom of God, 30 who will not receive manifold more in this time, and in the age to come eternal life."

Luke 13:22-30
22 He went on his way through towns and villages, teaching, and journeying toward Jerusalem. 23 And some one said to him, "Lord, will those who are saved be few?" And he said to them, 24 "Strive to enter by the narrow door; for many, I tell you, will seek to enter and will not be able. 25 When once the householder has risen up and shut the door, you will begin to stand outside and to knock at the door, saying, 'Lord, open to us.' He will answer you, 'I do not know where you come from.' 26 Then you will begin to say, 'We ate and drank in your presence, and you taught in our streets.' 27 But he will say, 'I tell you, I do not know where you come from; depart from me, all you workers of iniquity!' 28 There you will weep and gnash your teeth, when you see Abraham and Isaac and Jacob and all the prophets in the kingdom of God and you yourselves thrust out. 29 And men will come from east and

those who will miss the way.

Using the vehicle of another parable, Jesus warned that many would put off honest commitment too long and their window of opportunity for salvation would be closed.

Those shut out would try in vain to receive one more opportunity. They would plead they had eaten and drank in Jesus' presence while he taught in their streets. Their plea was self-centered and was rejected because they had no redeeming commitment to faith. Again Jesus said, you think you are to be first in God's kingdom. But you will find yourself left out and your place taken by strangers who come from the four corners of the earth.

west, and from north and south, and sit at table in the kingdom of God. 30 And behold, some are last who will be first, and some are first who will be last."

Go and tell that fox

Luke 13:31-33
31 At that very hour some Pharisees came, and said to him, "Get away from here, for Herod wants to kill you." 32 And he said to them, "Go and tell that fox, 'Behold, I cast out demons and perform cures today and tomorrow, and the third day I finish my course. 33 Nevertheless I must go on my way today and tomorrow and the day following; for it cannot be that a prophet should perish away from Jerusalem.'

Go and tell that fox

Luke 13:31-33

Comment

Was this a legitimate warning or were they trying to frighten Jesus into silence? Remember, not all Pharisees were Jesus' enemies. These came to warn him against Herod's treachery. The avowed threat of Herod was to see Jesus dead. Calling Herod Antipas "An old fox" was a dangerous insult because foxes were considered creatures of low cunning. Obviously these Pharisees had access to Herod Antipas. Jesus would not abandon his Ministry on the threat of being killed.

The mention of three days obviously refers to Jesus' pending death. Today and tomorrow mean for the immediate future Jesus would continue his teaching and

At dinner they were watching Him

Luke 14:1-6

1 One sabbath when he went to dine at the house of a ruler who belonged to the Pharisees, they were watching him. 2 And behold, there was a man before him who had dropsy. 3 And Jesus spoke to the lawyers and Pharisees, saying, "Is it lawful to heal on the sabbath, or not?" 4 But they were silent. Then he took him and healed him, and let him go. 5 And he said to them, "Which of you, having a son or an ox that has fallen into a well, will not immediately pull him out on a sabbath day?" 6 And they could not reply to this.

---

healing ministry. His death would come after he reached Jerusalem.

At dinner they were watching Him

Luke 14:1-6

Comment

The only time signature with this passage is on a "Sabbath" day.

The location was a dinner at the home of an unnamed Pharisee, who was a ruler in the Temple. There was a man present, who suffered from dropsy.

Jesus was being critically observed by the other guests, namely the scribes, (lawyers), and Pharisees. Jesus asked a rhetorical question, "Is it lawful to heal on the Sabbath or not?" He knew their answer would be, "no" because they considered healing an act of work. Jesus did not verbalize his answer; rather he demonstrated it by healing the man on the spot. Then, before the lawyers and Pharisees could recover, Jesus said, you won't allow healing on the Sabbath but if your son or your livestock fell into an open well you would not hesitate to pull them out!

Jesus remarked on how they selected the place of honor

Luke 14:7-11

7 Now he told a parable to those who were invited, when he marked how they chose the places of honor, saying to them, 8 "When you are invited by any one to a marriage feast, do not sit down in a place of honor, lest a more eminent man than you be invited by him; 9 and he who invited you both will come and say to you, 'Give place to this man,' and then you will begin with shame to take the lowest place. 10 But when you are invited, go and sit in the lowest place, so that when your host comes he may say to you, 'Friend, go up higher'; then you will be honored in the presence of all who sit at table with you. 11 For every one who exalts himself will be humbled, and he who humbles himself will be exalted."

Jesus remarked on how they selected the place of honor

Luke 14:7-11

Comment

As Jesus observed the seating arrangements at the meal he addressed an issue that was very much on the minds of most of the guests. They were concerned about who would receive the most valued places at the table. Jesus warned them not to think of themselves so highly that they overlook one who may be given the seat of honor. If they had selected for themselves a more elevated position they could be asked to move to a less notable seat.

This is the way to select

Luke 14:12-24

12 He said also to the man who had invited him, "When you give a dinner or a banquet, do not invite your friends or your brothers or your kinsmen or rich neighbors, lest they also invite you in return, and you be repaid. 13 But when you give a feast, invite the poor, the maimed, the lame, the blind, 14 and you will be blessed, because they cannot repay you. You will be repaid at the resurrection of the just." 15 When one of those who sat at table with him heard this, he said to him, "Blessed is he who shall eat bread in the kingdom of God!" 16 But he said to him, "A man once gave a great banquet, and invited many; 17 and at the time for the banquet he sent his servant to say to those who had been invited, 'Come; for all is now ready.' 18 But they all alike began to make excuses. The first said to him, 'I have bought a field, and I must go out and see it; I pray you, have me excused.' 19 And another said, 'I have bought five yoke of oxen, and I go to examine them; I pray you, have me excused.' 20 And another said, 'I have married a wife, and

This is the way to select

Luke 14:12-24

Comment

Matthew relates a similar story found in *The 8 days of Holy Week*, the chapter entitled "Wednesday."

Jesus would have the host consider an entirely different guest list. If they follow Jesus' advice the results would constitute an unexpected gift of alms to those who could never repay such an act of kindness.

Someone at the table made a very pious statement, "Blessed is he who shall eat bread in the Kingdom of God!" Jesus could not resist responding with another parable.

It is the parable of the man who gave a great banquet and invited many people to come. When the time came, he sent his servant to tell the invited guests that everything was ready and waiting for them. But unbelievably, they all made excuses as to why they could not come.

therefore I cannot come.' 21 So the servant came and reported this to his master. Then the householder in anger said to his servant, 'Go out quickly to the streets and lanes of the city, and bring in the poor and maimed and blind and lame.' 22 And the servant said, 'Sir, what you commanded has been done, and still there is room.' 23 And the master said to the servant, 'Go out to the highways and hedges, and compel people to come in, that my house may be filled. 24 For I tell you, none of those men who were invited shall taste my banquet.'"

The householder was angry and humiliated at the rejection of his guests, so he sent his servant back into the streets again to bring in the poor, blind, and lame.

Soon his servant came to him and reported they had done as he wished and there was still room to be had. Again he sent his servant out to the highways to compel people to come in that his house might be filled.

Kingdom of Heaven is like ... workers in a vineyard

Matthew 20:1-16

1 "For the kingdom of heaven is like a householder who went out early in the morning to hire laborers for his vineyard. 2 After agreeing with the laborers for a denarius a day, he sent them into his vineyard. 3 And going out about the third hour he saw others standing idle in the market place; 4 and to them he said, 'You go into the vineyard too, and whatever is right I will give you.' So they went. 5 Going out again

Kingdom of Heaven is like ... workers in a vineyard

Matthew 20:1-16

Comment

This is an independent Parable found only in Matthew.

The owner needed additional workers to gather his crop. The system for doing this was quite simple. Workers would gather at a specific place somewhere in their village. Those needing additional laborers knew where

about the sixth hour and the ninth hour, he did the same. 6 And about the eleventh hour he went out and found others standing; and he said to them, 'Why do you stand here idle all day?' 7 They said to him, 'Because no one has hired us.' He said to them, 'You go into the vineyard too.' 8 And when evening came, the owner of the vineyard said to his steward, 'Call the laborers and pay them their wages, beginning with the last, up to the first.' 9 And when those hired about the eleventh hour came, each of them received a denarius. 10 Now when the first came, they thought they would receive more; but each of them also received a denarius. 11 And on receiving it they grumbled at the householder, 12 saying, 'These last worked only one hour, and you have made them equal to us who have borne the burden of the day and the scorching heat.' 13 But he replied to one of them, 'Friend, I am doing you no wrong; did you not agree with me for a denarius? 14 Take what belongs to you, and go; I choose to give to this last as I give to you. 15 Am I not allowed to do what I choose with what belongs to me? Or do you begrudge my generosity?' 16 So the last will be first, and the first last."	to find them. The normal day's wage for a laborer was one denarius. After some haggling, the agreement was reached.

Around 9 a.m., the owner decided he needed more help. Returning, he found more men eager for work. This time, the owner promised to treat them fairly and pay them what was just. Around noon and again at 3 p.m., the owner acquired more help.

Late in the afternoon, about 6 p.m., the owner returned to look for more help. He sent these to his field also. As the sun set it was time to pay the laborers for their days work. The owner instructed his steward to start with the latest ones to come to work and give them a denarius for their day's labor. It was unbelievable. The other workers couldn't believe they had been given a full day's wage for just a few hours work.

When the men who had worked all day also received a denarius, they were very dissatisfied. They complained bitterly that the owner had mistreated them. The owner defended his position, |

telling them he had not cheated them, but had dealt with them fairly. He had promised them a denarius and that is what he gave them. These workers were unsatisfied with his answer. The owner replied, "You begrudge my generosity. It is my choice that the last were treated equally with the first."

Through this parable, Jesus delivered a great truth concerning the Kingdom of God. Those who entered the kingdom first would have no greater joy than the very last to enter.

Chapter 20

Jesus is going to Jerusalem

We are going up to Jerusalem!

**Mark 10:32-34;
Matthew 20:17-19;
Luke 18:31-34**

Mark 10:32-34
32 And they were on the road, going up to Jerusalem, and Jesus was walking ahead of them; and they were amazed, and those who followed were afraid. And taking the twelve again, he began to tell them what was to happen to him, 33 saying, "Behold, we are going up to Jerusalem; and the Son of man will be delivered to the chief priests and the scribes, and they will condemn him to death, and deliver him to the Gentiles; 34 and they will mock him, and spit upon him, and scourge him, and kill him; and after three days he will rise."

Matthew 20:17-19
17 And as Jesus was going up to Jerusalem, he took the twelve disciples aside, and on the way he said to them, 18 "Behold, we are going up to Jerusalem; and

We are going up to Jerusalem!

**Mark 10:32-34;
Matthew 20:17-19;
Luke 18:31-34**

Comment

Setting the scene: Passover was drawing near. Passion for freedom and the hope of the Messiah were beginning to stir the soul of the people of Israel.

Jesus and his Inner-Circle were headed for the city of Jericho. Following a centuries old custom of the rabbis Jesus was teaching as they walked. Suddenly, his words landed with a lethal force.

The disciples drew in their collective breath. They thought they knew what Jesus meant. Why in the world was he tempting fate by going right back into the hotbed of hostility and hatred? Surely he had not forgotten the threats upon his life so quickly. Without

the Son of man will be delivered to the chief priests and scribes, and they will condemn him to death, 19 and deliver him to the Gentiles to be mocked and scourged and crucified, and he will be raised on the third day."

Luke 18:31-34
31 And taking the twelve, he said to them, "Behold, we are going up to Jerusalem, and everything that is written of the Son of man by the prophets will be accomplished. 32 For he will be delivered to the Gentiles, and will be mocked and shamefully treated and spit upon; 33 they will scourge him and kill him, and on the third day he will rise." 34 But they understood none of these things; this saying was hid from them, and they did not grasp what was said.

question this was absolutely what they did not want to hear.

James and John want top spots

Mark 10:35-45
35 And James and John, the sons of Zeb'edee, came forward to him, and said to him, "Teacher, we want you to do for us whatever we ask of you." 36 And he said to them, "What do you want me to do for you?" 37 And they said to him, "Grant us to sit, one at your

James and John want top spots

Mark 10:35-45

Comment

Jesus had scarcely finished speaking when James and John approached him. They were bold enough to ask for what they wanted, POWER!

right hand and one at your left, in your glory."

38 But Jesus said to them, "You do not know what you are asking. Are you able to drink the cup that I drink, or to be baptized with the baptism with which I am baptized?" 39 And they said to him, "We are able." And Jesus said to them, "The cup that I drink you will drink; and with the baptism with which I am baptized, you will be baptized; 40 but to sit at my right hand or at my left is not mine to grant, but it is for those for whom it has been prepared." 41 And when the ten heard it, they began to be indignant at James and John. 42 And Jesus called them to him and said to them, "You know that those who are supposed to rule over the Gentiles lord it over them, and their great men exercise authority over them. 43 But it shall not be so among you; but whoever would be great among you must be your servant, 44 and whoever would be first among you must be slave of all. 45 For the Son of man also came not to be served but to serve, and to give his life as a ransom for many." | Jesus was astounded and replied, "You do not know what you are asking for." Jesus summed up the entire event of his arrest and crucifixion as he said, "Can you drink the cup that I must drink? Can you be baptized with my baptism?" Mistakenly assuming Jesus would allow the request they responded almost joyfully, "We are able!"

Jesus said, you will drink the cup that I drink, and you will be baptized with my baptism, but to give you the left and right-hand spots are not mine to give. When the remaining ten heard this they were greatly upset.

Jesus summed up the conversation by saying, "He who would be greatest among you must be your servant and your slave." |

Mother of John and James wants top spots for her boys

Matthew 20:20-28

20 Then the mother of the sons of Zeb'edee came up to him, with her sons, and kneeling before him she asked him for something. 21 And he said to her, "What do you want?" She said to him, "Command that these two sons of mine may sit, one at your right hand and one at your left, in your kingdom." 22 But Jesus answered, "You do not know what you are asking. Are you able to drink the cup that I am to drink?" They said to him, "We are able." 23 He said to them, "You will drink my cup, but to sit at my right hand and at my left is not mine to grant, but it is for those for whom it has been prepared by my Father." 24 And when the ten heard it, they were indignant at the two brothers. 25 But Jesus called them to him and said, "You know that the rulers of the Gentiles lord it over them, and their great men exercise authority over them. 26 It shall not be so among you; but whoever would be great among you must be your servant, 27 and whoever would be first among you must be your slave; 28 even as the Son of man came not to be

Mother of John and James wants top spots for her boys

Matthew 20:20-28

Comment

Except for the introduction this passage is identical to that found in Mark. Matthew says it was the mother of James and John who petitioned Jesus for the top spots in his coming kingdom.

served but to serve, and to give his life as a ransom for many."

At Jericho Blind Bartimaeus

Mark 10:46-52:
Luke 18:35-43

Mark 10:46-52
46 And they came to Jericho; and as he was leaving Jericho with his disciples and a great multitude, Bartimae'us, a blind beggar, the son of Timae'us, was sitting by the roadside. 47 And when he heard that it was Jesus of Nazareth, he began to cry out and say, "Jesus, Son of David, have mercy on me!" 48 And many rebuked him, telling him to be silent; but he cried out all the more, "Son of David, have mercy on me!" 49 And Jesus stopped and said, "Call him." And they called the blind man, saying to him, "Take heart; rise, he is calling you." 50 And throwing off his mantle he sprang up and came to Jesus. 51 And Jesus said to him, "What do you want me to do for you?" And the blind man said to him, "Master, let me receive my sight." 52 And Jesus said to him, "Go your way; your faith has made you well." And immediately he received his sight and followed him on the way.

At Jericho Blind Bartimaeus

Mark 10:46-52:
Luke 18:35-43

Comment

There is a very unique and important aspect to this particular healing. Matthew gives us the name of the blind man and his father's name. By giving these names, the early Christian community could check the validity of this story with the actual eyewitnesses.

When blind Bartimaeus called out to Jesus, those around him told him to shut up, but Jesus halted and said, "Call him over to me." Jesus honored his request for healing and told him that his faith had made him whole.

Luke 18:35-43

35 As he drew near to Jericho, a blind man was sitting by the roadside begging; 36 and hearing a multitude going by, he inquired what this meant. 37 They told him, "Jesus of Nazareth is passing by." 38 And he cried, "Jesus, Son of David, have mercy on me!" 39 And those who were in front rebuked him, telling him to be silent; but he cried out all the more, "Son of David, have mercy on me!" 40 And Jesus stopped, and commanded him to be brought to him; and when he came near, he asked him, 41 "What do you want me to do for you?" He said, "Lord, let me receive my sight." 42 And Jesus said to him, "Receive your sight; your faith has made you well." 43 And immediately he received his sight and followed him, glorifying God; and all the people, when they saw it, gave praise to God.

Jesus at Jericho	*Jesus at Jericho*
Luke 19:1-10	**Luke 19:1-10**
1 He entered Jericho and was passing through. 2 And there was a man named Zacchae'us; he was a chief tax collector, and rich. 3 And he sought to see who Jesus	**Comment** We are told Zacchaeus was a chief tax collector. This meant

was, but could not, on account of the crowd, because he was small of stature. 4 So he ran on ahead and climbed up into a sycamore tree to see him, for he was to pass that way. 5 And when Jesus came to the place, he looked up and said to him, "Zacchae'us, make haste and come down; for I must stay at your house today." 6 So he made haste and came down, and received him joyfully. 7 And when they saw it they all murmured, "He has gone in to be the guest of a man who is a sinner." 8 And Zacchae'us stood and said to the Lord, "Behold, Lord, the half of my goods I give to the poor; and if I have defrauded any one of anything, I restore it fourfold." 9 And Jesus said to him, "Today salvation has come to this house, since he also is a son of Abraham. 10 For the Son of man came to seek and to save the lost."

he had control over a district for tax collection for the government. He would have had a number of tax collectors working for him. He would also receive a percentage of all the taxes they collected. This would have made him a very rich man indeed.

Zacchaeus was small in stature and a creative thinker. His size made it impossible for him to see Jesus walking along the roadway. Therefore, he climbed up into a tree to get a better look. This would also protect him if he were caught in the crowd. He knew all too well the danger he would face if the crowd surrounded him. He had no desire to feel the sharp elbows and swift knees from the pushing and shoving throng of onlookers. He was too smart to let the crowd have any free shots at himself. He knew there were always those who would love the opportunity to inflict pain on any tax collector.

Meeting with Jesus was the greatest event of his life. He was so profoundly changed by this encounter that he declared he would give one half of all his goods to the poor. He went even

	further and said if anyone felt he had defrauded them he would repay them four times over.
	In response Jesus declared that salvation had come into his house.

What do we really know about Zacchaeus?

What do we really know about Zacchaeus? For starters he was a man in the grip of greed. His entire life had been wrapped up in the idea of accumulating all the wealth possible.

We also know he was curious, why else would he want to see Jesus? We are not told, but perhaps he was also a friend of Matthew. If this were true it is also possible Matthew alerted him that Jesus would soon be in Jericho.

We should also notice this is the first time Jesus invited himself into someone's home. It should be no surprise that the observing Pharisees were grievously offended that Jesus would enter his home and eat with this sinner.

Parable of the Nobleman	*Parable of the Nobleman*
Luke 19:11-27	Luke 19:11-27
11 As they heard these things, he proceeded to tell a parable, because he was near to Jerusalem, and because they supposed that the kingdom of God was to appear immediately. 12 He said therefore, "A nobleman went into a far country to receive a kingdom	**Comment** The people pressed Jesus constantly to know when the Kingdom of God would be present on earth. On this occasion, he told the parable

Jesus and the Gospel Timeline   445

and then return. 13 Calling ten of his servants, he gave them ten pounds, and said to them, 'Trade with these till I come.' 14 But his citizens hated him and sent an embassy after him, saying, 'We do not want this man to reign over us.' 15 When he returned, having received the kingdom, he commanded these servants, to whom he had given the money, to be called to him, that he might know what they had gained by trading. 16 The first came before him, saying, 'Lord, your pound has made ten pounds more.' 17 And he said to him, 'Well done, good servant! Because you have been faithful in a very little, you shall have authority over ten cities.' 18 And the second came, saying, 'Lord, your pound has made five pounds.' 19 And he said to him, 'And you are to be over five cities.' 20 Then another came, saying, 'Lord, here is your pound, which I kept laid away in a napkin; 21 for I was afraid of you, because you are a severe man; you take up what you did not lay down, and reap what you did not sow.' 22 He said to him, 'I will condemn you out of your own mouth, you wicked servant! You knew that I was a severe man, taking up what I did not	about a nobleman, who was planning to take an extended trip. The nobleman called ten of his most trusted servants together and gave each of them an equal amount of money, ordering them to trade with this until he should return. Verse fourteen poses problems to understanding and continuity of the passage. We are told that the citizens hated him, meaning the nobleman. They sent an emissary after him, saying that they did not want the man (the nobleman) to reign over them. Verse fifteen tells us the man returned to receive his kingdom. He called for an accounting of his servants. The first man came and presented the nobleman with an amount double the original investment. The noblemen explained. You have done a wonderful job. I will place you over ten cities. The second servant came with a 50 percent profit on the noblemen's investment. You have done well you shall have authority over five cities.

lay down and reaping what I did not sow? ²³ Why then did you not put my money into the bank, and at my coming I should have collected it with interest?' ²⁴ And he said to those who stood by, 'Take the pound from him, and give it to him who has the ten pounds.' ²⁵ (And they said to him, 'Lord, he has ten pounds!') ²⁶ 'I tell you, that to every one who has will more be given; but from him who has not, even what he has will be taken away. ²⁷ But as for these enemies of mine, who did not want me to reign over them, bring them here and slay them before me.'"	The third servant came bringing only what had been entrusted to him without any interest. He explained that he was afraid of the nobleman and was afraid he might lose the investment. The nobleman responded, "You are a worthless servant. Why didn't you at least give my money to the bank so that I would have the interest on it?" He ordered those standing nearby to take the investment from this servant and give it to the first servant. Rather than immediately complying with his word they question why he would give that individual more on top of what he already had. The noblemen explained, because those who have most will be given more, and those who have less will lose even that. Verse twenty-seven is a brutal statement reminiscent of an eye for an eye and tooth for a tooth. The complainers mentioned in verse fifteen are now given harsh treatment being considered enemies of the nobleman.

Two Blind men at Jericho

Matthew 20:29-34
29 And as they went out of Jericho, a great crowd followed him. 30 And behold, two blind men sitting by the roadside, when they heard that Jesus was passing by, cried out, "Have mercy on us, Son of David!" 31 The crowd rebuked them, telling them to be silent; but they cried out the more, "Lord, have mercy on us, Son of David!" 32 And Jesus stopped and called them, saying, "What do you want me to do for you?" 33 They said to him, "Lord, let our eyes be opened." 34 And Jesus in pity touched their eyes, and immediately they received their sight and followed him.

Mary and Martha send for Jesus

John 11:1-4
1 Now a certain man was ill, Laz'arus of Bethany, the village of Mary and her sister Martha. 2 It was Mary who anointed the Lord with ointment and wiped his feet with her hair, whose brother Laz'arus was ill. 3 So the sisters sent to him, saying, "Lord, he whom you love is ill."

Two Blind men at Jericho

Matthew 20:29-34

Comment

This is an independent statement found only in Matthew.

There is one major difference between this occurrence, and the one previously mentioned in Matthew 20:17-19. The major difference is this healing takes place as Jesus was leaving Jericho. There is a minor difference also in that Matthew mentions two blind men. Otherwise the stories are the same.

Mary and Martha send for Jesus

John 11:1-4

Comment

The story opens telling us that a man named Lazarus is ill. He lives with his sisters Mary and Martha in the town named Bethany. John then identifies Mary as the woman who anointed Jesus' feet and

⁴ But when Jesus heard it he said, "This illness is not unto death; it is for the glory of God, so that the Son of God may be glorified by means of it.'	dried them with her hair. (Ref. Luke 7:36-50 in chapter 14 for more details about the anointing incident.) The sisters decide Lazarus' illness was serious enough to send for their friend Jesus to come and use his healing power to make their brother well. They gently reminded Jesus that he "whom you love" needs you. When Jesus received the message his response was that this wasn't serious but rather an illness that would serve to glorify God. This is a marvelous story of intrigue and suspense. When Jesus heard that one of his dearest friends was about to die he seemed to be indifferent. He delayed until after his death and then ventured to the home of the bereaved sisters, Martha and Mary. Jesus finally arrived and was prepared to grant their hope, but they were not prepared for how he would do it. Martha was concerned about the condition of Lazarus' body when they opened the tomb. She was concerned about the offense this would bring to their friends, relatives, and neighbors. Jesus showed his compassion as he wept at the tomb.

All of the emotions of losing a loved one are enshrined in this momentous story. It speaks loud and clear of God's love. God loves you!

Jesus delays

John 11:5-8

5 Now Jesus loved Martha and her sister and Laz'arus. 6 So when he heard that he was ill, he stayed two days longer in the place where he was. 7 Then after this he said to the disciples, "Let us go into Judea again." 8 The disciples said to him, "Rabbi, the Jews were but now seeking to stone you, and are you going there again?"

Jesus delays

John 11:5-8

Comment

Jesus did not immediately move toward Bethany to comply with their urgent message. Jesus delayed for two days before making any move. The delay has led some to speculate this was a calculated move, waiting to feel the assurance of God's timing before he acted. Jesus' immediate response to the request of Martha and Mary greatly confused the Inner-Circle.

After two days Jesus announced that he was now ready to go to Bethany. Again the Inner-Circle was upset by Jesus' decision. They pointed out the obvious that Jesus had received death threats from the authorities and now he was going to walk back into their midst. Jesus knew the dangers that lay before him and he knew it would be more

	than just telling Lazarus to be well. He would be raising him from the dead and Jesus never worked a miracle from human motivation.

Where was he when he said this?

Where was he when he said this? Jesus and the Inner-Circle were at the place where John had first baptized, at Jordan across from Jericho.

Note how many times *death threats* are mentioned [John 8:39; 10:31; 11:9; Mark 14:1; Matt. 26:4; Luke 13:31; at Nazareth].

A confusing comment	*A confusing comment*
John 11:9-10	**John 11:9-10**
9 Jesus answered, "Are there not twelve hours in the day? If any one walks in the day, he does not stumble, because he sees the light of this world. 10 But if any one walks in the night, he stumbles, because the light is not in him."	**Comment** This is another very confusing statement by Jesus. This was a roundabout way of saying he knew with absolute certainty what he was doing. For the Inner-Circle it was like walking a strange path in the darkness of night.
Lazarus has fallen asleep	*Lazarus has fallen asleep*
John 11:11-16 11 Thus he spoke, and then	**John 11:11-16**

	Comment
he said to them, "Our friend Laz'arus has fallen asleep, but I go to awake him out of sleep." 12 The disciples said to him, "Lord, if he has fallen asleep, he will recover." 13 Now Jesus had spoken of his death, but they thought that he meant taking rest in sleep. 14 Then Jesus told them plainly, "Laz'arus is dead; 15 and for your sake I am glad that I was not there, so that you may believe. But let us go to him." 16 Thomas, called the Twin, said to his fellow disciples, "Let us also go, that we may die with him."	Jesus' lack of immediate response to the request of Martha and Mary had been at best confusing to the Inner-Circle. In a sad way it was also comforting to them because they feared for his safety. The Inner-Circle took Jesus literally when he said Lazarus was only ill. If he was just ill he would recover. Why then should they go to Bethany? Realizing how confused the Inner-Circle was Jesus then spoke plainly, "Lazarus is dead!" Only Thomas comprehended the immediate gravity of this decision. Thomas then turned to the other members of the Inner-Circle and said let us go and die with him.
<u>Four days after burial</u>	*<u>Four days after burial</u>*
John 11:17-27	**John 11:17-27**
17 Now when Jesus came, he found that Laz'arus had already been in the tomb four days. 18 Bethany was near Jerusalem, about two miles off, 19 and many of the Jews had come to	**Comment** Jesus arrived at Bethany four days after the burial of his friend Lazarus. Many mourners

Martha and Mary to console them concerning their brother. 20 When Martha heard that Jesus was coming, she went and met him, while Mary sat in the house. 21 Martha said to Jesus, "Lord, if you had been here, my brother would not have died. 22 And even now I know that whatever you ask from God, God will give you." 23 Jesus said to her, "Your brother will rise again." 24 Martha said to him, "I know that he will rise again in the resurrection at the last day." 25 Jesus said to her, "I am the resurrection and the life; he who believes in me, though he die, yet shall he live, 26 and whoever lives and believes in me shall never die. Do you believe this?" 27 She said to him, "Yes, Lord; I believe that you are the Christ, the Son of God, he who is coming into the world."

had come from Jerusalem and the surrounding area to bring comfort to Mary and Martha. Hearing Jesus was on his way Maratha met him on the road outside Bethany. Mary remained at home with her tears.

Martha had not lost hope, she knew Jesus could do something. Jesus responded, your brother will live again. Martha thinks he is talking about the resurrection. Jesus affirms her belief saying, "I am the resurrection." Then eye to eye straightforwardly, Jesus asked, "Do you believe this?" She responded, "Yes Lord I believe."

But this was not simply a matter of resuscitating a person on their deathbed as he had done with Jairus' daughter (Mark 5:22-43) or the widow's son at Nain (Luke 7:11-17). Lazarus had been dead and buried for four days.

Teacher is calling for you

John 11:28-37
28 When she had said this, she went and called her sister Mary, saying quietly, "The Teacher is here and is calling for you." 29 And when she heard it, she rose

Teacher is calling for you

John 11:28-37

Comment

Why did Jesus weep? Not because Lazarus had died or

quickly and went to him. 30 Now Jesus had not yet come to the village, but was still in the place where Martha had met him. 31 When the Jews who were with her in the house, consoling her, saw Mary rise quickly and go out, they followed her, supposing that she was going to the tomb to weep there. 32 Then Mary, when she came where Jesus was and saw him, fell at his feet, saying to him, "Lord, if you had been here, my brother would not have died." 33 When Jesus saw her weeping, and the Jews who came with her also weeping, he was deeply moved in spirit and troubled; 34 and he said, "Where have you laid him?" They said to him, "Lord, come and see." 35 Jesus wept. 36 So the Jews said, "See how he loved him!" 37 But some of them said, "Could not he who opened the eyes of the blind man have kept this man from dying?"

despair over never seeing him alive again. Perhaps a better answer is Jesus realized his own humanness and the end of his earthly life was rapidly approaching. As a human being he had experienced hunger and thirst, he had known loneliness and pain. He knew all of these things were coming to the supreme culmination in the torturers that awaited him in Jerusalem.

The tomb was a cave

John 11:38-44
38 Then Jesus, deeply moved again, came to the tomb; it was a cave, and a stone lay upon it. 39 Jesus said, "Take away the stone." Martha, the sister of the dead man, said to him, "Lord,

The tomb was a cave

John 11:38-44

Comment

Rich people built tombs for their final resting place. Small caves served the same purpose for the

by this time there will be an odor, for he has been dead four days." ⁴⁰ Jesus said to her, "Did I not tell you that if you would believe you would see the glory of God?" ⁴¹ So they took away the stone. And Jesus lifted up his eyes and said, "Father, I thank thee that thou hast heard me. ⁴² I knew that thou hearest me always, but I have said this on account of the people standing by, that they may believe that thou didst send me." ⁴³ When he had said this, he cried with a loud voice, "Laz'arus, come out." ⁴⁴ The dead man came out, his hands and feet bound with bandages, and his face wrapped with a cloth. Jesus said to them, "Unbind him, and let him go."

poor. A stone of suitable size to cover the opening was placed to keep away the wild animals.

Maratha and Mary both understood the death process and were honest in saying, "Lord, by now, after four days, he must stink." That is exactly why Jesus did not come sooner. He did not come to do a human favor, but to declare his authority over life and death. Before acting, he made clear to Martha what this event really meant. In stating, "I am the resurrection!" He explained everything about this powerful story!

Jesus gave thanks to God for already answering his prayer that would allow Lazarus to walk out of the tomb. Jesus then called for Lazarus to come forth. Lazarus emerged from the tomb looking like a walking mummy.

What are we to do?

John 11:45-54

⁴⁵ Many of the Jews therefore, who had come with Mary and had seen what he did, believed in him; ⁴⁶ but some of them went to the Pharisees and told them what Jesus had done. ⁴⁷ So the

What are we to do?

John 11:45-54

Comment

Many of the mourners gathered at the tomb believed in Jesus. Others quickly made their way

chief priests and the Pharisees gathered the council, and said, "What are we to do? For this man performs many signs. ⁴⁸ If we let him go on thus, every one will believe in him, and the Romans will come and destroy both our holy place and our nation." ⁴⁹ But one of them, Ca'iaphas, who was high priest that year, said to them, "You know nothing at all; ⁵⁰ you do not understand that it is expedient for you that one man should die for the people, and that the whole nation should not perish." ⁵¹ He did not say this of his own accord, but being high priest that year he prophesied that Jesus should die for the nation, ⁵² and not for the nation only, but to gather into one the children of God who are scattered abroad. ⁵³ So from that day on they took counsel how to put him to death.

⁵⁴ Jesus therefore no longer went about openly among the Jews, but went from there to the country near the wilderness, to a town called E'phraim; and there he stayed with the disciples.

to inform the Pharisees about what Jesus had just done. A council meeting was quickly called. The primary topic of business was simple, "What shall we do about this man?" There was no doubt among them Jesus did indeed perform signs (miracles).

They further believe, "If we let him go on thus, every one will believe in him, and the Romans will come and destroy both our holy place and our nation." The flaw in their reasoning was as follows: they believed Jesus would be the Christ in the form of a priestly warrior. They could not understand that a peaceful coexistence was possible between the holy place, (Temple Authority) and the Roman Empire or any other in power for that matter. Jesus understood when the Kingdom of God was fully in place it did not matter who ran the political scene.

The constituents of this meeting were beginning to become rattled so Caiaphas the high priest took charge. His attitude was imperial and condescending as he looked at the gathering. He pointed out clearly that one man should die rather than allow these calamities to engulf their nation. That one man was known as Jesus of Nazareth!

John interprets Caiaphas' statement to be that of an unbidden prophecy of Jesus' role as savior of the nation and the world. The decision of Jesus' death was now made. All that remained was the actual carrying out of a developed plan.

Passover was at hand

John 11:55-57

55 Now the Passover of the Jews was at hand, and many went up from the country to Jerusalem before the Passover, to purify themselves. 56 They were looking for Jesus and saying to one another as they stood in the temple, "What do you think? That he will not come to the feast?" 57 Now the chief priests and the Pharisees had given orders that if any one knew where he was, he should let them know, so that they might arrest him.

Passover was at hand

John 11:55-57

Comment

The time for Passover was very close. Many pilgrims had already arrived and completed the purification process. As they congregated in the temple precincts they asked the question, "Do you think Jesus will come to this feast?"

The chief priests and the Pharisees had already put the word out that anyone who knew Jesus' whereabouts should immediately inform the authorities so that Jesus could be arrested.

Study Guide

Book I

The Beginning

Chapter 1

- Why did Matthew and Luke include a "Family Tree" in the beginning of their writings?

- What are the major differences between these two reports?

- Name the women listed in the family tree.

Chapter 2

- Discuss the Herod family. How many are found in the Gospels? How many of them had contact with Jesus? What was the outcome of their contact with Jesus?

- Why was Zechariah in the Temple?

- Was there some sort of conflict during their meeting? If so, what was it?

- What could Zechariah have done differently?

- Why did Mary journey to her cousin Elizabeth?

- Did Mary travel alone?

- Why did she remain in seclusion during part of her pregnancy?

- Why was Elizabeth's child so unique?

Chapter 3

- Consider and discuss the feelings and reaction of Mary at the announcement.

- The angel Gabriel tells Mary that Elizabeth is pregnant and Mary goes to celebrate with her, why?

- Why did Joseph consider divorcing Mary?

- What affect did the decree issued by Caesar Augustus have on Joseph and Mary?

- The birth of Jesus includes Swaddling cloths, Shepherds, and Wise Men. What have you learned about the significance of these?

- Herod hears about the birth of Jesus and is alarmed.

- What reactions do you have with the story of Jesus at age twelve?

Chapter 4

- What is your definition of the word *wilderness*? What is the New Testament definition of *wilderness*?

- Consider the geopolitical regions, and their impact on Jesus.

- Discuss the kingdom of heaven. What emphasis do you put on the word?

- What was God's plan for John the Baptist?

- Discuss the three Torah Schools and their particular theological viewpoints.

- Would John's preaching be relevant for today?

Chapter 5

- Discuss Jesus' baptism. Why was Jesus baptized? Why did he choose John to administer the baptism? What was the Divine response?

- Why do we say the moment of destiny for Jesus had come?

- Discuss the "Wilderness." What is your first thought? How does it fit with the biblical definition?

- Discuss the term "Forty Years."

- Why was John reluctant to baptize Jesus?

- Discuss John's statement, "Behold, the Lamb of God." What is the significance of the title?

- Discuss the temptations Jesus faced. What two letter word does Satan use and why did he use it?

- Who are the four men who leave their livelihood? And why did they do it?

- Discuss the events of the Sabbath at Capernaum.

- Why is the mention of "sundown" important?

- Think about the implications and message of the, "next morning."

- Discuss the wedding at Cana.

Chapter 6

- Why did the Jews always take a "Circuitous route" when they went from Galilee to Judea?

- What is important about the Decapolis?

- Discuss the Galilee.

- Why did Jesus cleanse the Temple? What was the response of the authorities?

- Why did Jesus and Nicodemus meet at night?

- Discuss John's disciples having a dispute with the Jews about purifying.

- Discuss the "Plan of Salvation," "He who believes in the Son has eternal life."

- Why is the story of The Samarian Woman important?

- Discuss Herod Antipas having John the Baptist arrested and the reasons why.

Chapter 7

- Jesus heals the Leper and orders him to tell no one. Why did Jesus tell him to tell no one?

- As Jesus entered Capernaum a Centurion ask him to heal his servant. What is so unusual about this story?

- Discuss the Centurion's display of faith that was unlike any Jesus had yet seen.

- At Nain Jesus raises the son of a widow from the dead. What does this tell us about Jesus' ministry?

- At home (Nazareth) he heals a paralytic. What makes this healing so memorable?

- Reflect on the story of Matthew and his leaving a lucrative business to follow Jesus.

- Discuss the business of Tax Collecting.

- Discuss what this encounter is really all about as John's disciples question Jesus about fasting. John is now in prison.

Chapter 8

- What was so important about Jesus healing the man with the withered hand?

- Who were the Herodians? And what, if any, power did they possess?

- Why was Jesus concerned about "crowd control?"

- Discuss Jesus' interaction with the demons.

- Why did Jesus sometimes instruct a person receiving healing to say nothing about the healing and at other times he gave no such prohibition?

- Discuss the "follow me" comment and the naming of the Inner-Circle.

- Why would the leaders of Judaism say that Jesus healed by the power of Satan?

- What is the unforgivable sin? How would one commit this sin?

- How do you feel realizing Jesus and his family experienced times of conflict?

- Discuss "The Kingdom Of God."

Chapter 9

- Discuss the storm at sea and Jesus' calmness.

- How would you have felt if you had seen Legion running at you?

- How do we account for the swine being raised on the shores of the Sea of Galilee?

- Why were the people from the town so upset?

- Who is the first Gentile convert commissioned by Jesus in the Gospels?

- Discuss the story of the woman who had the flow of blood.

- Discuss the parable of the Sower.

- Discuss the far reaching impact of the parable of the Good Seed and the Weeds.

- Discuss what the Kingdom is like?

Chapter 10

- Discuss Jesus' comments about John the Baptist.

- Why did Jesus tell the people they have rejected both him and John?

- Why did Jesus refuse to be a judge for the man and his brother?

- Discuss the meaning of the parable about the greedy farmer. How does the teaching apply to us today?

- What does Jesus mean in the parable of the good tree and the bad tree?

- While in Jerusalem and on the Sabbath Jesus healed a man who could not compete with the healthier people who could get themselves into the pool. What is the power of this story? Why did it get Jesus in so much trouble?

- Discuss what Jesus taught about those who died before he came to earth.

- Discuss "The sign of Jonah."

Chapter 11

- Discuss the mission of the Inner-Circle and their effectiveness.

- What was the big deal about not washing their hands before eating?

- Discuss Jesus saying the Pharisees were hypocrites.

- Discuss the interaction between Jesus and the Lawyers.

- What was "Corban?"

- Who were the "blind guides?"

- Why are temptations necessary?

Chapter 12

- The Sermon on the Mount is found no where else in Scripture. However, the Gospel of Luke does contain many companion passages.

Chapter 13

- Why did the birthday party turn into an execution? Who were the chief persons involved?

- Was Herod Antipas a king or not?

- Discuss the story of Jesus being invited to the home of a Pharisee and the woman who came in uninvited.

- What do we learn from the parable about the two men who could not repay their debts?

- Who is the woman from the streets?

- Why were these women mentioned by Luke important to Jesus?

- Discuss the feeding of the 5,000. How did the crowd guess where Jesus was heading? Who got to the spot first, Jesus or the crowd? Did Jesus expect the Inner-Circle members to feed the crowd? How were they feed?

- Discuss Jesus walking on the water. Why did Peter begin to sink?

- When Jesus proclaimed he was the bread of life, why did it result in an ugly dispute?

Chapter 14

- Why did Jesus refuse to go with his brothers to the Feast of Tabernacles?

- How serious was the threat to kill Jesus?

- In what way did the Pharisees break the Sabbath? Did they suffer any sanctions for breaking the Sabbath?

- Why was it so important to establish where Jesus came from to be or not be the Messiah?

- Discuss the Officers being ordered to arrest Jesus and their reporting back to the Chief Priest.

- Discuss the story of Jesus and the woman caught in the act of adultery.

- What is at the heart of the "Abraham is our father" confrontation?

- Discuss the story of the man born blind.

Chapter 15

- Discuss the meaning of Jesus' contact with the Syrophoenician mother.

- Discuss the feeding of the 4,000.

- What is the importance of the story of the ten lepers?

- What is the sign of Jonah?

- Discuss the importance of the account of the Galileans and those who died at the Tower in Siloam.

- Who was the "Ruler" and what was his job?

- What makes Jesus' healing of the blind man at Bethsaida unique among all the rest of his healings?

Chapter 16

- What do we know about Caesera-Philippi? Did Jesus ever visit the city?

- Who proclaimed Jesus the Christ?

- Discuss what the meaning of *upon this rock* is that Jesus would build his church?

- Who holds the Keys?

- Why did Peter rebuke Jesus?

- Why did Jesus turn on Peter?

- Discuss the Transfiguration.

- Why couldn't any of the eight disciples left at the base of the mountain exorcize the demon?
- Discuss the inherent message found in the story of Jesus paying the Temple tax.

Chapter 17

- What is at the heart of the Inner-Circle's argument?

- Discuss salt that has lost its flavor.

- Discuss Jesus' position on child abuse.

- Why did the Samaritans refuse Jesus entry into their city?

- Discuss the sending on mission the seventy.
- Discuss the details of the story of the Good Samaritan.

Chapter 18

- Discuss the parable of the Prodigal Son, including the older brother.
- Discuss the parable of the dishonest servant in light of a modern day "White Collar Crime."
- Consider the parable of the Judge that had no fear of God.
- Discuss the problem of your brother sinning against you.
- How do you respond to the King that reversed his judgment? What might that look like today?
- What did Jesus mean when he said he was the door?

Chapter 19

- Discuss Jesus' teaching on divorce.
- Discuss the story we call The Rich Young Ruler.
- Discuss the parable of The Rich Man and Lazarus.
- Discuss the peril of being rich. What do you consider as being rich?
- Who can be "Saved?"
- Discuss "That Old Fox."

- Jesus suggests a radical way to select one's guest for a party or celebration.

- Discuss the actions of the vineyard owner. How does this parable reveal a dimension of God's mercy?

Chapter 20

- Discuss Jesus saying they were going up to Jerusalem.

- Discuss James and John's grab for power.

- You have heard stories about Zacchaeus from your childhood; now discuss what the Gospels really say.

- Discuss the parable of the nobleman who went on a long trip.

- Why did Jesus delay when the sisters of Lazarus sent for him?

- Discuss the Lazarus story.

- Discuss the council's deliberation and decision.

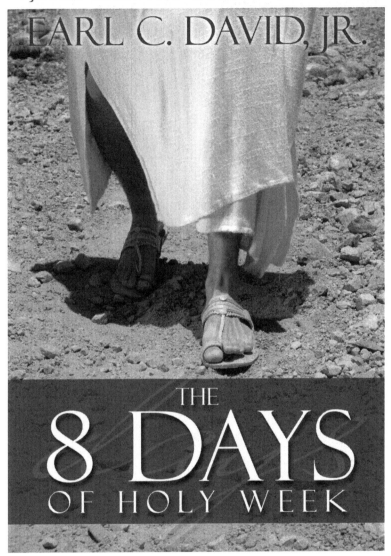

To order a signed copy of *The 8 Days of Holy Week*,
contact us by email at: the8days@bellsouth.net.

Do you need a speaker?

Do you want Earl C. David Jr. to speak to your group or event? Then contact Larry Davis at: (623) 337-8710 or email: ldavis@intermediapr.com or use the contact form at: www.intermediapr.com.

Whether you want to purchase bulk copies of *Jesus And The Gospel Timeline* or buy another book for a friend, get it now at: www.imprbooks.com.

If you have a book that you would like to publish, contact Terry Whalin, Publisher, at Intermedia Publishing Group, (623) 337-8710 or email: twhalin@intermediapub.com or use the contact form at: www.intermediapub.com.